WHAT THE
BIBLE SAYS
ABOUT
MISSIONS

WHAT THE
BIBLE SAYS
ABOUT
MISSIONS

Robert E. Reeves

College Press Publishing Company, Joplin, Missouri

Library of Congress Catalog Card Number: 89-081454
International Standard Book Number: 0-89900-264-1

DEDICATION

To Rosella, who has been my companion
and co-worker for thirty-eight years
in a ministry of mission.

Table of Contents

INTRODUCTION 11

1. "IN THE BEGINNING . . ." 53

2. PROMISE TO THE PATRIARCHS 77

3. THE PEOPLE OF GOD AND THE PEOPLE
   OF THE WORLD 87

4. THE KINGDOM OF ISRAEL AND THE
   KINGDOM OF GOD 113

5. THE POETRY OF THE KINGS 127

6. THE PROPHETS SPEAK 159

7. JESUS, GOD'S PERSONAL MISSIONARY 181

8. THE PARABLES OF JESUS 205

9. HE TOUCHED ME 231

10. THE PRINCIPLES OF MISSION PRACTICE 245

11. THE STRATEGY OF MISSION PRACTICE 267

12. ANTIOCH: THE MODEL MISSIONARY CHURCH 217

13. LETTERS TO MISSION CHURCHES 295

14. FINANCING MISSIONS 325

15. THE ACTS OF THE ALMIGHTY .333

CONCLUSION 353

BIBLIOGRAPHY 357

INDEX OF SCRIPTURES 363

PREFACE

This book is not a theology of missions, even though its theological nature may cause the reader to view each chapter as a theology of missions as found in the books of the Bible covered in that chapter. And the book does interact with some of the theologies of missions that have been advocated in recent years.

This book is an attempt to determine, as the title states, what the Bible says about missions. The method is to take a book, a portion of a book, or a group of books of the Bible that "belong" together; and examine the words and concepts found in them that relate to missions. The content is comprehensive although not exhaustive, which is to say that the attempt has been to thoroughly examine the Scriptures, although a few verses may have been missed or by-passed as redundant.

The reader will immediately observe that nearly half of the book is devoted to missions in the Old Testament. This may come as a surprise, since many see missions as a Christian enterprise. I believe I have written a lot about the Old Testament because the Old Testament say a lot about missions. In view of the fact that two-thirds of the Bible is Old Testament, having half of a book about the Bible devoted to the Old Testament does not seem excessive. Most of the books about Bible and missions give only one chapter to the Old Testament. Perhaps *What the Bible Says About Missions* will bring a balance to this approach.

"Missions" is one of the most misunderstood and abused words in the vocabulary of church leaders and members. For that reason, and for the reason that we need to have a common, and biblical, definition of "missions,"the introduction, perhaps excessively long, is devoted to defining "missions." Since the twelve Greek words examined there are from the Great Commission, no separate study of Jesus' last words on the first priority is undertaken in this work. This neglect may not be significant for two reasons: one, the Great Commission has been treated at length in many other places. And, two, after perusing this book you may reach the conclusion that the Christian mission has a much broader base, and as important as the Commission is, if it were cut out of the Scriptures, the mission of the church would still have a solid biblical foundation.

It is my hope that the reader after finishing this book will have developed "mission eyes," with the ability to see God's purpose and plan for His people in passages that heretofore had no mission significance.

More importantly, I hope that each reader will have a greater understanding of, commitment to, and involvement in the mission of Christ and His church.

A special thanks is due to two colleagues, Dr. John Castelein and Tom Friskney, who have corrected many errors. They are, however, not to be held responsible for the contents.

All Scripture quotations, except as otherwise noted, are from the *New International Version*.

INTRODUCTION

DEFINITION

The words "mission," "missions," and "missionary" are not in the popular English translations of the Bible. How then can we write a book entitled *What the Bible Says About Missions*? Is missions a false concept? Are missionaries extrabiblical or even antibiblical church leaders?

Quite the contrary. Missions is a biblical concept, for there are words in the Greek text that can be translated mission and missionary. And the concept of mission runs throughout the Scriptures as we shall seek to demonstrate.

To add to our confusion 95% of the churches have never defined missions.[1] One consequence is that there seems to be

---

1. *The Local Church Can Change the World*. (Pasadena: Association of Church Missions Committees, 1977), p. 16.

nearly as many definitions of missions as there are people. Money designated for missions has been used to replace the carpet in the parsonage and pay the league fees for the church softball team. Without a clear definition of missions anything can be missions; and when everything is missions, nothing is missions.

Perhaps we should defer any attempt at defining missions until after we have studied all the Bible says about missions. The weakness of this approach is that if we have a false or inadequate view to begin with, we might have a distorted view of what the various texts say. So we have chosen to put the definition of missions at the beginning of our study of the topic under discussion. Thus the definition is not arrived at arbitrarily but comes as a result of an in-depth word study of twelve key words from the five occurrences of the Great Commission.[2]

I. Send — *apostello* — John 20:21

Missions and its various correlaries came from the Latin *mitto* which means "to send." The Latin speaking Roman church introduced *missio* in the Sixteenth Century when the Jesuit and Carmelite orders sent out hundreds of "missionaries." Although *missio* was consistently used by Ignatius Loyola and others, the Latin never completely replaced the older Greek "apostolate."[3]

Interestingly, the Protestants, while rejecting the Latin church, adopted this Latin term almost exclusively for their efforts to propagate the gospel among the heathen. And they rarely used the Greek, "apostolate."

Mitto is the equivalent of the Greek *apostello*. The logical starting place for our study, then, is this verb which Jesus used

---

2. The Greek language of the First Century provided an adequate vocabulary for the use of the New Testament authors. Most words they used in the same sense as their contemporaries, some they modified with new Christian meaning as in the case of *agape*. Only one new word is coined, Christian, which we will consider in detail in Chapter 12.

3. Johannes Verkuyl, *Contemporary Missiology* (Grand Rapids: William Eerdmans Publishing Co., 1978) p. 2.

when He told the Twelve, "As the Father has *sent* me . . ." (John 20:21).

It is of interest to note that when the first two church-sent missionaries, Paul and Barnabas, were sent by the congregation at Antioch, Luke used the same word when he wrote, "they . . . *sent* them off" (Acts 13:3).

The noun form, *apostolos*, usually translated apostle, can also be translated, "missionary."

Rengstorf tells us,

apostellein in its basic meaning "to send forth" . . . expresses the fact that the sending takes place from a specific and unique standpoint which does not merely link the sender and recipient but also, in virtue of the situation, unites with the sender either the person or the object sent. To this extent it is only logical that *apostellein* should also carry with it the significance that the sending implies a commission bound up with the person of the one sent.[4]

In secular Greek *apostellein* is used to express the authority with which the messengers were sent,

Already the formula *apostelmanoi upo tou basileos* links with the thought of sending the further thought of the associated authoriza tion of the one sent. The men thus described are representatives of their monarch and his authority.[5]

Reflecting the seafaring origin of the word, *apostellein* also can refer to the material that is sent. The Greek grain ships were "filled" with grain, and the Greek navy was "prepared" for battle by being supplied with equipment.

The religious use of *upostellein* is made by such men widely separated by geography and calendar as Epictetus, Irenaeus, and Philo. Rengstorf writes,

---

4. *Theological Dictionary of the New Testament,* s.v. "*apostello,*" by Karl Heinrich Rengstorf.
5. Ibid.

13

We can hardly overestimate the significance of this fact for the linguistic expression of the early Christian awareness of mission.[6]

In the LXX (Septuagint, the Greek translation of the Old Testament), *apostellein* which is used to translate *shalach* "is a technical term for sending a messenger with a special task"[7] (Gen. 27:42; I Kgs. 20:20; Ezra 4:14; 5:17; Neh. 2:5; Gen. 31:4; 41:8 etc.).

By the time the New Testament authors picked up their pens *apostellein* for them "rests on the commission linked with it."[8]

And,

[in] relation to the general use of *apostellein* in the NT we must say finally that the word does begin to become a theological term meaning "to send forth to service in the kingdom of God with full authority (grounded in God)."[9]

However, the commission of Jesus raises a question. When he adds, "I am *sending* you," he uses a different word, *pempo*. Both in secular and New Testament Greek the emphasis in *pempo* is on the sending whereas in *apostellein* the emphasis rests upon the commission that is linked with it.[10] This distinction is probably not significant in view of the fact that those who were sent (*pempo*) were called apostles (*apostoloi*).

This brings us to the use of the noun *apostolos*.

In the Greek world *apostellos* belongs to seafaring terminology and more especially is a naval term. It is not a term used for an emissary, as it later became in the New Testament. This is due, in part, because the Greeks had many other words to ex-

---

6. Ibid.
7. Ibid.
8. Ibid.
9. Ibid.
10. Ibid.

press that idea. "Thus its later Christian usage was an innovation to Gk. ears or to those familiar with Gk."[11]

Apostolos only occurs once in the LXX, I Kings 14:6. It is important to note that here apostolos is "the messenger of God in the technical sense."[12] However, in century before Christ, as the sheluchim of Judaism travel farther from home, the authorization for their sending is the significant factor in their mission.

> In its legal basis the whole circle of ideas bound up with the shaliach goes back to the Semitic law of the messenger as presupposed in the OT. Here the messenger fully represents in his person the one who sends him, usually the king; and this is the original meaning of the sending of a plenipotentiary.

> On the other hand, it must be emphasized most strongly that Jewish missionaries, of whom there were quite a number in the time of Jesus, are never called sheluchim, . . . their work took place without authorisation by the community in the narrower sense, and it thus had a private character, though without detriment to its scope and significance.[13]

With this background of apostle we arrive at the New Testament use of the word. We may say it is a term used almost exclusively by Paul and his traveling companion Luke, for, of the the 79 occurrences, 29 are in Paul's epistles, and 34 are in Luke's twin volumes, for a total of 80% of the usage. Thus their use of apostello is particularly significant in establishing the meaning.

Bringing together the form of the word from Greek and the content from Hebrew we find the New Testament "always denotes a man who is sent, and sent with full authority."[14] Thus Paul can write, "We are therefore Christ's ambassadors" (II Cor. 5:20).

---

11. Ibid.
12. Ibid.
13. Ibid.
14. Ibid.

Popular use of apostle today is limited to refer to the Twelve and Paul. Further confusion is created because the New Testament calls Barnabas (Acts 14:4,14), James (Gal. 1:19), Junias (Rom. 16:7), and Andronicus (Rom. 16:7) apostles. They are not numbered with the original Twelve. How can they be apostles?

The key is in the account of the commissioning of Barnabas and Saul (Acts 13:1-3). They were sent by the church at Antioch and hence were apostles *of the church*. The Twelve were sent by Christ and hence were apostles *of Christ*. Paul indeed may be considered both an apostle of Christ and of the Church. It may be assumed since James, Junias, Andronicus, and perhaps many other unnamed apostles were not sent by Christ yet were called apostles, that they were sent by a local church.

Still another distinction needs to be examined: what is the difference between disciples and apostles? The meaning of disciple will be examined later in this introduction, but at this point we can point out that there is a significant difference in meaning and use of the terms, although there is some overlap. That is, all the apostles are disciples but not all the disciples were called to be apostles.

The difference, of course, is in the fact that the apostles were sent on a mission with authority (Matt. 28:18). Matt. 10:1-2 describes the change in roles with the consequent change in names,

> He called his twelve *disciples* to him and gave them authority to drive out evil spirits and to heal every disease and sickness. These are the names of the twelve *apostles*. . . .

The commission was expanded to a world-wide missionary enterprise after the death and resurrection of Jesus when the apostles were able to grasp the essence of the message they were to deliver (I Cor. 15:1-3).

One conclusion of this word study is that the terms apostle (in the general usage) and missionary are interchangeable and, similarly, the words apostolate and mission are equivalent in meaning.

In summary, a missionary is one sent by one in authority, either by Christ personally, or by Christ acting through a local church, with a specific message to deliver.

II. Make Disciples — *matheteuo* — Matt. 28:19

The verb in Matthew's account of the commission of Christ is "make disciples" (*matheteuo*). Consequently, our next key word for investigation is *matheteuo*. The verb only occurs four times in the New Testament (Matt. 13:52; 27:57; 28:19; and Acts 6:7).

The important fact that this verb discloses to us is that it is possible for people to become disciples of Jesus. Discipleship is not limited to race, nationality, heredity, intelligence, or other arbitrary physical factors. There are conditions of discipleship, of course, but they are actions which the potential disciple can choose or reject.

Another significant contribution to our understanding of making disciples comes from the frequent use (over 250 times) of the noun disciple (*mathetes*). The use of *mathetes* in the Greek world indicates that the disciple is more than a learner or student but is one who has a special relationship with his mentor.

The Greeks used the word in three different situations, but the emphasis on relationship is always present. The disciple was engaged in education, but he was learning with a set plan and, therefore, with a teacher. There was no disciple where there was no teacher.

In an almost technical sense the disciple was dependent upon the one with superior authority, and was in a relation that could not be broken. For instance, *mathetes* is the usual word for apprentice.[15]

---

15. *Theological Dictionary of the New Testament*, s.v. "*mathetes*," by Karl Heinrich Renstorf.

This relation could exist even if there was a gap of centuries between *didaskalos* and *mathetes*. As it was said, "Socrates is the true *mathetes* of Homer because he is his *zelotes* (enthusiast) and imitates him."[16]

The Jews in the time of Jesus use *mathetes* in this same way. John reports them as saying, "We are disciples of Moses" (9:28).

> The significant thing here is the way *mathetes* is expanded in terms of *mimeisthai* (imitate, follow). . . . The inner fellowship between the two (*mathetes* and *didaskalos*) and its practical effects and this to such a degree that the latter is basic to the whole relationship. This is not without considerable significance to the development of the Christian use of *mathetes*.[17]

The disciples who gathered around each of the philosophical masters in ancient Greece were joined together in a strong fellowship not only because of their common commitment to the master, but also because of their commitment to the truth as taught by the master and to their obligation to propagate this truth.

Consequently the master's sayings were carefully preserved and transmitted.

Given the obvious importance of the Greeks' use of disciple to Christian thought it is curious that *mathetes* does not even appear in the Old Testament. And the Hebrew equivalent, *thalmid*, only occurs once. This absence is striking.

Similarly, the Master-Disciple relation is missing from the Old Testament. And those instances that might superficially appear to involve a Master-Disciple relationship, on close examination, clearly do not. For instance, Joshua who succeeded Moses is consistently called his aide (Exod. 24:13; 33:11; Num. 11:28). And he is publicly appointed his successor by a specific command

---

16. Ibid.
17. Ibid.

18

from God (Num. 27:15-23), and not because he had been a disciple of Moses but because he had "the spirit."

The prophets, likewise, had assistants but no disciples. And although some of the prophets were organized into guilds (II Kgs. 6:1ff), these guilds can in no way be considered schools in the Greek sense, although in English they are sometimes called schools.

The reason for this absence is that

> [t]he religion of Israel is a religion of revelation. Here, then, the religious speech of man is simply the means which God uses to make known Himself and His will. . . . Their (agents and representative) whole work is based upon the divine commission which they have received. God has given them knowledge of His will, and put His word on their lips.[18]

As might be expected, the Jewish Rabbis who did not have personal revelations given to them, but were concerned with studying and teaching the Scriptures did have students (talmidim). Although lamad was used for learning a trade, the rabbis did not use talmidim for trade apprentices, but used it exclusively for those studying the Scriptures and religious traditions.

Perhaps the closest modern equivalent of mathetes is in India,

> where the disciple chooses a particular guru and proceeds to attach himself to his person, living under his roof, sitting at his feet, eating at his table, listening to his words, walking and talking with him in the bazaar or the marketplace, even helping with the household chores. In a word he shares the total life of the guru. In the give-and-take of this intimate fellowship the disciple gradually takes on the character of his guru. Before long he finds himself thinking, talking, acting like him. When he gets through he is a carbon copy of the guru. That is discipleship.[19]

---

18. Ibid.
19. J. Herbert Kane, *Christian Missions in Biblical Perspective.* (Grand Rapids: Baker Book House, 1976), p. 147.

19

This brings us to the New Testament where we find that *mathetes* is found only in the gospels and Acts and with few exceptions is confined to referring to those who have accepted Jesus as their Master.

As in the Greek world "*mathetes* always implies the existence of a personal attachment which shapes the whole life" of the *mathetes*.[20] For instance, the disciples of John fast; whereas, the disciples of Jesus do not. Further, this control extends to the inner life of the disciples. Accordingly, the disciples of John have a prayer; whereas, the disciples of Jesus ask to be taught to pray.

> This is what our Lord had in mind when He said, "Take my yoke upon you and learn from me." It is not enough to confess Christ as Savior. We must go on to acknowledge Him as our Teacher. We must attach ourselves to His person, enroll in His school, listen to His words, and walk in His way, surrender to His will.[21]

Although Luke drops *mathetai* in reference to the disciples of Jesus at Gethsemane (22:45), he resumes using it in Acts 6:1, where it is used of all Christians.

In the Gospels the disciples were personally called by Jesus into discipleship. There were other disciples besides the Twelve. The Gospel writers do not make it clear whether they, too, were called by Jesus or whether they attached themselves to Him. The statement that can be made is that it was Jesus who both knew and determined who belonged to Him (John 6:60-71).

Jesus' choice of a tax-collector (Mark 2:13ff), who was regarded by the religious people as a sinner (Luke 15:1f), and therefore unwelcome in their fellowship, establishes for the Christian era a different set of qualifications for discipleship.

The allegiance of the disciples was in their loyalty to the person of Jesus more than in their acceptance of His teaching. This is

---

20. Ibid.
21. Ibid.

seen particularly after the crucifixion. As the two walk along the road to Emmaus (Luke 24:13-49), in deep depression, they talk about "him" *not* His teaching:

> . . . it is nowhere stated or even hinted that after the death of Jesus His teaching was a source of strength to His followers, or that they had the impression of having a valuable legacy in the Word of Jesus.[22]

This personal relation is the factor that separates the disciples of Jesus from those of the Jewish rabbis. The disciples of the rabbis sought to find knowledge. Those who were called by Jesus were called into a personal relationship. They were taught many facts by the Master but their lives were controlled by faith in the Master not in the confidence that comes from knowledge. The resulting attitude was the difference of being legalistic or free.

In summary, the principle function of the missionaries is to make disciples, that is, to call people into a personal relationship of faith to the Master, and to develop them to the point that they are like Christ, and, in turn will be able to call still others into this unique relationship

III. Sending the Good News — *evangelion* — Mark 16:15

The word translated "gospel" or "good news" was already in use when the New Testament authors penned their books, although, as with other words, they infused it with new meaning. The history of *evangelion* helps us to understand its content.

The Greeks used *evangelion* for the *message* of a victory in battle that was brought home by a messenger who came by ship, horse, or runner. The declarations of the emperor, who was a god in the imperial cult, were also considered good news,

Because the emperor is more than a common man, his or-

---

22. Ibid.

dinances are glad messages and his commands are sacred writing. What he says is a divine act and implies good and salvation for men.[23]

Evangelion is only used six times in the Old Testament (II Sam. 4:10; 18:20,22,25,27; II Kgs. 7:9). In each case the good news is of a secular not religious nature and adds little to our understanding of the good news in the New Testament.

However, the Hebrew word *bashar* is used more frequently and does add to our understanding. In Accadian, Ethiopic, and Arabic as well as in Hebrew and Aramaic the stem has a sense of joy. So generally in the Old Testament there is the "bringing of good news" (II Kgs. 1:42; Jer. 20:15).

It is Isaiah who gives eschatological significance to the good news as he announces that the Messiah comes with good news (40:9 etc.). This good news includes the fact that Yahweh will be the God of the nations as well as of Israel (40:5; 45:23-25; 49:1; 51:4; 60:6). This is indeed good news for the whole world.

Rabbinic Judaism also contributed to the meaning eventually given to *evangelion* by the Christians. Friedrich informs us that the Rabbis generally understood the news (*bashar*) to be good news without even adding good (*tobah*) to news.[24] They did not conceive that the New Age with the Messiah would bring a new message, inasmuch as what would be proclaimed had been known from the time of Isaiah. Their desire was that the message would be proclaimed. Thus the preacher, and the act of proclamation, was more anticipated than the message itself. From this blending of the noun and the verb comes the idea in the New Testament of *evangelion* as the act of proclamation as well as the message proclaimed.

Jesus came to preach the gospel to the poor (Luke 4:18;

---

23. *Theological Dictionary of the New Testament*, s.v. "*evangelizomai*" by Gerhard Friedrich.
24. Ibid.

Matt. 11:5; Luke 7:22). This announcement at Nazareth and the answer to John the Baptist indicate

> that the longed for time is now dawning, that escatological good news expected from the days of Dt. Is. is now being proclaimed, and that the word has power and brings into effect what is spoken. Word and miracle, the proclamation of the glad tidings and the resurrection of the dead, are signs of the Messianic age.[25]

The message He brought was the Kingdom of God (Luke 4:43; 16:16), and that entrance into the kingdom brought joy.

The Twelve during their internship were assigned the task of preaching the Kingdom of God (Luke 9:1-6). As fully commissioned apostles they continued this ministry of Jesus after Pentecost as they preached Christ and the Kingdom of God (Acts 5:42; 8:12,35).

The proclamation of the good news was not an end in itself. The purpose was to bring salvation (Eph. 1:13; I Cor. 15:2; Rom. 1:16), peace (Eph. 6:15), new life (I Cor. 4:15; I Pet. 1:23; James 1:18), and hope (Col. 1:23).

Some unnamed disciples preached the good news on a consistent basis to non-Jews for the first time (Acts 11:20). Paul the apostle to the Gentiles continued to deliver the good news to them (Acts 14:7; 15:21; 16:10; 17:18; Rom. 15:20; I Cor. 15:1-2; II Cor. 10:16; 11:7; Gal. 1:8,11; 4:13).

One could almost say with Alan Richardson,

> The fundamental idea of these words (evangelizesthai, katangellein, and kerussein) is the telling of news to people who had not heard it before — 'evangelization.' For the NT preaching has nothing to do with the delivery of sermons to the converted, which is what it usually means today, but always concerns the proclamation of the 'good tidings of God' to the non-Christian world.[26]

---

25. Ibid.
26. Alan Richardson, *A Theological Wordbook of the Bible*. (New York: The Macmillan Company, 1955), pp. 171-172.

However, on one occasion, Paul says that he wants to preach to the Christians in Rome (Rom. 1:15). On the other hand, Baumgartel reads too much into the texts when he declares that Rom. 1:11; I Cor. 9:12-18; Gal. 4:13; and II Tim. 4:2 are to be construed as preaching in church. Baumgartel's conclusion is

> [t]he same Gospel is proclaimed in both missionary and congregational preaching. Paul makes no distinction. God Himself speaks in preaching and He does not speak to Christians or to heathen, but to man as such, revealing Himself to him in grace & judgment through the Word.[27]

The truth is somewhere in between these extreme statements. True, the good news is for both Christians and non-Christians, but the normal use of good news or proclaiming the good news in the New Testament is to the non-believer because they are the ones who have not yet received.

In summary, evangelization is the proclamation of the good news about Jesus Christ to those who have not heard it with a view to persuading them to become believers.

From *evangelion* the next logical word to study is *kerusso*.

IV. Sending a Herald — *kerusso* — Mark 16:15

"Go into all the world and *preach* the good news to all creation."

Kerusso means to herald, and in the noun form is a herald. The *kerux*, herald, in the royal period in the Greek world was to proclaim the king's messages. He was a free man not a slave. He had a place in the royal court, he had both religious and political significance, he carried a sceptre as a symbol of his royal dignity and majesty, he was highly regarded, yet he performed menial tasks, such as killing bullocks, assisting the maids in preparing meals, and harnessing the king's horses.

---

27. Ibid.

Further, the gods, like the kings, had special heralds to deliver their messages to men. When the herald served at religious festivities, he was considered under the protection of a deity; he offered prayer in the assemblies, participated in sacrifices, and served as herald of the gods.

By the time of the Stoics, when philosophy had become a religion, the Stoic had the understanding that God had revealed his secret to him and his task was to bear witness to it.

> Through him God Himself speaks. His teaching is revelation, his preaching the word of God. To despise his word and refuse to follow his teaching is to do despite to God. It is with this claim to be heard that he comes before man. As *kerux tou theou* he goes through the world and accepts all kinds of sufferings. He knows neither family, home, nor country. With only a scrip and a staff, he proclaims that there is no lack, comforting the weak, warning the wealthy, concerned for the salvation of all. On the streets and market-places he teaches men concerning good and evil, chiding errors and summoning to emulation. He even dares to compete with the imperial cult. The peace which the philosopher proclaims is higher than that which the emperor can grant.[28]

The similarity between these Greek preachers and the Christian missionaries has often been noted. Their activity is much the same. So much so, in fact, that Paul in Thessalonica is accused of being a peripatetic philosopher (I Thess. 2:3ff). The differences between them are in the message and the God who sent them.

Strangely, *kerux*, which seems to fit the Christian preacher, was only used three times in the New Testament (II Tim. 1:11; 2:7; II Pet. 2:5). Why did the inspired writers avoid using it? It is hazardous to speculate, but it appears that there was an emphasis in *kerux* they did not want to perpetuate. The Christian messengers were not under the protection of the king. In fact they

---

28. *Theological Dictionary of the New Testament*, s.v. *kerux*, by Gerhard Friedrich.

were often persecuted. But more importantly, "[t]he Bible is not telling us about human preachers; it is telling us about the preaching."[29] So we turn to *kerusso*, the declaring of the event.

The verb form does not occur as often as the noun in ancient Greek. Most often it is transitive and describes the activity of the herald in the discharge of his office.

Since the early Christians took their language not from contemplative philosophy but from common usage in public life, some uses of *kerusso* have special significance. For instance, at the games the honors and victors were proclaimed (*kerusso*). Of special interest is the occasion when the announcement was made (*ekeruxen*) at the game that the Greeks had defeated Philip of Macedon and consequently were a free and autonomous people.

In Greek religion *kerussein* occurs frequently. For instance, a devotee of Imouthes-Aesculpius, attempting to translate into Greek an ancient Egyptian papyrus, came to the account of the acts of the gods. He stopped his translation because "it is permitted to gods alone, not mortals, to describe the mighty acts of the gods." He then was given a vision to complete the task.

> The devotee of Imouthes-Aesculpius recognizes that we cannot understand *kerussein* of ourselves. We learn it when we put ourselves in the service of the deity and occupy ourselves with its demonstrations of power. Like Moses (Ex. 4:10), Jeremiah (1:6) and Jonah, he first resists the divine command. But when he has learned to know the greatness of God in his own life, he declares it. He tells of what God has done for him. He thus became a missionary for his religion.[30]

The thirty-three occurrences of *kerussein* in the Greek Old Testament are used to translate a variety of Hebrew words that

---

29. Ibid.
30. *Theological Dictionary of the New Testament*, s.v. *kerusso* by Gerhard Friedrich.

basically have the idea of cry, loud cry, and call.

The action of the herald who ran before the royal chariot and calls the attention of the crowd to the one who approached is *kerussein*. This heralding was done for Joseph (Gen. 41:43), Mordecai (Esther 6:9,11), and Daniel (Dan. 5:29). The orders of the king (II Chron. 4:29), Moses (Exod. 36:6), and Aaron (Exod. 32:5) were heralded to the populace. Most of the references, however, were to cultic decrees (Exod. 32:5; II Chron. 20:3; Jonah 3:5). In time the decrees were written (II Chron. 36:22) and the sense of "to cry," or "to proclaim orally" was lost.

Kerussein is seldom used of the proclamations of the prophets. Is this because the nature of their messages so frequently involved judgment against Israel? Or is it because their messages from God were designed for those who had not yet heard them? In those few cases where the action of the prophets is described as *kerussein* we have either a message for the Gentiles (Jonah 1:2; 3:2) or an eschatological announcement of the Kingdom of God (Isa. 61:1; Joel 2:1; Zeph. 3:14; Zech. 9:9).

> When we survey the use of *kerussein* in the OT we may conclude that it does not have here the predominant role which it comes to have in the NT. Mention of the most important references enables us to see the similarity and the difference between OT and NT *kerussein*. The preacher's call for repentance, the announcement of the Day of God, the word which brings fulfilment and the proclaiming of the ruler — all these remain in the NT. But nowhere do we find *kerussein* in the sense of Zeph. 3:14 and Zech (9:9).[31]

The Jewish rabbis often referred to the "criers" who made announcements throughout a town, spoke in courts, declared the decisions of the councils, wakened priests, and declared the judgments of the rabbis.

Although English has other words available for proclamation,

---

31. Ibid.

preaching is the nearly universal choice for translating *kerusso* and the other thirty-two New Testament words.

> Our almost exclusive use of 'preach' for all of them is a sign, not merely of poverty of vocabulary, but of the loss of something which was a living reality in primitive Christianity.[32]

Further, preaching as practiced today is not the *kerussein* of the New Testament. *Kerussein* does not mean "the delivery of a learned and edifying or hortatory discourse in well-chosen words and a pleasant voice. It is the declaration of an event"[33]

As noted in the section on the noun forms, the emphasis on the verb is also the act of preaching. However, I think Friedrich goes too far when he says, "Emphasis does not attach to the *kerugma*, as though Christianity contained something decisively new in content — a new doctrine, or a new view of God, or a new cultus."[34]

Although the concept of redemption through Christ was formed in the mind of God before the creation (Eph. 1:4) and was foretold throughout the Old Testament, the events of the incarnation, crucifixion, and resurrection, with their attendant meanings, were new and without this content the action of proclamation would have had no effect.

Jesus stated that the purpose of His earthly ministry was to preach (Mark 1:38; Luke 4:18-19,43-44). In the synagogue at Nazareth

> [h]e proclaims, like a herald, the year of the Lord, the Messianic age. When heralds proclaimed the year of jubilee throughout the land with the sound of the trumpet, the year began, the prison doors were opened and debts remitted. The preaching of Jesus is such a blast of the trumpet.[35]

---

32. Ibid.
33. Ibid.
34. Ibid.
35. Ibid.

The Synoptists spoke of Jesus as the herald who proclaimed the Word but John, who does not use *kerusso*, called Jesus Himself the Word through whom men come to God.

Jesus chose, trained, and commissioned the disciples specifically to herald His message to the whole world. Whereas He taught them in secret they were to proclaim publicly and fearlessly the message they had received from the Master (Matt. 10:27). The content of this message was enlarged after the resurrection. During the lifetime of Jesus they were to proclaim the same message as that given to John the Baptist and Jesus: repentance (Mark 6:12) and the nearness of the kingdom (Matt. 10:7). Beginning at Pentecost, they included the resurrection, baptism, forgiveness of sin, and the gift of the Holy Spirit (Acts 2).

The commission could exist only after the resurrection for two reasons. The obvious reason is that only then was Jesus present to renew the command to preach. But virtually as important, there was no message and hence no need for the command to herald without the resurrection. The disciples were to declare the message to the people (Acts 10:42); but beginning with Cornelius, they are to go to the whole world.

For the Gospel is not an esoteric doctrine nor the concern of a secret society. It belongs to the public. The message is to ring out on the streets and from the roof-tops. In season and out of season (2 Tim. 4:2) it must be boldly and constantly proclaimed to all men and situations. When the whole world has heard the Word of Christ, the commission of the risen Lord will be executed and the end will come (Mt. 24:14). The preaching of the apostles is part of God's saving plan for men, like the death and resurrection of Christ. It is not enough that Christ has lived and died, and that He is risen. These saving facts must be proclaimed in order that they become saving reality for individuals. . . . Sinful men are commissioned by God to declare this message to men. These men are neither miracle-workers nor philosophers. They are neither profound scholars who can convince all by their learning nor skilled orators who can bind men by their powerful speech. They are heralds — no more (1 C. 1:22f; 2:4). It is not their moral

29

blamelessly nor their Christianity which decides the worth or efficacy of their preaching. Otherwise the Word of God would be dependent on men.[36]

The New Testament preacher is not a reporter who tells his own experiences. He is not a philosopher who gives his own opinions. He is a herald, sent by a higher power, to proclaim a divine message.

The purpose of this preaching is to produce faith (I Cor. 2:4; Rom. 10:4).

Jesus linked sending (*apostellein*) and preaching (*kerussein*). This He did in His own ministry (Luke 4:18,43), in the ministry of the Twelve (Mark 3:14-15; Luke 9:2; Matt. 10:7), and in the Great Commission (Mark 16:15). Paul makes the same connection (Rom. 10:15). Paul further makes the same point as he sees himself as "a herald and apostle" (I Tim. 2:7; II Tim. 1:11).

Inherent in *kerussein* is the idea of sending, although the emphasis is on proclamation. The basic idea of *apostellein* is the sending, but it is inconceivable that there would be a sending without a purpose, a commission without a message to proclaim. It is thus inevitable that sending and proclamation should be linked. So much so is it true that we would have to make the connection even if the inspired writers had not joined the actual words together.

In summary, preaching is the divinely appointed way of proclaiming the good news about Jesus Christ to those who have not heard it.

V. Sending a Witness — *martureo* — Acts 1:8

"Ye shall be my witnesses." Four questions need to be answered about this text. Who can be a witness? To whom do they witness? What is the subject of their witnessing? How do they witness? These answers can be found in the meaning and use of

---

36. Ibid.

martus, martureo, marturia, marturion.
Martus and its cognates probably come from *smer*, "to bear in mind," "to remember," "to be careful."

> Hence *martus* was probably 'one who remembers, who has knowledge of something by recollection, and who can thus tell about it.' i.e., the witness.[37]

In secular Greek one may be a witness in two contexts. A witness is one who can and does testify as to the facts in a trial or legal transaction. A witness is also one who can give evidence to confirm a fact or statement to a third party in a non-juridical setting.

The four Greek words are used over 300 times in the LXX. In most of these occurrences they have the same popular or legal meaning as in secular Greek. In the Old Testament, however, witness takes on a religious sense in some passages.

One of the more interesting developments is in Isa. 43:9-13 and 44:7-11. Here is a kind of trial before the nations, who are at the same time spectators, advocates, witnesses, and ultimately judges of their gods. The nations are to witness to the deity of their gods, but they have nothing to say. Israel is told three times, "You are my witnesses." In this trial it is Israel's responsibility to "declare to the nations of the world the uniqueness, reality, and deity of God."

> The content of the witness is thus a religious truth of which the witness is convinced on the basis of his experience. It is a religious certainty whose content he emphatically represents, for whose acknowledgement he strives, but for the correctness of which he cannot give any rational proof or present any empirical demonstration. It is grounded, then, on the prophetic experience of revelation which is original, and which by nature is not subject

---

37. *Theological Wordbook of the New Testament, s.v. martus, martureo, marturia, marturion* by H. Stratham.

to rational control. This is certainty to the prophet. It is also certainty to Israel in so far as it follows the spiritual leadership of prophecy. The witness of this reality of God which is believed and experienced in faith bear the character of a religious confession advanced with the claim to recognition.[38]

Elsewhere we have reference to the "ark of the Testimony"
(Exod. 25:15,22). Since neither the tent nor the ark can be said
to give witness, the reference must be to the ten commandments,
or revelation, which is contained in the ark and were called the
"tablets of the Testimony" (Exod. 31:18; 32:15).

Thus the Old Testament adds to the meaning of witness the
fact that Yahweh is the subject of the witnessing and that man's
knowledge of Yahweh and his testimony to Yahweh comes from
revelation.

In the New Testament we find that the concept of witness
follows both senses found in secular Greek. This is, witness is
both personal knowledge of observable truths, and making these
facts known to others. In the sense of eyewitnesses we find *martus* in Matt. 15:63; Acts 6:13; Heb. 12:1; etc. It is found in the
sense of confessing witness, but this is found most meaningfully in
its development in Luke. Luke is responsible for giving an addi-
tional sense to witness. With him it takes on a unique Christian
meaning. "You are witnesses of these things" (Luke 24:48).
"These things" are not only the facts of the death and resurrection
but also include the significance of these events, specifically,
repentance and remission of sins. With Luke a person was
qualified to be a witness because he was present and could give
an eyewitness account of events that actually occurred in
historical time and place (Luke 24:47; Acts 1:8,22-26). But the
declaration of raw facts is insufficient to bring about God's
kingdom on earth. It is also necessary to know the meaning of
these facts through revelation. And this which was hinted at in

---

38. Ibid.

Luke is further developed in Acts (1:8; 10:42).

Paul, who was not an eyewitness of death and resurrection of Jesus, could be a confessing witness to what he had seen and heard on the Damascus road. Whether the things Paul "heard" included reports from the apostolic eyewitnesses is impossible to decide.

Witnessing (martureo), preaching (kerusso), and sending (apostello), are linked in Acts 10:42. Preaching exists because of the fact of the resurrection of Jesus. And it is to this fact that the preachers testify. Had there been no resurrection there would have been no content to the preaching and subsequently no preaching. Naturally Jesus sent them first to Israel. But now they are to go to all nations. All men, without distinction, are to hear the message (Col. 1:23; Mark 13:10; 16:15-20).

The sense of witness as martyr did not develop until after the New Testament age. Neither is the telling of one's personal religious experience called witnessing in the New Testament.

In summary, the Christian witness, then, is one who has knowledge of the facts of the gospel, either as an eyewitness or from revelation, and who bears witness to those facts with their attendant meanings.

VI. Send to Effect Change — metanoeo — Luke 24:47

The definition one gives to metanoeo and metanoia is going to influence one's theology and will impact significantly on one's evangelistic/missionary activity. For instance, metanoeo has been variously understood to mean, feel sorry, remorse, change your mind, do penance, change your ways, and be converted.

We receive very little help in understanding the New Testament use of metanoeo from classical Greek. Metanoeo is rarely used before the New Testament writers appropriate it and is even then limited to "regret," and "remorse."

Metanoeo is seldom used in the LXX. Although in the Old Testament we can see a move from the sense of "remorse" in the early sections toward a sense of "convert" in the later portions.

33

And in Jewish tradition *metanoia* carried the meaning of "feeling of remorse," "gesture of sorrow," "works of penance," and "self mortification." None of these concepts carried over in the Christian understanding or use.

In the New Testament *metanoeo* and *metanoia* are more frequently used in the Gospels, especially in Luke. The verb form occurs twelve times in Revelation. Paul uses the verb only once and the noun four times.

Except for Luke 17:3f and II Cor. 7:9f *metanoia, metanoeo* can only mean change of mind, to change one's mind, conversion, to convert.[39] Convert here is used in the sense of changing one's ways, changing one's religion.

John the Baptist called on his auditors to change their life (Mark 1:4, parallels; Matt. 3:2; Acts 13:14; 19:4; Luke 1:16).

> What John advances is the ancient prophetic summons for conversion, for a break with the ungodly and sinful past, for turning to God, because God, active in history, turns to man.[40]

Jesus also linked the imperative, repent (*metanoeite*) with the kingdom (Mark 1:15; Matt. 4:17). However, Jesus, unlike John declares that the kingdom is already present in His person.

Several concepts are associated with the required change. Every one must change (Acts 17:30; 20:21; II Pet. 3:9), not just the flagrant sinners (Luke 3:11). Gentiles are to change (Luke 3:14; Acts 11:18; 26:20). Certain religious leaders needed to change (Matt. 3:7-10). It was not just a change from the former way of life. It was also a surrender to the Lordship of Christ and willingness to do all that the reign of God requires. This kind of change can not take place solely by man's will or effort (Matt. 18:3). At the same time it requires man's effort (Acts 2:38; 3:19;

---

39. *Theological Dictionary of the New Testament*, s.v. *metanoeo, metanoia* by J. Behm.
40. Ibid., p. 1000.

8:22; 17:30; 26:20).

This religious change was associated with baptism. It was both expected and normal that anyone who repented would also be baptized (Matt. 3:6,11; Mark 1:4; Acts 2:38; 13:24; 19:4).

Repentance was turning from something (Acts 8:22; 3:26; Heb. 6:1; Rev. 2:22a; 9:20; 16:11). At the same time it was turning toward God (Acts 20:21; 26:20; Rev. 16:9; I Pet. 2:25).

This mandated change of life is serious and final. Once man has turned from evil to God there can be no going back (Heb. 6:4-6). In so turning away from God (Heb. 3:12) knowingly and deliberately (Heb. 10:26) no human effort can turn him around, and no further sacrifice has been provided. This change does not cause despair over leaving the old life or grief from performing penitential works of righteousness. On the contrary, the new lifestyle brings joy and peace because the convert is doing the will of God and is free from condemnation in the court of the Almighty.

Summary. The Christian herald is to proclaim the necessity of a changed life in order for one to enter the kingdom of Christ and receive the forgiveness of sin. This repentance is a complete change of one's life, climaxed in baptism, to prepare one for life in the new Kingdom of Christ.

VII. Send to Grant Forgiveness — aphesin — Luke 24:47

The root aphienai, means to "send off" and was used by the Greeks in a wide variety of ways. It meant "to hurl," "to let go," and "to release." It is natural it came to be used in legal contexts. So a person could be released from marriage, debt, office, or obligation. However, the Greeks never used aphienai in a religious sense, that is, for the forgiveness of sin.

Since aphienai had such a broad spectrum of application the translators of the LXX used it for several Hebrew words denoting meanings as diverse as release, surrender, leave, etc. Of special interest to us it is used for words of remission (Gen. 4:13; Exod. 32:32; Psa. 24:18; 31:5; Lev. 4:20; 5:10,13; Num. 14:19;

15:25f; Isa. 55:7; 22:14). And it is most frequently used of remission of sin (amartia). In the Old Testament it is God who forgives. The Greeks never spoke of God forgiving. Another disparity needs to be noted. In the Hebrew the verbs for forgiveness expressed a religious base for the forgiveness of sin, whereas the Greek word used to translate them had a legal sense.

As in secular Greek the New Testament writers use aphienai in a variety of ways, but it is also used for forgiveness of sin (Mark 2:5ff; Luke 7:47ff; John 20:23; etc.)

Forgiveness in the New Testament has a new and distinctive feature: forgiveness comes through the saving act of the death of Christ on the cross. Forgiveness is conditioned upon one's willingness to forgive (Matt. 6:12,14ff; 18:21-34; Luke 17:3f; Mark 11:25), and willingness to change (Luke 24:47; Acts 2:38). Baptism (Acts 2:38; I Pet. 3:21), confession of sin (I John 1:8), and the Lord's Supper (Matt. 26:18) are all associated with the forgiveness of sin.

The New Testament concept of forgiveness based on Christ's sacrifice for sin and man's willingness to obey God keeps intact the concept of Yahweh as Judge, man as sinner, redemption through an act of a gracious God, and an eschatological hope for man.

In summary, apostolic (missionary) preaching is to proclaim forgiveness of sin for sinful man, based on God's act of redeeming love at Calvary, and man's acceptance of that sacrifice. This is a forgiveness that assures man that there is therefore now no condemnation to the forgiven sinner in the day of judgment.

VIII. Send to Generate Faith — pistis — Mark 16:16

"Faith" came into use because Christianity was a missionary religion. "All missionary preaching demanded faith in the deity proclaimed by it."[41] As in secular Greek, pisteuein means "to rely

---

41. Rudolph Bultman, pisteuo, VI:181.

36

on," "to trust," "to believe."[42] *Pistis* can mean "faithfulness" or "trust" but is seldom used in the sense of faithfulness in the New Testament.

Believing comes as a result of the proclamation of God's word (Rom. 10:14,17), and is belief in God's word (John 2:22; Acts 24:14; Luke 24:25; Acts 26:27, etc.). It, then, is the acceptance of the message (Rom. 1:5; 3:25; 10:17; 1 Cor. 15:14,17; 1 Th. 1:8). *Kerugma*, then, is both the cause and content of faith. *Kerugma* and faith always go together (1 Tim. 3:16).[43]

The content of faith is the acknowledgment that Jesus rose from the dead and that He is Lord (Rom. 10:9). The resurrection made it possible for Jesus to be seated on His throne as Lord.

This faith is closely allied to hope. In Hebrews 11 the heroes of faith are "strangers and pilgrims on earth" (Heb. 11:13) not yet having received the fulfillment of their hope. Faith is the "hope of things not seen" (Heb. 11:1) which, for the Christian, is in the heavenly kingdom.

Faith always contains the notion of obedience. In Hebrews 11, for instance, each of the people who is cited as an example of faith, demonstrated that faith is obedience to God's word.

This accounts for the close connection between faith and baptism in the Commission of Jesus (Mark 16:15-16), and in the apostolic preaching (Acts 2:36-38; 8:12-13; 34-38; 9:18; 10:44-48; 16:14-15; 22:14-16). Martin Luther, who added "only," to "faith" in Rom. 1:16 did not separate baptism from faith. Baptism, for Luther, was the "obedience of faith."[44]

IX. Send to Evoke Action — *baptizo* — Matt. 28:19

Bapto and *baptizo* mean to dip in or under, to immerse. In

---

42. Ibid., p. 203.
43. Ibid., p. 209.
44. Hilton C. Oswald, ed., *Luther's Works*, vol. 25, Lectures on Romans (Saint Louis: Concordia Publishing House, 1972) p. 54.

early secular Greek there was as yet no religious significance to dipping and so is used of dyeing cloth by dipping, ships sinking, and people drowning.

Religions in Greece, Egypt, Rome, Babylon, Persia, and India all had sacred washings in which cultists were baptized. There seem to be two primary meanings attached to these baptisms. First, was the idea of cleansing, the washing away of guilt. Second, and especially in the Egyptian cults, was the attainment of immortality through baptism in the sacred Nile. In Egypt, where the Nile was literally the water of life, immortality was thought to be granted because of the sacredness of the river. So much so, that Herodotus tells that if a person, either Egyptian or foreigner, were drowned (immersed) in the Nile he must be embalmed as "one who is more than an ordinary being."

Baptein is used infrequently (19 times) in the LXX for dipping. In Lev. 11:32 the dipping is to cleanse unclean objects. In one of the more interesting events, Naaman is instructed to dip (*baptizo*) seven times in the Jordan to have his leprosy removed (II Kgs. 5:14).

By the time of John the Baptist it is generally agreed that the Jews were practicing the baptism of proselytes. Although John also apparently baptized Gentiles (Luke 3:14) his focus was ethical (repent) and preparatory (the kingdom of heaven is near), not cross-cultural.

The new development in John's baptism is the linking of the Messianic prophecies (e.g. Isa. 1:15ff; Ezek. 36:25; Isa. 4:4; Jer. 2:22; 4:14; Zech. 13:1; Psa. 51:7) with the opportunity to be initiated into the gathering Messianic community.[45]

The baptism of Jesus by John both raises a difficult question and at the same time gives a very helpful insight into the purpose of Christian baptism. John's baptism required repentance, but since Jesus had no sin for which to repent the question is, why

---

45. *Theological Dictionary of the New Testament*, s.v. *bapto* by Albrecht Oerke.

was Jesus baptized? A common answer, to set an example, although no doubt true, really is not a very successful answer.

Oscar Cullman helps us understand Jesus' baptism when he points out that the words of the heavenly voice, "This is my Son, whom I love; with him I am well pleased" (Matt. 3:17; Mark 1:11), are from the Suffering Servant section of Isaiah (42:1).[46] Jesus, here, then, is submissively accepting the role of the Suffering Servant, specifically His death on the cross. "[B]aptism was for Him a dedication as the Messiah."[47] This, further, gives meaning to Jesus' reply to John, "it is proper for us to do this to fulfill all righteousness" (Matt. 3:15). For it was through His death on the cross that righteousness was brought to sinful man (Rom. 5:18-19).

Baptism, then, for both Jesus and His followers is an acceptance of His death. Jesus in His baptism looks forward to His death on the cross. The believer in baptism looks backward to Jesus' death on the cross (Rom. 6:1-6).

"Baptizing," along with "going," and "teaching" are participles in Matthew's record of the Great Commission. This has led some commentators to say that they are subordinate to the verb, "make disciples." However, as Tom Friskney has pointed out, these are circumstantial participles that have the same force as the main verb.[48] The command (and the verbal forms are in the imperative mood) is to go, to baptize, to make disciples, and to teach.

The disciples clearly understood the commission to include baptizing penitent believers. Peter at the close of the first public proclamation after the resurrection and commision declared, "repent and be baptized, every one of you, in the name of Jesus Christ for the forgiveness of your sins. And you will receive the

---

46. Oscar Cullman, *Baptism in the New Testament*, trans. J.K.S. Reid (Chicago: Alec R. Allenson, 1950), pp. 14-15.

47. Oerke, ibid.

48. Thomas E. Friskney, Personal interview.

gift of the Holy Spirit" (Acts 2:38-39). This practice is continued throughout apostolic history inasmuch as in each case of conversion recorded in Acts baptism is specifically mentioned as the act of compliance that ushered the believer into this new fellowship.

> Because God is the only source of real life, and His holiness excludes sin, the basic conception both of Paul and of the NT generally in relation to baptism is that of the cleansing bath (I Cor. 6:11; Eph. 5:26; Heb. 10:22; cf. Acts 2:38; 22:16). The significance of baptism thus depends on the fact that it is a real action of the holy God in relation to sinful man. Hence both a superstitious and also a purely symbolical understanding are excluded.[49]

In summary, baptism is a command of Christ. It is included in the Great Commission because it is the act of obedience that initiates one as a disciple. Further, it has a rich variety of associations. It is the acceptance of, and identification with, the essential elements of the Gospel: the death, burial, and resurrection of Christ. This act of faith provides the forgiveness of sin, promises the gift of the Holy Spirit, and incorporates the believer into the Church.

X. Send to Teach — *didasko* — Matt. 28:20

Didaskein has the comparatively straightforward meaning of to teach, whether it is imparting information, passing on information, or acquiring skills.

In the LXX although *didaskein* is used for such diverse instructions as the use of weapons (II Kgs. 22:35) and the practice of a song (Deu. 31:19,22), has its "particular object . . . the will of God in its declarations and demands" (Psa. 93:10).[50]

In secular Greek the purpose of *didaskein* is to develop talents and abilities. From the Greek, then, we learn something about

---

49. Ibid.
50. Ibid., s.v. *didasko* by Karl Heinrich Rensdorf.

the method of teaching. However, from the Hebrews we gain insight into the emphasis on the content of the teaching. "In the LXX (OT), on the other hand, the concern is with the whole man and his education in the deepest sense."[51] The instruction in the Old Testament has as its object not the imparting of revelation or prophetic messages but the communication of a revelation that is already in place.

Teaching in the Jewish concept was the exegesis of the text. This can be further seen in the fact that the word, talmud, derives from the Hebrew word translated by *didaskein*.

Two-thirds of the 95 occurrences of *didasko* in the New Testament are found in the Gospels and the early chapters of Acts. One may conclude that it is a term in common use in the early Jewish congregations but one that did not gain favor in the later Gentile congregations. Thus we may expect a strong Hebrew flavor in the meaning of the word.

Jesus, Himself, was so influenced. His teaching in the synagogues followed the Jewish pattern of reading the Scripture while standing and expounding the text from a seated position (Luke 4:16ff). Jesus did not, however, restrict Himself to the exposition of the Scriptures. As the Word of God incarnate He had a teaching to deliver (John 8:28). In all instances He was "advancing the claim of God to the whole man."

The Master/Disciple relationship was normative in the early church. An exception to this principle occurs when the believer has certain spiritual gifts. John told his readers that since they have the *charisma* to teach them they do not need a human teacher (I John 2:27).

In Acts we see the disciples both preaching and teaching in the same context (4:2,18). The difference seems to be the method used not necessarily in the audience addressed. Perhaps *didaskein* includes proving the Messiahship from the Scriptures,

---

51. Ibid.

for when speaking to a Jewish audience it was appropriate both to proclaim the good news and prove its validity from the Hebrew Bible. In the Gentile context (Acts 28:31) the two words may have been used as synonyms.

From Matthew's account of the commission we are tempted to say that the normal distinction is that the evangelist announced the message to the world and taught the disciples. Paul seems to support this idea (Rom. 12:7; Col. 1:28; 3:16).

In any case the importance of teaching after baptism is heavily stressed both in the New Testament and missiology. Some have gone so far as to say the teaching done after baptism is more important than that done before.

A missionary in Tanzania went to several villages once a week for a year teaching them about Christ. At the end of the year they were asked to decide whether or not to follow Christ. Most of the villages chose to follow Jesus. The missionary baptized them and left.[52] Unfortunately he did not return for further teaching. I have heard that some time later another, examining his work, visited those "Christian" villages and found no trace of the churches. The disappearance of these infant churches was attributed to the lack of teaching after baptism.

We must give some attention to the difference between making disciples and teaching. Years ago the Great Commission was interpreted as teach, baptize, teach. As we have seen this is a great oversimplification of the text.

Recent missiologists have more accurately explained the difference as making disciples and perfecting disciples.[53]

Christian educators have confused the issue by popularizing the term discipling for programs of developing those who are already disciples. These programs are needed but there would be

---

52. Vincent J. Donovan, *Christianity Rediscovered*, (Maryknoll: Orbis Books, 1978).

53. Donald McGavran, *Understanding Church Growth*, (Grand Rapids: William B. Eerdmans Publishing Co., 1970), pp. 212, 359.

less confusion if they called these activities perfecting or teaching and left discipling for the specific process of making disciples.

In summary, baptism is not the end but the beginning of Christian growth. Those who have become disciples are to be taught all those things contained in the Scriptures that Jesus taught the first group of disciples.

XI. Send to others — *Ethne* — Matt. 28:19

Who is to be discipled? Perhaps there was a time when one could give a simple answer to this question. One could simply say, "all the nations" and assume the answer was adequate. However, recent studies by social scientists and statements by leading missiologists require us to examine nations (*ethne*) more carefully.

We again must begin our examination with the Hebrew Bible and the Greek words used to translate it. Two principal Hebrew words are used for people in the Old Testament, *am* and *goy*. *Am* came to be used for the holy people and *goy* for the non-Jewish or Gentile people. The LXX almost always translates *am* with *laos* and *goy* with *ethne*. There is a large number of instances in the Old Testament where the distinction between the two is clearly differentiated; e.g., Exo. 33:13; Deut. 7:6.

When we come to the Messianic prophecies the LXX understands the mission of the servant of the Lord is to the Gentiles (Isa. 49:6).

There is no evidence that either the Hebrews or the Greeks had a sociological definition of ethnic groups and used either *goy* or *ethne* of such groups. "The word is used non-sociologically to describe all the individuals who do not belong to the chosen people."[54] Nor is there any reason to think that nations refers to countries as would be expected in English.

In the New Testament *ethnos* "Means 'mass' or 'host' or

---

54. *Theological Dictionary of the New Testament*, s.v. *ethnos*, by Georg Bertram.

'multitude' bound by the same manners customs or other distinctive features."[55] It is found in this sense in Acts 17:26, "From one man he made every nation of men."

There are sixty-four places where *ethnos* or *ethne* occurs without the sense of being an "other" people as found in *goy*. For instance it is used of the Jews (Luke 7:5; 23:2; John 11:48,50,51,52; 18:35; Acts 10:22; 24:2,10,17; 26:4; 28:19; and I Pet. 2:9). *Ethnos* is used interchangeably with *laos* (John 11:50; Acts 4:25,27; 15:14; Rom. 15:11). And the fact that both Jews and Gentiles are meant is stated in the expression, *panta ta ethne* (all the nations) found in Matt. 24:9,14; 25:32; 28:19; Mark 11:17; 13:10; Luke 21:24; 24:27; Rom. 15:11; and Gal. 3:8.

Later Jewish writers, Philo and Josephus, both use *ethnos* of all people including the Jews.

There are one hundred places where *ethne* is clearly used of the Gentiles in contrast to the Jews (e.g., Matt. 6:32). And additionally there are several places where the word may not be the technical word for Gentile but the context indicates it is the Gentiles who are to be understood (e.g., Rom. 15:11).

Apparently the Jews saw the rest of the world as "others," much as the Greeks described foreigners as *ethne*. In this framework of "otherness" it should be pointed out that *ethne* can also be translated "sinners."

From the perspective of evangelism the important point is that the nations are those who "do not know God" (I Thess. 4:5; Jer. 10:25).

In summary, nations in the Old Testament generally had the idea of Gentiles. The New Testament authors reflect this Hebrew influence inasmuch as 25% of the occurrences of *ethne* refer to the Gentiles. But the preponderance of the usages reflect more nearly the original meaning of *ethne* which refers to peoples who have distinctive language and cultural differences. It is in this

---

55. Ibid., s.v. *ethnos* by Karl Ludwig Schmidt.

sense that Jesus used nations in the Great Commission. The breadth of the commission is underscored by the addition of *all* to the nations (*panta ta ethne*). None are to be neglected or bypassed in the evangelization of the world.

It is this understanding that has led Donald McGavran to identify nations with the ethnic or people groups that exist in the Twentieth century.[56] He is not without his critics who insist that nations should be translated Gentiles.

McGavran is close to the meaning of *ethne*. But he seems to be giving *ethne* a Twentieth century scientific definition that is determined by the current social sciences, sociology and anthropology. It is unlikely that the New Testament authors had anything quite that precise in mind. McGavran is giving a "hard" meaning to a much "softer" understanding of the First century.[57]

In any case, nations, especially as combined with sending, requires the church to cross cultural barriers in their outreach programs.

The main point to be observed is that the commission of Jesus includes the specific direction to make disciples of "others," that is, people unlike ourselves.

XII. Send to all — *kosmos* — Mark 16:15

Although *kosmos* can mean the whole created world or even the universe it is obvious that the object of the commission is the inhabited world or perhaps the even more restricted world of the fallen humanity.

World is used in the sense of the inhabited world in places like Matt. 4:8; Luke 4:5; Rom. 4:13; Mark 16:15; Rom. 1:8; and I Pet. 5:9. Thus, "preaching to the whole world implies preaching

---

56. McGavran, Donald. *Understanding Church Growth*, revised ed. (Grand Rapids: William B. Eerdmans Publishing Company, 1980), Chapter Ten.
57. I am indebted to John Castelein, Ph. D., for the distinction of hard and soft meanings.

to 'all who dwell on earth.' "[58]

Herman Sasse further observes,

> When the term no longer denotes merely the dwelling-place of man or the theatre of human history, but the setting of God's saving work, then it takes on a new significance which is distinctive in the NT and for which there are no parallels either in the Greek world or in the Jewish.[59]

We find Jesus using *kosmos* in this way (Matt. 5:14; 13:38; 18:17). The disciples use *kosmos* of the race before the flood (II Pet. 3:6), the world of the ungodly (II Pet. 2:5), and the refuse of the world (I Cor. 4:13).

The New Testament also sees the world has a relationship with God. However, it is a relationship that is broken by sin (Rom. 5:12). Thus the inhabitants of the whole world are sinners before God (Rom. 3:19). And the purpose of the coming of Christ was to reconcile the world to God (II Cor. 5:19).

Luke sees "all the nations of the world" (*panta ta ethne tou kosmou*) as the "pagan" world (Luke 12:30). The *kosmos* in this sense is the world to which no true member of the people of God can belong.

However, in John this distinction does not occur. The explanation is that in this Gospel the Jews in their obduracy are equated with the *kosmos*, the evil world.

It is John who used *kosmos* in the most refined and theological way. It is the setting of the drama of redemption that is played out in the New Testament. God loves the world, (John 3:16), sends His Son to save the world (John 12:47). Jesus comes to the world as saviour (John 4:42), light (John 8:12), and life (John 6:33).

---

58. *Theological Wordbook of the New Testament*, s.v. "kosmos in the New Testament."

59. Ibid.

But *kosmos* meant more to John than just men. Since it was ruled by a certain prince who was not of the human race, world included a certain orientation, worldview, or mindset. To be dominated by Satan or his thinking made one "of the world." Being "of the world" may include being materialistic but it was much more. It was an orientation of life away from God and toward self. The disciples then at the same time were physically in the world (John 17:11) but were not a part of it. As a consequence the world (here its inhabitants both human and spiritual) hated them (John 15:18; 17:14). And the Christians looked forward to overcoming the world (I John 5:4-5). Thus Sasse could observe, "when the *kosmos* is redeemed, it ceases to be the *kosmos*."[60]

In summary the good news is to be taken to every person in the world who is alienated from God.

How can all this be summarized?

To make disciples is to bring men into a relationship with Christ as Master and the individual as an apprentice who is learning to reproduce the attitude and actions of Jesus in his own life which includes the ability of the disciples to make other disciples. A disciple, then, is not one who only learns some facts about the life of Jesus or one who believes in Him as the son of God.

The proclamation of the good news is the declaration of the events of the life of Jesus in a persuasive way so as to cause those who hear to accept Jesus as the Master of their lives. Inherent in evangelism is the concept that the messenger is sent and that the proclamation is not an end in itself but has the purpose in view of making disciples.

The messenger is a herald, who like the ancient Greek messenger, runs to relay the good news of victory, or announce the king's decrees. Such a messenger can never assume the responsibility on his own, he is one sent. And he has no message of his own but only that of his Master.

---

60. Ibid.

The essence of the gospel — the death, burial, and resurrection of Jesus Christ — is appropriated for one's own benefit in the surrender of both body and spirit in the act of Christian baptism. Baptism is not to be construed as a mechanical or magical act. It is effective only if it is accompanied by a changed life. Baptism then is the obedience of faith that results in the forgiveness of sin, the gift of the Holy Spirit, and entrance into the eternal kingdom of the Lord.

It is at this point teaching really begins. The disciple is to learn to obey all the things that Jesus taught. Learning means practicing the ethics of the kingdom and being obedient to the commission. Above all, it is emulating the attitude and actions of the Master.

This learning is critical to being a witness. The Twelve could testify about the things they saw and heard. All generations of disciples since then can only give the testimony found in the Scriptures.

Essential to the understanding of the commission is the fact that message was to be taken to the other peoples of the whole world. Specifically mentioned are those who are of people groups that are differentiated from those who are going. It is cross cultural evangelism.

The early missionaries, usually translated apostles, were sent either by Christ or the church. One may say that the Holy Spirit sends them through the church.

Twelve terms representing at least twelve concepts have been examined. From these ideas we arrive at the following definition of mission: Mission is the sending across cultural barriers by Christ through the church evangelists whose primary function is to make disciples of Jesus Christ by proclaiming the good news about Jesus. They require faith in Jesus as Lord, changed lives, and baptism of potential disciples. The disciples receive the promise of forgiveness of sin and entrance into the eternal kingdom. These disciples are to be taught the principles of the kingdom and in turn are to become evangelists, making other disciples.

INTRODUCTION

Let us simplify this definition further by classifying the terms we have studied. The twelve terms fall naturally in four categories:

To send
To make disciples
  The method
    Proclaim
    Evangelize
    Witness
  The condition
    Faith
    Repentance
    Baptism
  The benefits
    Forgiveness
    Gift of the Holy Spirit
To cross cultural barriers
  People groups
  World
To teach
  To observe all things
    Train new leaders
    Evangelize
    To meet human needs

A simple and workable definition of mission, using these four basic concepts, then, is:

(1) To send, (2) evangelists across cultural barriers, (3) to make disciples, (4) training them to reproduce themselves.

Kane summarizes more succinctly, "The missionary concept includes four ideas: the One who sends, the one who is sent, those to whom he is sent, and the message he is commanded to proclaim."⁶¹

George Peters' definition is similar,

> *Missions* is a specialized term. By it I mean the sending forth of authorized persons beyond the borders of the New Testament church and her immediate gospel influence to proclaim the gospel of Jesus Christ in gospel-destitute areas, to win converts from other faiths or non-faiths to Jesus Christ, and to establish functioning, multiplying local congregations who will bear the fruit of Christianity in that community and to that country.⁶²

McGavran's definition of mission is "an enterprise devoted to proclaiming the Good News of Jesus Christ, and to persuading men to become His disciples and dependable, reproductive members of His Church."⁶³

In what way is this different from evangelism?

There are three basic differences. Evangelism in the strict sense of the word refers to one phase of this process which is the persuasive presentation of the gospel with a view to lead men to become disciples of Christ. Two, evangelism does not necessarily imply the sending of evangelists for one may evangelize among one's own people without this sense of going. Three, it does not imply a cross-cultural ministry.

Three leading missiologists have defined missions/evangelism in contradictory ways.

McGavran⁶⁴ and Winter⁶⁵ define evangelism as the larger sphere that encompasses missions, (see chart, next page),

---

61. Kane, p. 149.

62. George W. Peters, *A Biblical Theology of Missions* (Chicago: Moody Press, 1972), p. 11.

63. McGavran, p. 34.

64. McGavran, Chapter Four.

65. Ralph D. Winter, "The Highest Priority: Cross-Cultural Evangelism," J.D. Douglas, ed., *Let the Earth Hear His Voice* (Minneapolis: World Wide Publications, 1975), pp. 213-225.

Peters,[66] on the other hand, defines missions as the larger sphere which encompasses evangelism.

66. Peters, p. 11-12.

I prefer to picture the two as separate but overlapping circles,

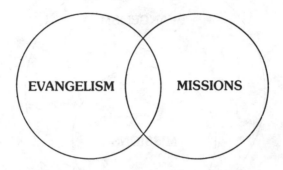

In current missiological studies the trend is to speak of mission in the singular, emphasizing the overall purpose of world evangelism.

What application does this definition have on the local level? It will revolutionize both the way we think and act in the mission program in the local churches.

It will mean rethinking and reworking our mission budgets.

If all twelve elements are not present in a program, that activity, no matter how worthwhile or Christian it may be, is not missions.

Softball league fees, carpet for the parsonage, church camps, Bible Colleges, retirement homes, and a host of other programs will need to be taken out of the missions budget and placed elsewhere in the church budget.

Now that we have a clear definition of missions, we may proceed to look at the contents of the whole Bible as a missionary book.

1

"IN THE BEGINNING . . ."

GENESIS 1-11

Missions does not begin with the Great Commission. Nor does it start with the inauguration of the Church on Pentecost. Although Paul and Barnabas may have been the first church-sent missionaries they did not launch the mission enterprise. It does not begin even with the birth of Jesus. Missions begins in the mind of God. Douglas Webster expresses our sentiment, "We begin, then, where missions begins, with God."[1] We believe, therefore, that the mind of God is revealed in the Scripture and that the concept of missions is found throughout the Bible.

Consequently, in this study we start our study in the first verse

---

1. Peters, p. 25.

of the Bible and pursue our examination to the last sentence.[2] This study, then, basically will follow the historical development of salvation history. The arrangement of the books of the Bible roughly follows this scheme making our study easier.

The first words are, "In the beginning God."

The Bible begins with God. And the first eleven chapters tell us a great deal about both God and man.

I. THE NATURE OF GOD

At least seven things are said about the nature of God that relate to missions:

1. He is the Creator.

We read that He created the universe, the world, and man. We are told of

the entire world . . . as a creation of God. This thought is so familiar that it no longer strikes us as being one of the most profound foundational principles of the doctrine of mission. And yet Genesis 1:1 is obviously the necessary basis of the great commission of Matthew 28:19-20.[3]

David writes,

The earth is the LORD's and everything in it, the world, and all who live in it; for he founded it upon the seas and established it upon the waters (Psa. 24:1-2).

---

2. Other authors begin elsewhere. Pentecost begins with Gen. 3:15. Edward C. Pentecost, *Issues in Missiology: An Introduction* (Grand Rapids: Baker Book House, 1982), p. 16. Stuhlmueller, influenced by source criticism, starts his study with Gen. 12:1-3. Donald Senior and Carroll Stuhlmueller, *The Biblical Foundations for Mission* (Maryknoll: Orbis Books, 1983), p. 9. Rowley begins with Moses, p. 11.

3. J.H. Bavinck, *An Introduction to the Science of Missions* (Grand Rapids: Baker Book House, 1960), p. 12.

However, to be a part of creation does not mean automatic access to God.

> Who may ascend the hill of the LORD?
> Who may stand in his holy place?
> He who has clean hands and a pure heart,
>   who does not lift up his soul to an idol
>   or swear by what is false (Psa. 24:3-4).

That God is Creator implies that He has jurisdiction over earth and its inhabitants. With that jurisdiction He begins to reveal Himself and His will to man.

> God commenced the disclosure of himself to his people as the sovereign Creator: loving, orderly and progressive in his activity, first in the universe and finally in man.[4]

Since the very first thing we learn about missions in the Bible is the authority of God as Creator, the question arises: "Did the early preachers use the creation as part of their persuasive preaching?"

The first time creation is mentioned in apostolic preaching is in Acts 17:24-31. Paul is speaking to the Athenians, who worshipped the gods of Greece, when he says, "The God who made the world and everything in it is the Lord of heaven and earth and does not live in temples made by hands."

Prior to this incident the New Testament preachers were either preaching to Jewish audiences, or to proselytes and god-fearers among the Gentiles. There is no record in Acts that reference to the creation was made in preaching to people with this background in Old Testament history.

Our conclusion is that the further the audience is from the knowledge of God revealed in the Hebrew Scriptures, the earlier in salvation history the preacher begins his message. For instance,

---

4. Arthur Glasser, *Theology of Mission I — Old Testament* (Pasadena: Fuller Theological Seminary, n.d.), p. 10.

the Jews had the Scriptures and believed in the coming of the Messiah. There was much common ground between Jews and Christians, but the Christians had little in common with the Gentile world and the one religious meeting ground was the common belief in the God of creation.

2. God is a person.

As a person God desired the fellowship of other persons.

"Then God said, 'Let us make man in our image, in our likeness . . .' " (Gen. 1:26).

James Weldon Johnson captures the spirit of this event when he writes, "And God stepped out into space, and said, 'I'm lonely, I'll make me a man.' "[5]

Later we are told,

> Then the man and his wife heard the sound of the LORD God as he was walking in the garden in the cool of the day, and they hid from the LORD God among the trees of the garden. But the LORD God called to the man "Where are you"? (Gen. 3:8-9).

The tense indicates that God's walking with man was a regular thing. On this occasion He is not just pursuing Adam and Eve because of their sin. Rather, God genuinely wants fellowship with man.

3. God has knowledge without sin.

"And the LORD God said, 'The man has now become like one of us, knowing good and evil' " (Gen. 3:22).

Man's acquisition of knowledge came through the sin of eating the forbidden fruit. God, on the other hand, by nature possessed this knowledge of right and wrong and neither sinned in its acquisition or as a consequence of its possession. God is without sin. This may seem obvious to the Christian. But many of the world's religions have made God in the image of man, warts and all.

---

5. James Weldon Johnson, "The Creation."

4. Therefore, God is holy.

Glasser said, "Nothing is so intolerable to the human race as God's holiness and nothing is so intolerable to God as human sinfulness."[6] Separation between God and man was the inevitable result of man's sin. The mission that follows is a prolonged and deliberate effort to remove the alienation and to reconcile man to God. Indeed, this is the theme of the entire Bible.

5. God hates sin.

It is sometimes said that God hates sin but loves the sinner. Whereas this is a beautiful sentiment it has little basis in the biblical record. The record in Genesis says the opposite: "the LORD God banished him from the Garden of Eden to work the ground" (3:23); "Now you are under a curse and driven from the ground" (4:11); "I will wipe mankind, whom I have created, from the face of the earth" (6:7); "I am going to put and end to all people . . . I will send rain on the earth for forty days and forty nights, and I will wipe from the face of the earth every living creature I have made" (6:11; 7:4).

With the strong emphasis on love and forgiveness in Christian theology God's wrath and anger are sometimes sublimated, ignored, or even denied. The significance of the wrath of God in the Old Testament can be seen in the fact that there are nine Hebrew words used for wrath.

> It is significant that the Bible does not use the false dichotomy of saying that his wrath was directed against man's sin whereas his love for sinners remained unchanged. He "hates all workers of iniquity" (Psa. 5:5).[7]

The concept of a God of wrath may need to be retained in missionary preaching. It is reported that in one culture the people

---

6. Arthur F. Glasser and Donald A. McGavran, *Contemporary Theologies of Mission* (Grand Rapids: Baker Book House, 1983), p. 39.
7. Glasser, p. 21.

believed in a God of high moral standards who punished the violators of the moral code. When the Christian missionaries came preaching a God of love and forgiveness the Anang people of Southeastern Nigeria accepted Christianity readily, but simultaneously they became very immoral in their behaviour. Their reasoning was, the Christian God would not punish them for their sin, but much preferred forgiving them.[8]

6. God is forgiving.

The foundation for the forgiveness of sin is laid on the occasion of the first sin. One phrase in the curse placed on the serpent holds out hope to all sinful men, "he will crush your head and you will strike his heel" (Gen. 3:15). This is clearly a prophecy of the crucifixion of Jesus. Satan in his attempt to destroy the Son of God will succeed in getting Him executed. But the death of Jesus will not be permanently fatal. It is rather like a wound to the heel from which He will recover. On the other hand, in the victory over death achieved in the resurrection, Jesus delivers a fatal blow, a blow to the head of Satan. Satan is not yet dead but is writhing from the agony of the death blow until the time that he is cast into the lake of burning sulphur (Rev. 20:7-10).

This prophecy, brief as it is, holds out at least three reasons for hope for man: 1) God has made provision for the forgiveness of sin through the sacrifice of His Son (Rom. 3:21-26). 2) God has made provision for victory over death through the resurrection (I Cor. 15:12-28). 3) God has made provision for man to live in the new Jerusalem (Rev. 21:1-4).

7. God is Faithful.

Johannes Blauw observed,

On the other hand — and this is even more important for the Biblical understanding of man in his religion — God does not give

---

8. John C. Messenger, Jr., "The Christian Concept of Forgiveness and Anang Morality," Smalley, William A., *Readings in Missionary Anthropology* (Pasadena: William Carey Library, 1974), pp. 180-186.

up His claim upon man. He, unlike man, is not unfaithful. Man remains for him the image of God and His creature. In other words, man's view of God may have changed, but God's view of man does not change. When man gives up service, God does not give up man as his servant. When man no longer considers himself a creature, God nevertheless treats him as His creature. When man hides himself from the presence of the Lord, God does not hide Himself from the presence of man.[9]

II. THE NATURE OF MAN

There can be no adequate theology of missions without a biblical understanding of the nature of man. The creation account in Genesis gives us a substantial beginning for developing a theology of man. Arthur Glasser has written:

The Creation account does not provide us with a comprehensive answer to the mystery of man's nature, but his significance is clearly underscored. He was created in the image and likeness of God (Gen. 1:26,27; 2:8,15,18-25). Although constituted with all other creatures as completely dependent upon his Creator, he also uniquely bears God's image and reflects his glory and majesty. Man is revealed as a psycho-physical organism, not a soul incarnated in a body.[10]

1. Man is made in the image of God (Gen. 1:26-27).
What does it mean to be in the "image of God?" Leslie Newbigin offers a helpful explanation.[11] He states that there are two kinds of images. First, there is the kind of image that is inherent in an ob-

---

9. Johannes Blauw, "The Biblical View of Man in His Religion," Gerald Anderson, ed., *The Theology of Christian Mission*, (New York: McGraw-Hill Book Company, Inc., 1961) pp. 33-34.
10. Glasser, p. 7.
11. Leslie Newbigin, *Sin and Salvation* (Naperville: SCM Book Club, 1956), pp. 16-18.

ject. For instance, the image of a king on a coin is imbedded in the coin. Or, in the animal world, a dog's dogginess is in itself.

Second, there is the kind of image that depends upon a relationship. For example, a near perfect image of the moon can be seen reflected on the surface of a smooth lake. But a slight wind or the passing of a boat can send waves that distort the image of the moon on the water.

Man's image of God, like the image of the moon on the water, depends on a relationship. Man reflects a perfect image only as he is in a perfect relationship with his Creator. But sin has distorted that image. It is important to note that it is distorted, not destroyed. Johannes Blauw said it this way, "Man's humanity *is* his relationship to God."[12]

2. Man is a spiritual being.

Man is capable of knowing God. To put it another way, the essence of man is that he is incurably religious. Augustine said, "Man is restless until he finds his rest in God." Or, as another put it, each man has a "God-shaped vacuum within."

Incidentally, whereas the evolutionary theory of man's origin may offer a possible explanation of the appearance of man's physical body on earth, it gives no satisfactory explanation for the spiritual dimension. There is no observable spiritual nature in other animals. And there is no demonstrable evolution from physical to spiritual qualities.

3. Man is to reproduce (Gen. 1:28).

"Be fruitful and increase." This is the one command that man has had little difficulty obeying. In fact in July 1987 the population of the world reached five billion people.

There are areas that some say are ovepopulated because the locale cannot support so many people in a healthy manner. Perhaps it is not so much a matter of overpopulation as of underproduction. Or, more accurately, inadequate distribution, for the whole world is still producing more food than it consumes.

---

12. Ibid., p. 32.

The growth of the human population has created a whole new set of ethical situations in the last half of the Twentieth Century that will continue into the first half of the Twenty-first. All of these impact on the mission of the church in these areas:

Quality of life. The larger the number of people, the less space, water, food, and material possessions are available for each. All people, Christian and non-Christian alike, are having to decide whether they are going to have fewer children with the hope each has a better quality of life.

Family planning. Because so few children grew to adulthood in the past, parents wanted several children so that at least a few of them would live long enough to take care of the parents in their old age. This practice is still the "Social Security" system in much of the Third World. But as missionaries bring better health care and, consequently, greater longevity, many parents are asking, "is it possible to limit the number of children we have?" So, for the first time, family planning has become an acceptable option to them.

Abortion. Although for centuries a few people have practiced abortion, the combination of modern medical technology, new laws, and the desire for limited or childless families has made abortion an ethical issue.

"Be fruitful and increase" is still a part of the divine mandate, but it has implications for missions today that were undreamed of even a generation ago.

4. Man is to rule the world.

> God blessed them and said to them, "Be *fruitful* and increase in number; fill the earth and *subdue* it. *Rule* over the fish of the sea and the birds of the air and over *every* living creature that moves on the ground" (Gen. 1:28, emphasis mine).

The Lord deliberately connects reproduction and ruling. It is a shocking statement to a person with a puritanical worldview. A moment's reflection provides a sensible explanation. Two individuals could hardly be expected to rule the whole earth with its myriads of animal inhabitants. Further, when human death entered the world, a new generation of men would be needed to carry on the work of the preceding one. Man has had little difficulty in obeying the first part of the command, to reproduce, but he has had great difficulty mastering the second, to rule.

What does it mean to "subdue," to "rule"?

> Subdue, the new word in the account of man's dominion, is *khabash*, and it differs from "have dominion" (rule) (*radhah*) in that its root rather implies "to knead" or "to tread," whereas the latter is the stronger according to parallel roots, meaning "to stamp down." Yet this difference is not to be pressed.[13]

The world to be ruled is to include the earth as well as the animals.[14] When we are tempted to think solely in otherworldly terms, and to consider our mission to be strictly of a spiritual nature, it is helpful to remember that the Lord's prayer, which includes, "thy kingdom come" also petitions for "our daily bread." We dare not become so heavenly minded that we are of no earthly use.

Given man's propensity to selfishness the attempt to rule the earth has frequently degenerated into controlling the world for one's own ends. However,

> "Subdue the earth" does *not* mean: "Create a rich, productive culture, create social perfection, transform unruly nature with your technology into the dwelling of civilization." . . . it means this instead: "When you put your stamp on creation, see to it that your human life and your culture do not become a sign of your

---

13. H.C. Leupold, *Exposition of Genesis* (Grand Rapids: Baker Book House, 1950), p. 95.

14. Keil and Delitzsch, *Old Testament Commentaries*, vol. 1: *Genesis to Judges 6:32* (Grand Rapids: Associated Publishers and Authors, n.c., n.d.), 1:50.

eternal restlessness and your blind titanism, but rather a thanksgiving and a response to him who gave you this earth."[15]

Thielicke puts our rule in perspective, and at the same time puts us in our place: "For, after all, we are not to rule and subdue the earth because we stand *above* the other creatures, but only because we stand *under* God and are privileged to be his viceroys."[16] Or, as D.T. Niles wrote, "Man is free to dress and keep and multiply and rule over what God has committed to him, but he is not free to decide by himself what is good and what is evil either for himself or for the world."[17]

The mandate to subdue, to rule, is clear. The question each Christian, and especially each missionary, must answer is, is this mandate included in the missionary mandate? Does "discipling the nations" include development? Does it mean teaching literacy, providing schools, promoting health, drilling wells, teaching agriculture and animal husbandry, and changing political systems?

The debate has been a long one. However, it came into sharp focus in the first half of this century as those who were known as theological liberals began practicing the social gospel only. The evangelicals reacted by saying, "our only task is to preach the gospel." During the last half of the Twentieth Century the pendulum, for the evangelicals, has swung back toward the middle. They have said, "we must treat the whole man, body and spirit." And so the cultural mandate of Genesis has entered the missionary mandate of Jesus. Many Christians perceive they are to rule this world as well as to prepare for the next.

Several economic issues are involved in this cultural mandate: *Technology.* The technology to "make the desert bloom" is

---

15. Helmut Thielicke, *How the World Began*, trans. by John W. Doberstein, (Philadelphia: Muhlenberg Press, 1961), p. 110.

16. Ibid., p. 67.

17. D.T. Niles, *Studies in Genesis*, (Philadelphia: The Westminster Press, 1958), p. 59.

available today. The problem is that this agricultural technology is mostly limited to those countries of the world that have highly developed technological societies. Can and should these technologies be transmitted to the people who are controlled by, rather than control, their environment? Much of the debate in mission has shifted from preaching the gospel versus the social gospel, to how much and what kind of human services will the evangelistic missionary render.

Distribution. Presently the world has enough material things for everyone. The problem is distribution. Some areas have more than enough. Many have too little. Few question that redistribution should take place. The issues are how, to what extent, at what cost?

Knowledge. It was once said that if you gave a man a fish he could eat for a day, but if you taught him to fish he could feed himself. It is now recognized that in time he will run out of fish, and we need to go a step further today and teach him to raise fish.

There are several religious issues:

Taboos. Virtually every society has religious taboos against eating certain foods. Perhaps best known is the Hindu refusal to eat beef, which exists in abundance in India. In other places pregnant mothers are forbidden to eat the very kind of food they need to produce healthy babies.

Spirits. The lives of animists the world over are controlled by their belief in spirits. For instance, the tribal people in Thailand will not plant a crop until approval is given by the spirits.

5. Man is a social being.

In Genesis 5:2 we read, "He created them male and female; at the time they were created, he blessed them and called them 'man.' "

This is an interesting play on words. Earlier in the text (Gen. 1:7) God had formed man (Heb. *adam*). This word also became his name (2:20; 3:17,20; 4:1; 5:1,3-5). But as the account of the creation of man is recounted at the beginning of the story of the flood Adam and Eve together were called "man" (Heb. *adam*). The implication, stated specifically in 2:18) ("it is not good for the man to be alone"), is that man is a social being and is not really complete as an isolated individual. His nature requires him to have social intercourse in order to be a whole man.

6. Man has a choice.

"And the LORD God commanded the man, 'You are free to eat from any tree in the garden; but you must not eat from the tree of the knowledge of good and evil, for when you eat of it you will surely die' " (Gen. 2:16-17).

Man was free to choose to sin. And in spite of commands, warnings, and possible punishment man did choose to disobey God.

Later in the Scriptures we will encounter the word, "predestination." As we seek to understand and define the concept of predestination, it must not exclude the fact that man is always free to choose between right and wrong. Whatever else it may mean it does not mean that the privilege of choice is taken from man.

7. Man was innocent, albeit only briefly.

"The man and his wife were both naked, and they felt no shame" (Gen. 2:25).

God made man pure. Every part of the human being — thoughts, body, sexuality, attitudes, motives, behavior — was free from sin. The only place we can see this pristine innocence today is in a new born baby.

8. Man is a sinner.

". . . she took some and ate it. She also gave some to her husband, who was with her, and he ate it" (Gen. 3:6).

It may appear to be a paradox that man is both innocent and a sinner. This may be explained by the fact that the Bible is an historical narrative and reading it may be compared to watching a movie. The movie may be stopped at any time on a single frame which will produce one event frozen in time. But the whole story can only be grasped as all the frames are viewed, and seen in the proper sequence. In Genesis 3 man is innocent in one frame and a sinner in the next.

This sin which alienated man from God also separated man from other men.

This separation is first of all personal.

> Cain said to the LORD, 'My punishment is more than I can bear. Today you are driving me from the land, and I will be hidden from your presence; I will be a restless wanderer on the earth . . . ' (Gen. 4:13-14).

Cain's guilt, resulting from his offering an unacceptable offering, created such a chasm between him and his brother that he was able to murder Abel. And the consequence of that sin separated him from the rest of his family.

Each sin causes a separation between the sinner and the one sinned against. Each of us has experienced that estrangement when we have wronged someone, or have been wronged. Only a forgiveness that really erases the sin will allow a return to a friendship and fellowship that can resume as if nothing had ever happened.

Separation resulting from sin can result in division into clans, languages, and nations. During the attempt to build "a tower that reaches to the heavens" the Lord said, "Come, let us go down and confuse their language so they will not understand each other" (Gen. 11:7).

III. THE NATURE OF SIN.

The primal paradise was characterized by *beauty, utility,* and the *moral test* (the "trees"). God's probation of innocent, free man was the provision of an alternative to discipleship. Would man choose to remain in the face-to-face relation with God as his vice-regent over the earth or would he choose a separate existence, to be "self-made" wrestling his knowledge, satisfactions and values

66

from the created world in defiance of the Creator? Man chose this later alternative.[18]

This choice is called sin.
1. The essence of sin.
Sin is disobedience.

The woman said to the serpent, "We may eat fruit from the trees in the garden, but God did say, 'You must not eat fruit from the tree that is in the middle of the garden, and you must not touch it, or you will die' " (Gen. 3:3).

But they disobeyed this command of God.
The next recorded sin is the sacrifice of Cain. It is a little more difficult to understand.

Now Abel kept flocks, and Cain worked the soil. In the course of time Cain brought some of the fruits of the soil as an offering to the LORD. But Abel brought fat portions from some of the firstborn of his flock. The LORD looked with favor on Abel and his offering, but on Cain and his offering he did not look with favor (Gen. 4:2-5).

Why was Abel's offering acceptable and Cain's not? The answer is given in Heb. 11.4, "By faith Abel offered God a better sacrifice than Cain did." But how did Abel achieve this faith? Paul explains, "faith comes from hearing the message, and the message is heard through the word of Christ" (Rom. 10:17). We can only conclude that God spoke to Cain and Abel, giving them instructions about the offering. Abel believed and obeyed. Cain did not. Again, disobedience is seen as the essence of sin.
But what were the directions that Cain disobeyed? There are two possibilities.
One, Abel brought "fat portions" of the "firstborn" of his flock

---

18. Glasser, p. 17.

whereas Cain only brought "some of the fruits." This can be understood as Abel bringing the best whereas Cain did not.

Two, Abel's sacrifice required the shedding of blood whereas Cain's grain offering did not.

2. The Consequences of Sin.

a. Man has a sense of guilt. "I heard you in the garden, and I was afraid because I was naked; so I hid" (Gen. 3:10).

b. Man has pain. "I will greatly increase your pains in childbearing; with pain you will give birth to children" (Gen. 3:16).

c. Man will be in submission to another. "Your desire will be for your husband and he will rule over you" (Gen. 3:16). Although the reference is first to a wife's submission to her husband it is also evident that the ultimate consequence is that each man is subservient to another.

d. Man is required to labor.

Cursed is the ground because of you; through painful toil you will eat of it all the days of your life. It will produce thorns and thistles for you, and you will eat the plants of the field. By the sweat of your brow you will eat your food until you return to the ground, since from it you were taken; for dust you are and to dust you will return (Gen. 3:17-19).

e. Man's length of life is limited. "For he is mortal; his days will be a hundred and twenty years" (Gen. 6:3).

f. Man will die.

For dust you are and to dust you will return. . . . And the LORD God said . . . He must not be allowed to reach out his hand and take also from the tree of life and eat, and live forever (Gen. 3:19,22).

Paul tells us that this death will come to all men, "just as sin entered the world through one man, and death through sin, and in this way death came to all men, because all have sinned"

(Rom. 5:12).

g. Man is out of intimate fellowship with God.

So the LORD God banished him from the Garden of Eden to work the ground from which he had been taken. After he drove the man out, he placed on the east side of the Garden of Eden cherubim and a flaming sword flashing back and forth to guard the way to the tree of life (Gen. 3:23-24).

3. Sin is virulent.

Like a rapidly spreading malignancy one sin begets another. Cain's bloodless sacrifice led to the shedding of Abel's blood.

And as man continued his journey his sin intensified. "The LORD saw how great man's wickedness on the earth had become, and that every inclination of the thoughts of his heart was only evil all the time" (Gen. 6:5).

Glasser commenting on the building of the tower of Babel writes,

His [man's] determination to build the tower points up his arrogance and his pathos: he strives for the impossible ("its top in the heavens"). Only man's sins will ever reach as "high as heaven" (Rev. 18:5).[19]

4. Sin does not mean total depravity.

Calvinism teaches that man is totally and hereditarily depraved as a result of the original sin. However, this view is impossible to document from the Scriptures. Sinful man is still capable of doing good, of obeying God's commands. As it is sometimes stated, "the cultural mandate was not abrogated." That is, the commands given to Adam and Eve are still in effect, and man is still capable of obeying them.

We can see that man retains his ability to provide food for himself and his family, to rule the world, to be faithful in marriage,

19. Ibid., p. 26.

t be creative, to administer justice, and to be forgiving. Paul even tells us that it is possible for "Gentiles, who do not have the law, [to] do by nature things required by the law" (Rom. 2:14).

5. Sin is a failure.

George Peters has an interesting insight about the failure of sin to accomplish its purpose,

> It is my conviction that the fall, though horrible in its historical and eternal consequences, was a disappointment for Satan. It had not accomplished all that the fall was intended to accomplish. Man had remained man and, as such, a salvable creature. The depth of the fall had not reached the core of the human being. It did not obliterate the image of God.[20]

IV. THE NATURE OF REVELATION

Revelation is communication from God. The normal form of this revelation is verbal. Frequently the text says, "And God said. . . ."

Fortunately, many of these communications from the Almighty have been written for our benefit. Paul tells us that "All Scripture is God-breathed and is useful for teaching, rebuking, correcting and training in righteousness, so that the man of God may be thoroughly equipped for every good work" (II Tim. 3:16-17).

We may speak of our search for God. But we will never find Him through our searching. As Harold Lindsell has said, "God is only to be found as he reveals himself."[21]

---

20. Peters, p. 78.
21. Harold Lindsell, *An Evangelical Theology of Missions* (Grand Rapids: Zondervan Publishing House, 1970), p. 45.

V. THE NATURE OF SALVATION

The first eleven chapters of Genesis do not give us the complete solution to sin. But they do give suggestions as to the nature of the salvation ultimately to be revealed.

1. The Promised Messiah.

The enigmatic and metonymic prophecy of Gen. 3:15 reads, "he will crush your head, and you will strike his heel." The picture is of conflict between Satan and the Messiah in the battle of the cross and the tomb.

In nailing Jesus to the cross it appeared that Satan had won the fight. The Son of God was dead and buried. "Right was on the scaffold and wrong on the throne." But the finality and permanence of the death of Jesus was in appearance only. The blow was only to the heel, not a fatal blow to the head. He was injured grievously, and suffered as much as any man who has died from crucifixion. Three days later, however, the hand of God reached into the tomb and raised Jesus from the dead. A fatal blow was delivered to Satan's head in the process. Although Satan is not yet dead he is writhing in his death pains from the blow of the resurrection of Christ. Someone has said, "Satan is alive and well." He may be alive, but he is not well. While it may appear the forces of righteousness are on the run, the decisive battle at Golgotha and the Garden assure us that Satan has been defeated and Christ is the victor.

John tells us, "The kingdom of the world has become the kingdom of our Lord and his Christ, and he will reign for ever and ever" (Rev. 11:15).

2. The Prefigured Messianic Community.

Noah was to build an ark. Specific directions were given for the construction of this giant boat. Only certain men and animals were to be taken on board (Gen. 6:14-7:24).

Christians have seen the ark as a type of the church — the divine institution of the New Testament that God is using to rescue His people from sin.

71

Peter has an interesting statement,

> in it (the ark) only a few people, eight in all, were saved through water, and this water symbolizes baptism that now saves you also — not the removal of dirt from the body but the pledge of a good conscience toward God (I Pet. 3:20-21).

3. The Sacrifice of the Messiah.
After the flood

> Noah built an altar to the LORD and, taking some of all the clean animals and clean birds, he sacrificed burnt offerings on it. The LORD smelled the pleasing aroma and said in his heart: "Never again will I curse the ground because of man, even though every inclination of his heart is evil from childhood. And never again will I destroy all living creatures, as I have done" (Gen. 8:20-21).

The principle of sacrifice is stated, "For the life of the creature is in the blood, and I have given it to you to make atonement for yourselves on the altar; it is the blood that makes atonement for one's life" (Lev. 17:11).

The life lost through sin was regained through the sacrifice of life (blood). Thus although certain grain and liquid *offerings* are specified, the *sacrifice* for sin was an animal sacrifice.

The fact that these sacrifices were repeated in large numbers indicates the lack of efficacy of animal sacrifices for human sin. This fact is specifically stated in the New Testament:

> The law . . . can never, by the same sacrifices repeated endlessly year after year, make perfect those who draw near to worship. If it could, would they not have stopped being offered? For the worshipers would have been cleansed once for all, and would no longer have felt guilty for their sins. But those sacrifices are an annual reminder of sins, because it is impossible for the blood of bulls and goats to take away sins (Heb. 10:1-4).

The perfect sacrifice awaits the coming of the Lamb of God.

3. The Covenant of the Messiah.

A covenant is an agreement. As used in the Bible it refers to an agreement between God and man. The first such covenant is announced after the flood and anticipates a series of covenants that will be made later.

> Then God said to Noah and to his sons with him: "I now establish my covenant with you and with your descendants after you. . . . Never again will all life be cut off by the waters of a flood; never again will there be a flood to destroy the earth" (Gen. 9:8,11).

This covenant is unilateral. It is made by God without man's participation. And there are no conditions. God promises unconditionally that He will not again destroy man with a flood. In this aspect the first covenant is unique. All later covenants are dependent upon man's observance of the conditions.

4. The Universal Messiah.

From the beginning salvation is regarded as universal, that is, it is for all men.

Three times the Scriptures make promises to Noah "and his sons" (Gen. 9). Since all men presently on earth descended from one of these sons the promise of deliverance is to all men.

In Gen. 9:27 Noah prophesied, "May God extend the territory of Japheth; may Japheth live in the tents of Shem." Japheth was the ancestor of the Philistines and Phoenicians. And it is conjectured that he was the progenitor of the Indo-European nations.

> Whereas the Old Testament is silent about Japhethites actually dwelling in Shem's tents, the New Testament repeatedly predicts a vast ingathering of Gentiles through the Gospel (Matthew 8:11; Ephesians 3:6; Revelation 5:9,10).[22]

Universalism may be the most neglected concept by the

---

22. Glasser, p. 26.

people of God. As we shall soon see, Israel, though her prophets, spoke often about the acceptability of the Gentiles (*goyim*) but rarely invited them into fellowship with God. And the controversy in the early church about accepting Gentile believers without circumcision would have never arisen if the Judaizers had grasped this universalism taught in Genesis.

Since the ouster from the Garden man has resisted universalism. One purpose in erecting the tower of Babel was "to make a name for ourselves" (Gen. 11:4). This was a kind of corporate selfishness that would prevent them from being "scattered over the face of the whole earth" (Gen. 11:4), and, at the same time, keep them uncontaminated by contact with other people.

This tendency exists today in nations that assume a hostile approach toward other nations, in cultures that assume an attitude of superiority over other cultures, and in churches that are ambitious for growth and prestige of their own congregation at the expense of a dynamic program of cross-cultural evangelism.

5. The Messianic Remnant.

Only eight people were saved in the ark. The rest of the world's population was destroyed. Although God does not wish that any be destroyed (II Pet. 3:9) the fact remains that the majority of men choose to lead a life that leads to destruction. And God throughout history has chosen a remnant, sometimes one person, or one family, through whom His purpose can be achieved.

SUMMARY

In the beginning chapters of Genesis we have found the foundation for Christian mission in the nature of God. We have seen God as the Creator who desires the fellowship of man. Although He condemns sin and man who sins, He is forgiving and has made arrangements to forgive man. Further, communication with Him is possible because He is a living, loving being.

Missions is necessary because man who was made in the image of God has distorted that image with sin. Although he has asserted his independence he still needs fellowship with God. His responsibilities include ruling the world, reproduction, and making choices.

The nature of sin includes disobedience as the essence of sin, the consequences of sin, and its virulent but not totally depraved nature.

The nature of Revelation is that God communicates with man though verbal messages recorded in the Bible.

The nature of salvation is portrayed in its seminal form in the first eleven chapters of Genesis. These components of salvation include the promised Mesiah, the figure of the ark as the type of the church, the blood sacrifices that anticipate the crucifixion of Christ, the covenants of God preparing for the ultimate promise of salvation to be given to all men.

In a sentence, God who cares for His creatures has provided for the forgiveness of sin which has separated mankind from God through the sacrifice of Christ which is to be proclaimed as the good news to all people.

"The rest of the Bible unfolds the manner in which God, while not condoning man's rebellious pride nor leaving man's sin unpunished, will seek the objective he had in view for man from the beginning.[23]

> I fled Him, down the nights and down the days;
>   I fled Him, down the arches of the years;
> I fled Him, down the labyrinthine ways
>   Of my own mind; and in the midst of tears
> I hid from Him, and under running laughter.
>   Up vistaed hopes I sped;
>   And shot, precipitated
> Adown Titanic glooms of chasmed fears,
>   From those strong Feet that followed, followed after.

---

23. Ibid., p. 18.

. . . .
    Halts by me that footfall:
    Is my gloom, after all,
  Shade of His hand, otstretched caressingly?
    "Ah, fondest, blindest, weakest,
    I am He Whom thou seekest!
Thou dravest love from thee, who dravest Me."[24]

24. Francis Thompson, "The Hound of Heaven," in Nella Bradley, ed., *The Standard Book of British and American Verse* (New York: Garden City Publishing Co., 1932), pp. 661-65.

2

PROMISE TO THE PATRIARCHS

GENESIS 12-50

The background of missions involving the nature of God, the nature of man, the nature of sin, and the nature of salvation has now been laid.

Preparation must be made for the coming of the Savior. From all the people of the world God must choose one person through whose line the Savior can come. He must prepare a people to take the message of redemption and reconciliation to alienated mankind. Beginning in Genesis 12 we see the specific actions of God to prepare the way for the sending of the Savior and the redemption of the entire world.

The promise of salvation to all nations was first made to Abraham.

I. ABRAHAM

Abraham is important to the biblical writers. Fourteen of the fifty chapters of Genesis are devoted to him. The New Testament authors refer to him more than to any other person in the Old Testament. The writer of Hebrews gives him more space than to any other in the Hall of Men of Faith.

1. Abraham was called.

"The LORD has said to Abram . . ." (Gen. 12:1). He didn't receive an invitation from the Canaanites to come to their land. He was not given an eviction notice by his neighbors in Ur. He did not even have a vision of what he could accomplish if he went west. God directed him to go.

His call, then, did not come from without. It did not come from within. It came from above. This was a divine mission. Later, in the New Testament apostles, we shall see a similar pattern.

Abraham was an historical person with an ancestry rooted in history (Gen. 10). As Gerhard von Rad has noted, there is no mythology attached to his primal history. He was born into a secular world, and the "future experience of God will be in the realm of secular history and, indeed according to Genesis 10, *in the realm of universal secular history.*"[1] This is not to say that Abraham and Israel did not have religious faith and ceremony but that the faith of the Old Testament was acted out in life on this earth.

2. Why Abraham?

It was not because he was the only man who worshipped the one true God. In fact he did not worship the true God at all (Josh. 24:2-3)!

It was not because he was in the right place, because he had

---

1. Gerhard von Rad, *Old Testament Theology*, 2 vols. (New York: Harper and Row, 1965), 2:342. Emphasis added, quoted in Stuhlmueller, p. 11.

to move when he accepted God's call.

It was not because he was an Israelite. There were no Israelites yet. In fact, he had the same genealogical chart as everyone else, which led back to Adam.

The rabbis pondered this same question. They considered him the first proselyte.[2] We are told by Eichhorn that Deut. 26:5 is quoted twice yearly in the synagogues today to remind the congregation that Abraham was not born an Israelite.[3]

Even the word "Hebrew" is not a proper name for a specific people, but a generic word for a resident alien, immigrant, refugee, uprooted person, or displaced person.[4]

Given the subsequent misbehavior of Abraham in accepting Hagar to produce an heir, and his passing off Sarah as his sister on two occasions, we may question God's judgment in selecting Abraham. Or, later, we may even wonder at his wisdom in choosing Israel. We are tempted to agree with Hillare Belloc's couplet,

> How odd of God
> To choose the Jews.

But when we turn to the New Testament we find an explanation. The choice is not as arbitrary as it first appears: "By faith Abraham, when called to go to a place he would later receive as his inheritance, obeyed and went, even though he did not know where he was going" (Heb. 11:8). The one quality Abraham possessed, according to the record, was faith. But we must note that this faith was not an abstract quality that he had before God

---

2. Richard R. DeRidder, *The Dispersion of the People of God*, (Kampen: J.H. Kok, Co., 1971), p. 24.

3. D.M. Eichhorn, *Conversion to Judaism*, p. 14; quoted in DeRidder, ibid.

4. Julius Lewy, "Origin and Significance of the Biblical term 'Hebrew,' " HUCA, XXIV (1957), pp. 1-13, quoted in DeRidder, ibid.

spoke to him. It was a faith "that came by hearing the word of God." It was when God called him that he believed and obeyed the message from God.

3. Abraham is called for a purpose.

"And all peoples on earth will be blessed through you" (Gen. 12:3). The promise to Abraham was universal — it was to embrace every human being. Abraham was to be blessed, but the whole purpose in the blessing was to bless others. Abraham was to be the beginning of a new people (goy), and the reason was so that through this one people all peoples could be blessed. God chose a particular people. But they were not to be exclusivistic. Although they were forbidden to intermarry with other races, and commanded to exterminate entire people groups, the ultimate goal was to include all peoples into the people of God.

Abraham was to be blessed by God. But that blessing was not primarily for Abraham's benefit. The benefits of a covenant relation to God were to be passed on to all the peoples of the earth. When Israel kept these benefits exclusively and selfishly for themselves, they fell short of God's purpose, and, as a consequence, became a sinful people.

Knofel Staton has correctly identified the paired concepts: privilege and purpose.[5] When the people of God are given a privilege it is always for a specific purpose: they have the responsibility to give the benefits to others.

4. Abraham is called to establish a people.

The rest of the Old Testament is the story of these people. They were to serve three important purposes in the evangelization of the world.

One, they were the people through whom Jesus, the Messiah, was to come. Matthew and Luke, recognizing the importance of this line, trace the genealogy of Jesus in the opening paragraphs of their gospels.

---

5. In an address given at the National Missionary Convention, Phoenix, Ariz., September, 1984.

Two, they were to provide the initial evangelists who were to take the message to the world. Not only were all the Apostles of Christ Jews, but virtually all the members of the church for the first decade were Jewish.

Three, they provided a bridge to the Gentile population. The Jews were scattered throughout the world of the First Century. Every city had a large Jewish enclave. The high ethical standards of their religion attracted many Gentiles who had become disenchanted with the pagan gods. As a consequence there were many proselytes and god-fearers attached to the synagogues.

Paul, the apostle to the Gentiles, incorporates this fact into his strategy of missions. He goes to the cities where there are concentrations of Jews, and consequently where there are synagogues. Although the Jews generally rejected his message of the resurrection, the converts he made from among the proselytes and god-fearers opened the door to the rest of the Gentile community. Thus, by the second generation of Christians, the church is composed principally of non-Jews.

5. Abraham is called to go to a place.

Why was he not allowed to remain in Ur, or even Haran? Why could not the Mesopotamian valley be the promised land? Why was he not permitted to establish his new family in familiar surroundings?

I am tempted to say that it is necessary for a person to go to another place, live in another culture, and to learn another language, in order to be a missionary. Consequently, it was necessary for Abraham, the father of missionaries, to cross a cultural barrier. However, there is another, eschatological, reason. It is not explicitly given in the Scriptures, but it can be induced from history.

The promised Savior and the promised land needed to be within the Roman Empire. Paul gave us a hint, "but when *the time had fully come*, God sent his Son, born of a woman, born under law, that we might receive the full rights of sons" (Gal. 4:4 emphasis mine).

81

What does it mean, when the time had fully come?" Time has to do with history: therefore, the time was historically ripe. Many factors had merged at the beginning of the First Century making it the right time to launch a new, world-wide, religion.

The *Pax Romana* provided an unprecedented period, uninterrupted by wars, that allowed the Christian missionaries to travel, unhindered, anywhere in the known world spreading their message. The Greek language, "regarded by some as the richest and most delicate the world has ever seen,"[6] had become the *lingua franca* of the world. This gave the missionaries two advantages. One, the concepts of Christianity could be stated in a precise way. Two, only one language had to be learned to preach anywhere in the world. The Roman government had built a network of paved roads throughout the empire. They did it so as to dispatch the army quickly to any trouble spot. But it also facilitated travel for the civilian missionary. The ubiquitous presence of the Roman army assured safe travel anywhere for the missionaries. Kane feels,

> [t]he dispersion of the Jewish people was the greatest single factor in preparing the world for the coming of the Messiah and the preaching of the gospel. . . . In A.D. 70 Strabo reported: "It is hard to find a single place on the habitable earth that has not admitted this tribe of men, and is not possessed by it."[7]

6. Abraham went.

Abram was a wealthy man. No doubt he had a pleasant position and a comfortable home in Ur. Travel was not easy in the Twentieth Century. To make matters worse he would have to cross the semi-desert Middle East. To complicate the matter further, he did not know his direction and did not have a road map. He had every excuse in the world not to go.

---

6. J. Herbert Kane, *A Global View of Christian Missions from Pentecost to the Present*. (Grand Rapids: Baker Book House, 1975), p. 4.
7. Ibid.

But Abraham went.

Someone has said that Moses was the first missionary. May I propose Abraham for that exalted position. He has the qualifications: God sent him, his purpose was to bless the nations, and he had to cross cultural barriers.

7. Abraham had to obey.

Abraham and Sarah were growing old and there seemed to be no possibility that God was going to keep His promise to make Abraham's descendants as innumerable as the stars of the heavens or the sands of the seas. He did not even have one child, much less the promised myriads.

Sarah meant well, but her suggestion for Abraham to have a child by Hagar was one of the most harmful made in the history of mankind. Ishmael's descendants became the constant enemies of Israel. The new religion, Islam, inaugurated by one of them, has also been the nemesis of the church. The Muslim armies sweeping across north Africa virtually eliminated Christianity where once it was strong.

Today one of the battlefields between Islam and Christianity is along the Sahel in Africa. In the past Christianity advanced northward, and the Muslim religion southward, toward the Sahel. Someone has observed that these religions were halted by the advance of the tsetse fly and the British government. Supposedly, the Arabs rode horses and moved southward until they came to a region infested with tsetse flies, which transmitted diseases that killed the horses and effectively stopped the advance of Islam. On the other hand, the British government, which controlled most of the land on the southern edge of the Sahel, did not want armed conflict between the Muslims and Christians, so forbade the missionaries to go any further north. Today, missionaries from both religions are going to the unreached animists in the region. It is apparent that the religion that is able to field the greatest number of effective missionaries will probably win the region's population to their respective cause.

If there is a lesson here, it is, to paraphrase Samuel, "obedience is better than innovation."

II. THE OTHER PATRIARCHS

The Bible frequently lumps together the three great patriarchs, Abraham, Isaac, and Jacob. However from a mission
viewpoint there is only one great patriarch, Abraham. Little is said
about the others that advances our understanding of God's purpose in the world. Consequently, we will examine only briefly the
life and lessons of the remainder of the patriarchs.

1. Isaac

Isaac, compared to the towering Abraham, the complex
Jacob, and the noble Joseph, is considered a weak character.[8]
Nevertheless the promise made to Abraham is renewed with
Isaac. A famine came on the land in the time of Isaac. He was
tempted to leave the promised land for Egypt. But the Lord asked
him to remain whereupon He reiterated the promise made to
Abraham (Gen. 26:1-6). Because of his miraculous birth, his only son status, his divinely given name, his persecution, and his
presentation as a sacrifice, he is considered to be a type of Christ.[9]

Further, Isaac's blessings of Jacob contain refrains from the
promise to Abraham (Gen. 27:29; 28:3-4) with the attendant
responsibilities to bless the world.

2. Ishmael

Ishmael is not strictly a patriarch and certainly is not in the line
to receive the blessings promised to Abraham (Gen. 21:11-13)
although he would be a great nation because he was Abraham's
son. More important to a study of missions is the fact that the conflict between Isaac and Ishmael continues today in the Arabic

---

8. *The Interpreter's Dictionary of the Bible,* 4 vols., (New York: Abingdon Press, 1962), s.v. "Isaac" by L. Hicks.

9. Victor E. Hoven, *Shadow and Substance* (St. Louis: The Bethany
Press, 1934), pp. 32-6.

Muslim opposition to the spread of Christianity.

3. Jacob

Jacob, the deceiver, has little about his character to be admired. However, on his return to his homeland confrontation with Esau, he wrestled with the angel of God. It was a continuation of the conflict with men and God that began in the womb. He insisted on a blessing. And as a part of that blessing he is given a new name, Israel, and begins a new life.

Jacob is the father of the twelve sons that are a genealogical foundation for the nation of Israel. These descendants are frequently called the "sons of Israel." More will be said about the lessons from Israel in the next chapter.

The writer of Hebrews calls Isaac and Jacob "heirs of the same promise" with Abraham (Heb. 11:9).

Jacob could see the fulfillment of the promise to bless all nations through his sons. In his deathbed blessing to Judah he predicted that the Messiah would come through Judah, and gave the most complete prophecy, until that time, of Jesus (Gen. 49:9-12). Further, he also promised that through Jesus all nations would come in obedience, and that the Messiah would rule over all the world.

> The scepter will not depart from Judah, nor the ruler's staff from between his feet, until he[10] comes to whom it belongs and the obedience of the nations is his (Gen. 49:10).

4. Esau

Esau, the man of this world, is the least significant of these early descendants of Abraham. His descendants come to our attention again as the Edomites who opposed the passage of Israel to the Promised Land.

5. Joseph

God through Joseph saved the lives of his father and brothers

---

10. "He" is "Shiloh" in Hebrew.

and welded together the sons of Israel in such a way that there was a more or less homogenous group for Moses to lead to the Promised Land. There is nothing in the Genesis record to indicate that Joseph is ever able to see beyond the establishment of Israel, to the people of God being a blessing for all nations.

Joseph, like Jesus, was humiliated then exalted for the divine purpose of saving his people. Thus Joseph, like Jacob, provided a picture of the Savior who was to come.[11]

SUMMARY

The promise to the Patriarchs is a promise and nothing more. The promise had two sides: the physical, the establishment of Israel in the Promised Land, with countless descendants; and the spiritual, the blessings to be conferred on the Gentiles.

The history from Abraham to Moses is checkered. There are a few high points but for the most part the descendants of Abraham are marked by selfishness and materialism. On occasion they even lost hope in the Promised Land and were willing to abandon the promise.

Still, God remained faithful. He would bless the nations through Abraham's seed, in spite of their behavior.

11. Hoven, pp. 4-51.

3

THE PEOPLE OF GOD AND THE PEOPLE OF THE WORLD

EXODUS - I SAMUEL

God had chosen one man, Abraham, through whom His blessing would come to the world. Approximately seven hundred years had passed. The promises made to Abraham remained unfulfilled. Abraham's descendants were not yet too numerous to count. Only a few, if any, of them were in the Promised Land. Most of them were in slavery in Egypt. No foreigners had received a special blessing. The Messiah had not come. Israel, the nation, was not yet in existence. If anyone possessed a record of, or historical memory of, God's promise to Abraham, it would have surely appeared that God had forgotten, or was unfaithful, or had a timetable that required eons to fulfill.

But now the time had come for God to take the next giant step toward keeping His promise. As He had chosen one man through whom to bless the world, He now had to choose one people to be His chosen nation. Israel had arrived at Sinai. The Lord instructed Moses to tell the people:

> You yourselves have seen what I did to Egypt, and how I carried you on eagles' wings and brought you to myself. *Now* if you obey me fully and keep my covenant, then out of all nations you will be my treasured possession. Although the whole earth is mine, *you* will be for me a kingdom of priests and a holy nation (Exod. 19:4-6 emphasis mine).

The Lord owns all the nations of the earth. Of all them He has now chosen Israel to be His "treasured possession" (Deut. 7:6; 14:2). Like silver or gold she is now to have special value to Yahweh. He has already shown His care for her by carrying her on "eagles' wings" from Egypt to Sinai. As an adult eagle flies with its fledgling and spreads its wings as a safety net to keep the young eaglet from crashing to death on the rocks below, in case of failure in flight, so God has taken Israel into His care (Deut. 32:11).

The purpose of this selection is not left as a mystery. Israel is to be "a kingdom of *priests* and a holy nation." The function of a priest is to serve as a mediator between God and man. Israel is to serve that function for the whole world. She is to mediate God's revelation and redemption to the other nations. The very reason for her being was to serve as a missionary nation.

Israel's God was holy, pure (*qadosh*), and demands holiness in His worshippers. Israel was not called because she was already pure any more than she was called because she was already a priest. She was called to be made pure — a purity that came through the expiation of her sins.

To be pure, and know one is pure, provides one with the opportunity to be tempted by pride, a sin Israel constantly had to contend with.

Because of the imperfect nature of the Hebrew religion, Israel could not provide an effective priesthood or real purity to the other nations (Hebrews 8,10). It remained for the Church to engage in this dual ministry of priesthood and purity (Rev. 1:9).

The dual event, the exodus and the giving of the law, constituted Israel a nation. It was, consequently, the single greatest event in her history. It meant freedom from Egyptian bondage (Deut. 13:5). It made Israel an identifiable nation instead of an undefined collection of slaves. It assured Israel a place in history. It gave them a place in God's plan for the world. The biblical writers often called Israelites back to their heritage by reminding them of this great event. The theological significance is noted by Paul,

> our forefathers were all under the cloud and that they all passed through the sea. They were all baptized into Moses in the cloud and the sea (I Cor. 10:1-2).

Traditionally in Christian theology, the exodus was seen as a type of deliverance from sin. Moses was a type of Christ. The crossing of the sea was a picture of Christian baptism. The law foreshadowed the gospel. The wilderness journey paralleled the Christian life. And the promised land was fulfilled in heaven.

The exodus took on a new significance in Christian theology beginning in 1968. A number of theologians, most of them in Latin America, most of them Roman Catholic, living in the terribly oppressive circumstances in Hispanic America, saw in the exodus from Egypt a hope for their deliverance from today's economic and social slavery. This led to a call for social change. Some liberation theologians argued for non-violent activity to bring about this change. Others promoted violent overthrow of existing structures.

Space does not permit a thorough presentation or analysis of liberation theology. But a few comments are in order. In liberation theology sin is seen as social evil. Salvation is deliverance from the evil social order. The kingdom of God is identified with political activity, and its success is achieved, not by the direct acts of God as in Egypt, but by human efforts to effect political change.

We encountered the word *goy* (nation) in the Introduction. Now that Israel is constituted a nation we must examine it a little more carefully. We may find, like many other ancient words, it doesn't have the constant and precise meaning we would like for it to have.

Goy is first used of the divisions of the descendants of Japheth, Shem, and Ham (Gen. 10:5,20,31). At this time *goy* has

> [t]he basic idea — that of a defined body or group of people or some specific large segment of a given body. The context will generally indicate the specific quality or characteristic which is to be understood.[1]

Nation then is indiscriminately used of Abraham's descendants (Gen. 12:2; 17:4-6,16,20; 21:8), Israel (Exod. 33:13), specific nations other than Israel (II Kgs. 6:18; Gen. 10:31; Jdgs. 2:23; Isa. 61:11; Zech. 12:3), and peoples in and around Canaan (Deut. 4:38; Josh. 2:21,23; 23:13).

With the development of Israel as the chosen nation in covenant relation with God the other nations are increasingly seen as "other" and so the term nation takes on in some contexts the meaning of Gentile, or heathen. Kane observes, "[t]he Hebrew word *goyyim*, as used in the Old Testament, is identical with 'heathen.' It carries with it a religious rather than a political connotation."[2] This is true in some contexts but not all.

We shall examine Israel as the people of the Lord, the law, and the land.

---

1. *Theological Wordbook of the Old Testament*, 2 vols. (Chicago: Moody Press, 1980), s.v. "goy," by R. Laird Harris, I:153.
2. Kane, p. 21.

I. THE GOD OF ISRAEL

Israel's existence depended upon Yahweh. Yahweh delivered them from Egypt. He constituted them a nation. He provided for their needs. He was present with them in their travels and battles.

Yahweh was unique. Israel's neighbors in Egypt, in the wilderness, and in Canaan had gods, lots of them. But Israel's concept of God was not borrowed from them. Rather, He revealed Himself to them through His words at Sinai and elsewhere, and through His actions in their corporate life. "Israel's religion rested in no abstract theological propositions, but in the memory of historical experience as interpreted by, and responded to, in faith."[3]

1. His name is Yahweh.

The importance that God attaches to the calling of Israel is seen in the fact that God for the first time gives His proper name. Until Moses He is only known by the generic term, god (elohim).

> God also said to Moses, "I am the LORD (*yahweh*). I appeared to Abraham, to Isaac and to Jacob as God Almighty, but by my name the LORD (*yahweh*) I did not make myself known to them" (Exod. 6:2-3).

The fact that we find Yahweh in Genesis does not contradict this statement. If Moses wrote Genesis, and I believe that he did, he is reflecting his post-Midian experience as he is writing the history of an earlier age.

Yahweh explains the meaning of His name, "I am who I am" (Exod. 3:14). Bright says,

> [i]t is likely, however, that Yahweh is a causative form of the verb "to be." Thus the enigmatic formula of Ex. 3:14, in its original

---

3. John Bright, *A History of Israel* (Philadelphia: The Westminster Press, 1959), p. 132.

third-person form (*yahweh asher yihweh*). would mean "He Causes to be what Comes into Existence;" i.e., Yahweh is the creator of all and the moving power in all.[4]

2. Yahweh alone is God.

"You shall have no other gods before me" (Exod. 20:3). "Before me" has the sense of "aside from me."[5] This is not admission that there are other gods, but rather that nothing else is to be treated as god. Unfortunately, throughout their history until the Babylonian exile, the Israelites did worship other gods. This was not condoned because Yahweh is a jealous god (Exod. 20:5).

"Hear, O Israel: The LORD our God, the LORD is one" (Deut. 6:4).

Yahweh sits on the throne alone. There is no pantheon. There is no consort. (Interestingly, Hebrew does not even have a word for "goddess.") And there is no offspring. As a consequence, Israel developed no mythology as did the Babylonians, Egyptians, Greeks, and others.

Yahweh's battles are not with other deities. There is a spiritual war with a fallen angel, but most of the text is concerned with conflicts with *earthly* beings, the Egyptian pharaoh, the Philistine armies, the Canaanite kings, etc.

3. He is a person.

He is not an idol. He is not an idea. He is a person who communicates with and who is responsive to man. He carries on conversations with Moses, Joshua, Samuel, and the prophets. One of the more insightful events disclosing the nature of God is Abraham's discussion (argument?) with God about the number of righteous men necessary to save Sodom (Gen. 18:16-33).

The concept of God as a person led to the widespread use of anthropomorphisms by the Hebrew people. There is no reason to believe that they ever understood these expressions were to be

---

4. Ibid., p. 137.
5. Ibid.

taken literally. God was very real. And the most real way they had to express this reality was to talk of His hands, feet, etc.

4. He is the Creator.

Aside from the possible understanding of Yahweh to mean the Creator, there is little in the period we are studying in this chapter that refers to the Creator. In fact, the only reference to the creation is in Deuteronomy 4:32 when the Lord challenged Israel to inquire "from the day God created man on the earth" if any god has done anything as great as God did for Israel when she was still in Egypt. There is a reference to the Creator when Moses sang of "your father, your Creator, who made you and formed you" (Deut. 32:6).

The historical event of the creation of Israel out of motley slaves was even more formative in Israel's development than their creation as men in the Garden. Later, we will also see in the New Testament, that the New Israel is more concerned with their creation as the church than in their creation of human beings.

5. He is invisible.

No one ever saw God (Deut. 4:12). There were symbols of His presence such as the pillar of fire, and pillar of cloud, and pre-eminently, there was the Shekinah in the Holy of Holies.

His invisibility provided several things to His people. God was not to be confined to a physical mass. He was omnipresent. He was not to be confined to a visible shape, color, or size. He was as great and diverse as faith allowed. He was not confined to a thing, an idol, or an icon, He was, however, in men.

This view of God confounded those who were accustomed to having tangible gods, but gave great comfort to those who believed in a living, non-material God.

6. He is the God of Action.

Israel's God was responsible for the things in the natural world, but was not to be identified with them. He used the clouds, the winds, the sea, the storm, the sun, the moon, and earthquakes to serve His ends, but He was not, as the pagan gods, known as the sun-god, rain-god, etc. The Creator did use His creation.

But He was far more identified with the unrepeatable actions in history. He led Israel out of Egypt, and through the sea. He gave them the tablets of testimony. He led them through the wilderness. He led them to military defeat of their enemies.

Later, in the New Testament, we see this same God who acts in history. Jesus was born of a virgin, He died on the cross, He was buried, and He was raised from the dead. Christianity is based on these historical events, not on God's control of nature.

7. He gave birth to Israel.

As I was growing up I gave my father many occasions to discipline me. Of all the times he punished me, the most painful occasion, and the most effective, was when he said, "Bob, we wanted you." I realized I was here because I was wanted. More than that I was wanted to be a certain kind of person. The fact that I had failed hurt my father deeply.

In a similar way Moses chastises Israel just before his death with these words, "[y]ou deserted the Rock, who fathered you; you forgot the God who gave you birth" (Deut. 32:18).

II. CHARACTERISTICS OF ISRAEL

"Israel" means God reigns. Although earlier used of the man who was the father of the twelve men who became the tribal heads, "Israel" was transferred to the children of Israel which in turn became the corporate community of the twelve tribes as they were constituted a nation. And it anticipated the time when God would rule in the Messianic Age.

The marks of Israel that distinguished them from the nations around them were at least six in number.

1. Yahweh is present in Israel.

While Moses was off on the mountain receiving the Ten Commandments, God appeared to be away also, and the Israelites made a golden calf. Their excuse was that they wanted "gods who will go before us" (Exod. 32:23). The Lord's reaction was to direct Moses to lead them to the promised place. An angel was to accompany them, but the Lord said, "I will not go with you . . . I might destroy you" (Exod. 33:3). After Moses' petition the Lord relented and replied, "My presence will go with you, and I will give you rest" (Exod. 33:14).

Yahweh's presence brought benefit to Moses. The argument Moses used with God that won this concession was, "You said, 'Lead these people,' and I don't even know where I'm going. You said, 'you know me,' but I don't know you." The Lord's response to be present and go with them also provided Moses with direction.

Jesus promised centuries later that "surely I am with you always, to the very end of the age." Paul found the promise to be true for the Lord's direction took him to the responsive missionary field, Macedonia, instead of to Bithynia.

Yahweh's presence brought benefit to Israel. When they knew He was present they more closely obeyed Him. And when He was present they could win the military battles where the odds were overwhelmingly against them.

The strength given to the Christian to resist temptation and to win spiritual victories is also the presence of God, "you will receive the gift of the Holy Spirit" (Acts 2:38). "You will receive power when the Holy Spirit comes on you" (Acts 1:8).

Yahweh's presence brought benefit to the nations. Moses had asked, "how will anyone know that you are pleased with me and your people unless you go with us?" (Exod. 33:16). Repeatedly, on the journey, and after entering the Promised Land, the Gentiles saw "the Lord was with Israel."

In the First Century the people, Jews and Romans, saw the effects of the presence of the Lord in lives of the missionaries and myriads of them also became Christians.

2. Israel is Monotheistic.

It is difficult for the Twentieth Century Christian to grasp the importance of the first two commandments. The west is strongly influenced by the Judeo-Christian heritage of monotheism. The Near East is dominated by the monotheism of Islam. We take it as a matter of course that there is only one God. It was not so in the days of Israel. They were surrounded on every side by polytheists. And there was much that was appealing in these religions. They appealed to the natural man. Religious prostitution was common. God was in the form of an idol that could be seen.

There had been one attempt about a century earlier to establish a monotheistic religion of one God in Egypt. Amenophis IV (ca. 1370-1353) declared Aten (the solar disk), a previously existing deity, to be the sole god. The pharaoh changed his name to Akhenaten in honor of his god. He built a new capital, Akhetaten, to show his support of his deity. Scholars have debated the degree to which this was true monotheism, since the pharaoh was still regarded as a god, and the status of the other gods was not made clear. Akhenaten faced great opposition to this monotheism, principally from the powerful priests of Amun. He died young and the new monotheism died with him.

Israel's monotheism existed alone in a sea of polytheism. And from time to time the Israelites succumbed to the attractiveness of the other gods. The Lord said,

> They made me jealous by what is no god and angered me with their worthless idols. I will make them angry by a nation that has no understanding (Deut. 32:21).

3. Israel is a Nation of Law.

There had been nations with laws earlier. For instance, one of the more famous sets of law was the Code of Hammurabi. The law of Israel was different. It had been given by Yahweh and was therefore a divine law, inspired in a way that no other law had been. It was a permanent law. The law did not change when a new king came into power. The law was just. Judges might be weak, or prejudiced, but men were tried by law not by whim.

It was particularly important that Israel have a law in the first two centuries of her existence. During this period there was no central government to give either cohesiveness to the nation, or uniformity to the legal system. The one thing that tied them together was the law they had in common.

The law of Israel, especially in the pristine form of the Ten Commandments, has had enormous effect on all the nations who have been touched by the Judeo-Christian influence.

4. Israel is a Nation of Ethics.

Six of the Ten commandments govern the behavior of a person's relationship with other people. Much of the detailed application found in Exodus through Deuteronomy is direction for ethical behavior. In our tendency to resist control over our lives we sometimes reject this moral code as artificial or irrelevent. We see such rules as restrictive rather than helpful.

5. Israel is a nation that sinned.

From the perspective of three thousand years after the events, it is a mystery why Israel sinned so repeatedly when it is so clear that disobedience leads to punishment and obedience leads to blessing. We say, "If I had been there, I would not have done that." Then we realize we have more revelation, and more help, and still we sin.

Paul addresses the same issue, "What advantage, then, is there in being a Jew?" (Rom. 3:1). Paul had just shown the Jew and Gentile will be judged impartially. That is, if the Gentile keeps the law, even without knowing the law, he is acceptable. But if the Jew, who has the law, does not obey the law, he will be condemned (Rom. 1,2). Israel has sinned. What advantage has she? There are two:

One, "they have been entrusted with the very words of God" (Rom. 3:2). However, merely possessing the oracles of God is not an amulet that assures their righteousness. And the "trust" they have is not to preserve but to obey the revelations placed in their care. But they did not always obey. "Will their lack of faith nullify God's faithfulness?" (Rom. 3:3). No, God is going to keep

97

His promise to bless the nations through Israel. God's faithfulness will require him to send Israel into captivity. But the unfaithfulness of the chosen People will not cause God to be unfaithful to His promises.

Two, "and from them is traced the human ancestry of Christ" (Rom. 9:5). The supreme purpose for Israel is to provide the channel through which the Messiah will come. God will not be diverted from His purpose by the sin of Israel.

6. Israel is a redeemed nation.

Among all the nations of the earth, Israel sustained a unique relationship to Jehovah. The other nations were made by Him (Ps. 86:9) and ruled by Him (Ps. 103:19), but only Israel is said to have been "redeemed" by Him: "Thus says the LORD, who created you, O Jacob, he who formed you, O Israel: 'Fear not, for I have redeemed you; I have called you by name, you are mine' " (Isa. 43:1). Thirteen times in the second half of Isaiah Jehovah is referred to as the "Redeemer" of Israel.[6]

7. Israel arrives in the Promised Land.

"The LORD said . . . get ready to cross the Jordan River into the land I am about to give . . . to the Israelites" (Josh. 1:2). The promise to Abraham, Isaac, and Moses had always included the possession of the Promised Land. Their presence there ultimately allowed the fulfillment of another prophecy,

But you, Bethlehem Ephrathah, though you are small among the clans of Judah, out of you will come for me one who will be ruler over Israel, whose origins are from of old, from ancient times (Micah 5:2).

The birth of Jesus made it possible for all nations to be blessed. Thus Israel's existence, and Israel's location, were major factors in the evangelization of the world.

---

6. Kane, p. 22.

III. THE RELIGIOUS LIFE OF ISRAEL

1. Sacrifices were necessary.

On the annual Day of Atonement the high priest was to sacrifice a bull for his own sins and a goat for the sins of the people (Lev. 16; 23:26-32; Num. 29:7-11; Exod. 30:10; Lev. 25:9). In addition, a ram and seven lambs were presented as burnt offerings. With these there were to be presented prescribed grain offerings. This was the yearly sacrifice to atone for the sins of the whole nation. It provided cleansing not only for the nation, but for the sanctuary itself. It was the highest atoning ceremony of the year in which blood was applied, not only to the altar, but also sprinkled seven times in the Holy of Holies in the presence of God.

Other animal sacrifices were offered daily (Exod. 30:38ff; Num. 28:1-8), and on holy days (Num. 28:9-10). Sacrifices were also made on any occasion when an individual sought relief from sin (Lev. 4:1-5:13) and guilt (Lev. 5:14-6:7). Two special occasions required a sacrifice: the consecration of a priest (Exod. 29:26-28), and the expiration of a Nazirite vow (Num. 6:13-20).

The value of the sacrifice required of an individual was determined by his position. For example, the priest who presided over the sacred things was required to bring the most costly animal, a bullock. The congregation was to bring the same. A ruler brought a male goat. The private person brought what he could afford ranging from a male goat, a female lamb, two turtle doves, to two young pigeons. If destitute, one could substitute a tenth part of an ephah of flour.

The rationale for the blood sacrifices is given:

> For the life of the creature is in the blood, and I have given it to you to make atonement for yourselves on the altar; it is the blood that makes atonement for one's life (Lev. 17:11).

Israel began its nationhood with the sacrifice of the passover lambs in Egypt (Exod. 12). It is assumed that sacrifices were offered also upon the receipt of the Ten Commandments to seal this new covenant, but there is no record of these having been made.[7]

Animal sacrifices were offered in virtually every ancient culture. However, the sacrifices of Israel's religion differed from those of their neighbors in several important ways.

Among the Hebrews many of the sacrifices were for the specific purpose of the expiation of sin. Atonement seems to have little or no part in the pagan sacrifices. Many other Israelite sacrifices were offered to express thanksgiving to God. There seems to be less of this among the heathen, and where gifts of the firstfruits are presented they seem to have the effect of "rent" to the god of harvest.

The Jewish sacrifices were not offered to control God, or to gain His favor, although this seems to be the major emphasis in the heathen sacrifices. Neither was food offered to God to feed Him, in contrast to Israel's neghbors who were concerned with feeding the god while he was away from home and from his food sources, as if it were their responsibility to sustain the god.

Human sacrifice was forbidden among the People of God, although it was practiced among Arabs, Carthaginians, Assyrians, Canaanites, and others.

The chief purpose of the animal sacrifices in the Old Testament was to prepare for the coming sacrifice of the Lamb of God. The writer of Hebrews saw both the priest and the sacrifice as types of Christ who "was sacrificed once to take away the sins of many people" (Heb. 9:28). "Many people" is not very specific. It is not clear from this text alone whether the writer to the Hebrews had the Gentiles in mind. But there is no equivocation in Paul's thinking: Christ died for the ungodly which includes both Jews and Gentiles (Rom. 5). Many tribes today still practice animal sacrifice. A few still make human sacrifices. The Christian mis-

7. Reeves, ibid.

sionary to these people needs a thorough understanding of the relationship of the sacrifices of the Old Testament to the death of Jesus. Those people who have blood sacrifices in their culture often will understand and accept the sacrifice of Christ on the cross, because they have the background to understand its significance.

2. Centered in the Sanctuary

Yahweh was invisible, but had a physical focal point in the religion of Israel. This focus was the ark, a piece of furniture of the tabernacle and later of the temple. As built under Moses' direction it was a wooden chest, approximately 2¼' by 2¼' by 3¾', covered with gold. Integral with the solid gold lid were two gold cherubim facing each other and looking at the mercy seat. It was, then, at the same time, a container for the tablets and a throne for Yahweh.

The ark was the only item of furniture in the cube-shaped Holy of Holies, which was the second room of the tabernacle. Only the high priest was permitted to enter this most holy place, and that only on the Day of Atonement. All of the other articles of furniture in the Tabernacle, and the services that were performed in association with them were related to the ark in some way.

The importance of the ark is further seen in the fact that after the tabernacle mysteriously disappeared after the arrival in the Promised Land, the ark survived and continued to represent God's presence even though there is no report of the Shekinah with it. Of special importance in understanding the place of the ark is I Sam. 4-7.

After Israel lost a battle to the Philistines they enlisted the help of Yahweh by bringing "the ark of the covenant of the LORD Almighty, who is enthroned between the cherubim" (II Sam. 6:2). Interestingly, the Philistines had the same understanding of the presence of the ark, for when

> they learned that the ark of the LORD had come into the camp,
> the Philistines were afraid. "A god has come into the camp," they

said (I Sam. 4:6-7).

The presence of the ark did not offset the sin of Israel, so the Philistines not only won the next battle but captured the ark. The presence of Yahweh, however, did not provide a blessing but a curse to the Philistines inasmuch as the population of the cities where it was placed were afflicted with disease and desolation, and their gods destroyed.

Does this mean that the Gentiles can not be included in the People of God? For the answer we must look at another feature of the tabernacle. Surrounding the tent of meeting was a courtyard. And the principal article of furniture in the court was the altar of Burnt Offering where the animals were sacrificed, and the blood sprinkled. No restrictions were given in the Old Testament as to who was permitted to enter the court. It is assumed that only those who had come to worship would enter, but Gentiles are not specifically excluded. Later we see provision for the Gentiles in Herod's Temple which had a Court of the Gentiles. Revelation 11:2 tells us the outer court has been given to the Gentiles.

Central in the court was the Altar, as the Ark was central in the Holy of Holies. A.R.S. Kennedy has provided a helpful diagram,[9] (on next page).

The symbolism is clear. Jesus, who is both the altar (Heb. 13:10-12) and the Lamb, provides the sacrifice for sin for Jew and Gentile alike. Then, provision having been made by the sacrifice once for all, sin is washed away at the laver, a type of Christian baptism (Titus 3:5; Eph. 5:26; Heb. 10:22 — where the Greek *louo*, laved, is translated washed), so that the worshipper can enter the holy place, the church, and ultimately into the Holy of Holies, heaven, into the presence of God Himself.

3. Conducted by priests

---

8. *A Dictionary of the Bible* (Edinburgh: T. & T. Clark, 1902), 5 vols., s.v. "Tabernacle," by A.R.S. Kennedy.

A special class of professionals was developed to conduct the sacrifices and religious ceremonies. The first group included Aaron and his four sons. In time, the tribe of Levi was designated to assist in the work relating to the tabernacle and religious rites (Num. 3-4). From them the priests were selected.

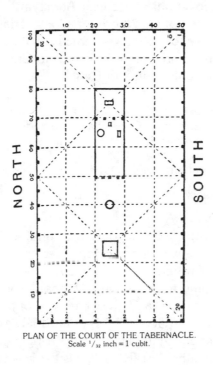

PLAN OF THE COURT OF THE TABERNACLE.
Scale $1/_{32}$ inch = 1 cubit.

4. Controlled by the Covenant

God had first made a covenant with Noah, and then one with Abraham. But the covenant that governed Israel's view of herself and her behavior was the covenant made at Sinai. This covenant was an acceptance by Israel of God's reign over them. Thus the notion of God's rule, or kingdom, begins here.[9]

---

9. Bright, p. 135.

This covenant, according to Jewish count, had 613 regulations governing the conduct of those who were a party to it. As a consequence it controlled the life of the individual and the conduct of the nation.

But, perhaps more important for our interests, it was an addendum to the covenant made with Abraham.[10] That covenant was for the purpose of blessing the nations. That purpose continues in the Mosaic form. Paul is particularly concerned to show that the "law was put in charge to lead us to Christ" (Gal. 3:24). The "us" includes both Jew and Gentile:

> You are all sons of God through faith in Christ Jesus, for all of you who were baptized into Christ have clothed yourselves with Christ. There is neither Jew nor Greek, slave nor free, male nor female, for you are all one in Christ Jesus. If you belong to Christ, then you are Abraham's seed, and heirs according to the promise (Gal. 3:26-29).

5. Rites of Israel

The rites fall into two categories: personal and corporate.

The personal rite was circumcision. Again it did not begin with Moses but with Abraham (Gen. 17:9-27). There it had the purpose of initiation into the covenant. Abraham was told, "You are to undergo circumcision, and it will be a sign of the covenant between me and you" (Gen. 17:11). Paul makes the point that Abraham was made righteous by faith, a righteousness signed and sealed by circumcision (Rom. 4). Israel was to continue this rite of initiation into the covenant (Lev. 12:3).

The three great annual feasts of Israel were Unleavened Bread (including Passover), Weeks, and Ingathering. These were important but it is difficult to accept Bright's statement, "Early Israel's cult, however, did not center in a sacrificial system, but in certain

---

10. Mont W. Smith, *What the Bible Says about Covenant* (Joplin: College Press, 1981), p. 2.

great annual feasts."[11] It seems to me that the sacrificial system
was the center of Israel's religious life. Without the sacrifices and
offerings even the annual feasts would have lost their meaning.
Israel could have survived without the feasts but she could not
have continued without the sacrifices. Further, the sacrifices met
the religious needs of the people between the feasts.

6. The Sabbath of Israel

There was nothing unique about circumcision. The same rite
could be observed among most of Israel's neighbors. Even today
it is a rite of passage for boys entering manhood in many tribal
societies, where it also has religious significance.

But the Sabbath was unusual. There were Sabbaths in
Babylonia and Assyria but both the days of observance and the
conditions of observance were different from that found among
the Israelites. Sabbath observances have not been found among
other nations of that period.

The Sabbath Year (Exod. 25:1-7; Deut. 15:1-18) and the
Year of Jubilee (Exod. 25:8-55) were established to rectify social
injustices and to wipe the slate periodically and give everyone,
poor and rich alike, a fresh start. These were probably the most
revolutionary laws ever enacted with respect to social justice.

Many today, especially among the liberation theologians, see
the law of the Year of Jubilee as a model to emulate in those nations where a very few rich people are exploiting the masses, the
poor. However, it is unrealistic to have as a missiological goal the
reinstatement of the Year of Jubilee. Such action would require
the same conditions prevail today as in ancient Israel; namely, a
theocracy with God as Supreme Ruler, universal commitment to
the Mosaic code, and an agricultural economy.

IV. THE POLITICAL LIFE OF ISRAEL

Israel came into existence in a period of history in which there

---

11. Bright, p. 149.

was no major political power threatening to capture or exterminate this infant nation. The days of Egypt's Empire were over. Assyria was in a century-long period of weakness. The Hittite Empire had vanished. The westward push of Phoenicia would not occur for some time. "Whatever crises the infant Israel had to face, she would be free to pursue her development without any threat from any world power."[12]

1. Israel was a theocracy.

Her God, Yahweh, was a living God who was to take an active part in ruling Israel. Throughout this period we find Moses, Joshua, and the judges consulting the Lord to ascertain the action He wanted Israel to take. It was when these leaders acted on their own authority, using what otherwise might be considered good judgment, that they discovered the Lord was not with them, and even punished them. The incident of Moses striking the rock at Meribah is a case in point (Num. 20:1-13).

2. Israel was an amphictyony.

An amphictyony is a loose association of tribes based on a common religious belief. It was Israel's faith that created the amphictyony, it was not the existence of the tribes that created the faith. It is incredible that this loosely connected collection of twelve tribes could function at all. The book of Judges gives us the explanation. From time to time as circumstances warranted "the Spirit of the LORD came" upon a man so that he became a judge. His authority was not hereditary, absolute, or permanent. It rested wholly upon Israel's perception that he possessed the Spirit of God and therefore that God, the king, was speaking through him. A woman could be a judge, as in the case of Deborah. The tribes were obligated to respond to the judge's call to arms, and were cursed if they did not (Jdgs. 5:15-17,23).

From a human point of view an amphictyony is a weak form of government. It was difficult to prevent intertribal war (Jdgs.

---

12. Ibid., p. 153.

12:1-6), or to bring to justice a member of one tribe who had commited a crime against a member of another tribe (Jdgs. 19,20). In time, Israel asked for a king, hopefully to correct these weaknesses.

3. Israel was not a state.

Israel lacked all the accoutrements of a national government. She had no king. She had no parliament. She had no national judiciary system. She really did not have a strong blood relation within Israel. From the beginning she had accepted the *goyim* into membership. The only things that bound her together were those things related to her religion: the covenant, the sacrificial system, the sanctuary, the priesthood, the Sabbath, and above all faith in Yahweh.

4. Israel had charismatic leaders.

The priests, who were not political leaders, were the only men who received their office by inheritance. Judges, prophets, and later kings, were *called by God* to serve. And those whom He called He also spoke to, giving them His directions for service. Further, Israel was not a democracy; there was no election of leaders.

Centuries later in the church, the New Israel, these same four components are found in the New Testament.

V. ISRAEL'S RELATION TO THE *GOYIM*

The attitude of God and the actions of Israel toward the Gentiles seem to be contradictory. On occasion Gentiles are invited into the family of God. On the other extreme, entire populations of Gentiles are to be exterminated. In fact, if anyone is spared, Israel is punished. How can we explain this anomaly and what does it teach us about mission?

1. Israel is told to separate herself from the *goyim*.

Upon the inauguration of Israel Moses is told, "Be careful not to make a treaty with those who live in the land." Neither we nor

Moses need to wonder about the reason for this restriction,

> for when they prostitute themselves to their gods and sacrifice to them, they will invite you and you will eat their sacrifices. And when you choose some of their daughters as wives for your sons and those daughters prostitute themselves to their gods, they will lead your sons to do the same (Exod. 34:15-16).

The issue is clear. The influence of unrepentant people will have a deleterious impact on Israel. Immorality and idolatry must not be tolerated because of the infectious nature of these influences.

Beginning with Jericho Israel was instructed to wipe out the entire population of the city to avoid their own destruction (Josh. 5:14-6:27). Nevertheless, one person, with her family, was saved because of her faith (Heb. 11:31).

2. Israel was told to accept *goyim* into her fellowship.

The first occasion was in Egypt upon the celebration of the Passover. The rule was that "No foreigner is to eat of it" (Exod. 12:43). However,

> [a]n alien living among you who wants to celebrate the LORD's passover must have all the males in his household circumcised; then he may take part like one born in the land (Exod. 12:48).

Egyptians, apparently, were a part of the original group that formed the people known as Israel (Lev. 24:10). Others from the areas they passed through joined the march to the Promised Land: Midianites (Num. 10:29-32; Jdgs. 1:16; 4:11), Amalekites (I Sam. 15:6), and Edomites (Josh. 14:13f; Jdgs. 1:10-20; Josh. 15:16-19; Jdgs. 1:11-15; Josh. 15:13).

In Canaan Israel absorbed, to a greater or lesser degree, Gibeonites (Josh. 9), Canaanites of Hepher and Tirzah (Josh. 2; Josh. 12:17,24), and Amorites of Shechem (Josh. 17; Gen. 34).

An Israelite warrior was permitted to marry a captured foreign woman (from the neighboring enemies, not from the Canaanites) after shaving her head, trimming her nails, disposing of her clothes, and mourning her parents for a month (Deut. 21:10-14). Shaving and washing were acts of purification on other occasions (Lev. 14:8; Num. 8:7) and are so to be understood here. Thus the woman was not coming into this marriage or into Israel bringing her idolatrous religion with her. One of the more interesting statements is "if you notice among the captives a *beautiful woman.*" The Lord, who made man, recognized his natural instincts. Nowhere in the Scriptures is there found the disparagement of beauty, or the injunction to be plain in appearance.

What does all this mean?

First, there has never been such a thing as Israel as a pure ethnic group. From the first there has been an infusion of bloodlines from other nations. At least two of them, both women, Rahab and Ruth, are in the blood line of the Messiah.

Second, the selection of Israel over the nations is not to be interpreted as rejection of the nations by God. He created them (Psa. 86:9), will redeem them (Isa. 11:10), and ultimately grant them the promised blessings (Gen. 12:1-3).

Third, the nations' rejection of Yahweh did not remove them from God's reign (Dan. 5.18-24).

> But their rejection of Jehovah in no way removed them from His rule. Even as heathen nations, with their false gods and pagan practices, they were still under Jehovah's universal control. They belonged to Him and were accountable to Him whether or not they acknowledged the fact.[13]

Four, the principal purpose of the existence of Israel was to produce a Messiah who would bring salvation to the *goyim* (Isa. 42:1,6).

---

13. Kane, p. 21.

VI. THE PURPOSE OF ISRAEL

"God heard the groaning (of Israel in Egypt) and he remembered his covenant with Abraham, with Isaac and with Jacob" (Exod. 2:24). From that moment He began to put into effect the actions that would bring Israel into being. The Lord restates the purpose of Israel's existence in unequivocal and unmistakable terms,

> I have raised you up for this very purpose, that I might show you my power and *that my name might be proclaimed in all the earth* (Exod. 9:16 emphasis mine).

We are not to understand that this is an evangelistic commission in the sense of Matthew 28:18-20. "In fact, nowhere in the Old Testament was Israel 'sent' to the nations."[14]

Israel's role was to be accomplished through three short range objectives:

1. Israel was to be the vehicle for God's revelation. The entire body of Hebrew scriptures was written by the Israelites. Even the earlier history of man from the beginning, Genesis, was written by Israel's new leader, Moses. The prophecies of the Messiah, the promised hope for the nations, are all found in this inspired record.

2. Israel was to provide a People to propagate God's message. The concepts of a holy God, a monotheistic religion, an ethical life, a personal Savior, and an eternal hope were spread throughout the world by the dispersed Jews. And so the preparation was made for the coming of Christianity. And the Christian apostles were all Jews who came from the Israelite background.

3. Israel was to be the nation through whom the Messiah would come. Much more of this will be treated in "The Promise of the Prophets."

---

14. Peters, p. 21.

SUMMARY

Israel was selected by God, not for her own benefit, but to bless the nations. She was constituted a nation of priests to accomplish this very purpose. The history of Israel is the history of redemption. The nations also belong to Yahweh, but they are mentioned in this history of redemption only in relation to Israel.

The deliverance of Israel from Egypt was not just an escape from slavery. They were saved in order to provide a world-wide ministry to the nations.

In spite of all the emphasis we have seen in Israel on the potential of evangelizing the Gentiles, we see very little outreach by the Israelites. In spite of their belief in One God who will brook no other, in an ethical religion that is superior to all others, and in a promised blessing that is to include all others, there are no missionaries from Israel, no overt attempt to convert their neighbors.

At this point we have to say that Israel was centripetal in its outlook, not centrifugal. If people came to Israel and to Israel's God they would accept them. But they had no concept that they were to go to others. That must wait until later. This was a time to prepare Israel, not to send Israel to the world.

4

THE KINGDOM OF ISRAEL AND THE KINGDOM OF GOD

I SAMUEL - II KINGS

Next to the Exodus and Giving of the Law the events in the lives of Saul, David, and Solomon are the most important in the development of Israel. In this relatively brief period we see the emergence of a world power out of a dozen refugee tribes. We see the change in government from the autonomous amphictyony of twelve tribes to a centralized government with an established dynasty. In religion we see a permanent sanctuary with the erection of the Temple to replace the Tent of Meeting. And we see a sense of fulfillment — of being settled, finally in the land promised to Abraham. This period is, as John Bright has said, "one of the most significant in Israel's entire history."[1]

---

1. John Bright, *A History of Israel*, (Philadelphia: The Westminster Press, 1959), p. 163.

It is in this period we begin to think of Israel as a kingdom. But this raises several questions. Is Israel of the Monarch Period the Kingdom of God? Is it a distortion of God's plans for Israel? To what extent, if any, does it foreshadow the Kingdom of God spoken of by Jesus? This chapter, combined with the chapters on the Prophets and Jesus, will attempt to address these questions. Since many perceive the principal motif of the Bible is kingdom it is important to understand exactly what the Bible says about kingdom.

As G.R. Beasley-Murray states, "the ultimate purpose . . . is the establishment of the kingdom of God. To what extent was this hope of the kingdom integral to Israel's thought, and how significant did it appear to the people?"[2]

But since our principal concern in this book is what the Bible says about missions, our interest in this chapter focuses on Israel's perception of her role in fulfilling God's purpose through Abraham's descendants, which is that "all the peoples on earth will be blessed through you" (Gen. 12:3). In what way does Israel fulfil this role? Are they even cognizant there is a role to fill?

As Stuhlmueller asks,

> what contribution to world mission could ever come from a people like Israel whose history separates them more and more from all the neighboring nations and whose sacred books developed an ethnocentric theology of being exclusively God's chosen ones? As a matter of fact, to this day Israel possesses no significant missionary program to proselytize non-Jews and so is uniquely different from Christianity and Islam.[3]

I. THE CHANGE FROM JUDGE TO KING

The first phase in the dramatic and traumatic transition was

---

2. G.R. Beasley-Murray, *Jesus and the Kingdom of God*, (Grand Rapids: William B. Eerdmans Publishing Company, 1986), p. 17.
   3. P. 9.

the replacement of the judges of Israel with kings. The change took place as a result of the request of the people for a king (I Sam. 8:6-9; 12:12-17). Samuel took it personally. The Lord comforted Samuel with the revelation, "it is not you they have rejected, but they have rejected me as their king" (I Sam. 8:7; 10:17-19).

This was not the first time Israel had asked for a king. The Israelites had asked Gideon to rule (*mashal*) over them after his defeat of the Midianites. He refused to be king, giving as his reason, "The Lord will rule over you" (Jdgs. 8:22-24).

There were two kinds of pressures bearing on Israel causing them to ask for a king, one internal, two external. According to the compiler of Judges Israel was in chaos because "[i]n those days Israel had no king and everyone did as he saw fit" (Jdgs. 17:6; 18:1; 19:1; 21:25). Many felt that the only way to bring order out of this disorder was to have a king.

There were external forces pressing for a king. One was example. All the nations surrounding Israel had kings, especially influential were those who were fighting Israel. The peer pressure of the successful contemporaries on these semi-nomadic ex-slaves, who were attempting to establish themselves as a respectable nation, was no doubt greater than we can imagine. But the greatest pressure was war. The judges had no power but the persuasion of their charismatic personalities to conscript an army from the scattered tribes. And the tribes, often remote from personal threat of invading enemies, found reason not to go to war. The increasing military conflict, especially by the Philistines, was motivation for some of the more threatened tribes to call for a king who would have the power to conscript an army sufficient to defend the young nation.

The idea of a king and kingship was not new to Israel. The innovation was the selection of a *human* king. Up to this point the descendants of Abraham thought of the Lord as king. Although the Old Testament does not use king (*melek*) to refer to Yahweh up to this point, Eissfeldt and Buber have pointed out that all

Semitic peoples thought of their gods as kings, and that these nomadic peoples thought of their king as the god who accompanied them on their journeys and led them to good pastures.[4]

At the outset in the establishment of the covenant at Sinai, Israel was to be "a kingdom of priests" (Exod. 19:6). Yahweh was to be king. And in the law a provision was made for a king. In fact it was predicted that Israel would ask for a king like the surrounding nations. Deuteronomy lists the qualifications of the king: he is to be one the Lord has chosen; he is to be a brother Israelite; he is not to accumulate horses; he is not to send people back to Egypt; he is not to become wealthy; and he is to read the law daily and obey it (Deut. 17:14-20).

This provision seems to be in direct conflict with the Lord's statement to Samuel that the people have rejected Him as king when they make a request for a king. Can this contradiction be resolved? The most important thing is that the Lord is absolute sovereign and that His will for the people be followed. God can rule through either judges or kings, if they will surrender to his will. It appears that the statement in Deuteronomy is a prophecy inasmuch as the Lord knew the Israelites would ask for a king. As in other instances, He made a concession to them. He could successfully rule directly through the charismatic leaders as He had demonstrated. Seemingly He would prefer this unique arrangement. But if they insisted on having a king, He would specify the conditions of the kingship — not an unreasonable demand. As Beasley-Murray suggests, "[t]he notion of kingship of God is flexible."[5]

The judges of Israel were men upon whom the Spirit of God came and enabled them to perform extraordinary deeds. For this reason they are called charismatic. The early kings of Israel also

---

4. O. Eissfeldt, "Jahwe als Konig," ZAW 5 (1928):81-105; Martin Buber, *Kingship of God*, trans. Richard Scheiman, (1967); cited by Bright, ibid., pp. 17-18.

5. Beasley-Murray, ibid., p. 18.

possessed this gift. It is recorded of Saul, "the Spirit of God came upon him in power" (I Sam. 11:6). The change from judge to king was ultimately a change from charismatic to dynastic leadership, but this was not an abrupt change, neither did the possibility of divine leadership pass completely away during the kingdom period.

But of all men, why Saul? In many respects Saul was a failure. His deterioration in his later years left the country in worse condition than he found it. He broke relations with Samuel. His insane jealousy of David nearly destroyed the nation. And at the last he attacked the sanctuary and destroyed the priests, the very representatives of Yahweh.

However, Saul had an auspicious beginning. He was an impressive man as he was a head taller than his fellows (I Sam. 9:2). He was a hero (*naqid*) (I Sam. passim). He had defeated the Ammonites. He was from Benjamin, the smallest tribe, and hence not a threat to the larger tribes. He lived close to the Philistines, the principle enemy of the day, with more at stake than most others. More importantly, he was elected by both prophetic approval and popular acclamation (I Sam. 10:1f; 11:14f).

The kingdom of Israel was not permanent or eternal. It existed by the grace of God and its continued existence would depend upon their king's obedience to God. The dynasty was always within one generation of extinction. At the same time the Lord promised Solomon,

if you walk before me in integrity of heart and uprightness . . . and do all I command and observe my decrees and laws, I will establish your royal throne over Israel forever. . . . *But* if you or your sons turn away from me and do not observe the commands and decrees I have give you and go off and serve other gods and worship them, then I will cut off Israel from the land and will reject this temple I have consecrated for my Name. Israel will then become a byword and an object of ridicule among all peoples (I Kgs. 9:4-7 emphasis mine).

117

II. THE CHANGE FROM AMPHICTYONY
TO NATIONAL STATE

Early in the conquest of Canaan the Twelve Tribes had remarkable success on occasion (e.g. the destruction of Jericho, and the second assault on Ai, etc.). Their victories did not continue, however, and the crushing defeat by the Philistines at Aphek with the capture of the Ark of the covenant and the death of 34,000 soldiers was the death knell of the amphictyony.

The Philistines, too, were without a central government. But somehow they were able to unite together in war. And with their iron weapons and chariots, and trained soldiers they overpowered the ill-trained, ill-equipped tribal conscripts.

Israel's solution was to elect a king.

It is not surprising then that Saul's entire reign was spent in armed conflict with Israel's neighbors (I Sam. 14:47-48,52).

Samuel had predicted that the appointment of a king would bring a national army, nationalized industry, nation-wide taxation, and personal slavery to the national government (I Sam. 8:10-17). This, however, did not have its complete fulfillment until Solomon.

Although Saul accepted the role of a king he made no known changes in the political structure of Israel.

Saul has "officials" but their names, positions, and functions are not given. We only know he has a general, his cousin, Abner (I Sam. 14:50). He conducted the official business under a tamarisk tree (I Sam. 22:6). He had no palace. He established no national bureaucracies. He did not return the ark to Israel, or establish a national shrine. Saul's one change in the government was to accept the position of king.

But his selection as king was the first in a series of steps that would bring Israel into a full-blown kingdom.

With the accession of David to the throne the development toward nationhood speeded up. With his selection by all twelve tribes (II Sam. 5:1-4) we have the unification of the twelve tribes and the joining of the North and South, Israel and Judah, under one political leader and as one nation. His selection of a central city, heretofore unoccupied by any tribe of Israel and hence neutral, gave a focal point to the national government. The transfer of the Ark of the Covenant to the new capital made it also the focal point of all religious expression.

III. THE CHANGE FROM INVADERS OF A LIMITED AREA TO THE CONTROLLERS OF A LARGE GEOGRAPHICAL AREA

The expansion of Israel's territory took place under David.

David, in the tradition of the charismatic leaders, from the time of his anointing by Samuel had the Spirit of the Lord in power (I Sam. 16:13). This was in contrast to the next verse that said, "[n]ow the spirit of the LORD departed from Saul, and an evil spirit from the LORD tormented him."

The men of Judah were the first to accept David as king (II Sam. 2:1-4). With Abner's help Ish-Bosheth (Eshbaal) is made king of Israel (II Sam. 2:8-10). The rivalry which had first political expression in these kings would result in a permanent political rift much later.

After the deaths of Saul and Ish-Bosheth David is elected king by all the tribes of Israel. They recognized his blood line, his military skill and experience, and his choice by Yahweh.

> We are your own flesh and blood. In the past, while Saul was king over us, you were the one who led Israel on their military campaigns. And the LORD said to you, "You will shepherd my people Israel, and you will become their ruler" (II Sam. 5:2).

And so the shepherd-boy became the shepherd-king.

David began consolidating his territory while still king of Judah. His rule included the Simeonites, Calebites, Othnielites,

Jerahmeelites, and Kenites (I Sam. 27:10; 30:14; Jdgs. 1:1-21). The unanimous election of David by the tribes of Israel further consolidated the position of the new king. The first military action was to drive the Philistines from the mountains near Jerusalem (II Sam. 5:17-25; 23:13-17; I Chron. 14:17). After this victory David went on to conquer all of Philistia (II Sam. 8:1,12; I Kgs. 4:24).

The next move was to capture the Jebusite city (II Sam. 5:6-10) which provided him an appropriately located capital from which he could rule the whole nation.

The various Canaanite cities located in Philistia were annexed to Israel with the local government officials now becoming subjects of King David.

Now Israel, for the first time since Joshua led them across the Jordan, controlled all of the Promised Land. But they did not occupy it exclusively. Many Canaanite groups were within the political jursidiction, but few, if any, were integrated into Israel's tribes, culture, or religion. The Hebrew Scriptures make no claim that the promise to Abraham was now fulfilled, but no doubt many Israelites had that feeling (Gen. 12:1-3; 15).

It was now time for David to pursue his expansionist ambitions. He captured Ammon to the east of the Jordan River, then the army advanced southward and captured Moab and Edom. To the north he conquered the Arameans of Syria. Israel's territory now roughly was the equivalent of Egypt's hegemony in Asia at the height of the Empire.

Israel now was a world power. No other country had the military strength to fend her off or to compete with her. The stage was set for the next phase of her development.

IV. THE CHANGE FROM A SLAVE STATE
TO AN ECONOMIC POWER

A third stage in the development of Israel's monarchy occurred with accession of Solomon to the throne. The Lord had promised David through Nathan, that his house and kingdom would be established forever (II Sam. 7:11-16). This assured that David's rule would become a dynasty. David later sent Solomon to the priest, Zadok, and prophet, Nathan, to be anointed king (I Kgs. 1:28-52). This action completed the progression from theocracy to kingdom. For the first time in Israel's history a man was chosen to be the ruler because of his ancestry rather than his charismatic quality.

Inheriting the throne of a strong nation with no serious threat from enemy political or military powers, Solomon both had the responsibility to maintain the empire established by his father and the opportunity to develop Israel into a significant nation of international trade. As a result of his economic sagacity he was able to make Israel a wealthy state.

Solomon created alliances with many neighboring states. Many of these were sealed by his marriages to women of the royal families of these states. These actions, which may have been wise politically, were in violation of the laws of Moses and brought into the royal house of Israel both foreign and pagan influences. This ultimately brought about the downfall of Solomon and the end of the Davidic dynasty (II Kgs. 2:1-13).

Economically, his most important alliance was with Tyre of Phoenicia. The westward expansion of the Phoenicians by sea was at its height. Solomon took advantage of their sailing and trading and imported hardwoods for his building projects, and exported wheat and olive oil to Tyre to finance his programs. Further, he used Phoenician shipbuilders and sailors to build and sail his fleet from Ezion-geber through the Red Sea to distant and exotic ports (I Kgs. 9:26-28; 10:11f,22).

Solomon also exploited the overland trade routes through Arabia. In addition to the trade Israel conducted with the eastern nations, these roads terminated in Israel, giving Solomon the opportunity to collect large amounts of taxes and duties from the traders (I Kgs. 10:15).

A giant copper industry was also developed by the king. Copper mines had existed throughout the Arabah for centuries, but Solomon made the maximum use of these resources by building the world's largest refinery at Ezion-Geber. The production not only met all the needs of Israel but gave the government large surpluses to export. Important as this development was financially it is not mentioned in the Bible.

One of the more interesting trading ventures was the import and export of horses and chariots. The text (I Kgs. 10:26-29) that tells us of this trade is unclear. The translation by Bright clarifies the matter.

> And Solomon's import of horses was from Kue (Cilicia); the king's merchants would bring them from Kue at the current price. And a chariot was brought and delivered from Egypt for six hundred shekels of silver, and a horse from Cilicia for one hundred fifty. And so they were delivered through their agency (i.e., of Solomon's merchants) to all the kings of the Hittites and of Aram.[6]

Solomon was the first Israelite king to utilize chariots in any number. Perhaps he was the first to have the opportunity to do so since the Israelites did not breed horses and did not build chariots. In his ingenuity he saw the possibility of importing chariots from one place and the horses from another (following Bright's explanation). Ultimately he had a stable of 12,000 horses and 1,400 chariots. He was entrepreneur enough to see that the neighboring nations needed similar transportation and would pay well for it.

In spite of the tremendous income from these various sources, the expenses of Solomon's reign outran the income. Samuel's prophecy of the cost of kingship was fulfilled. David had used conquered peoples for slave labor (II Sam. 12:31). But Solomon conscripted citizens of Israel to work in labor gangs for

---

6. Ibid., p. 195.

his building projects (I Kgs. 5:13-18). Even though this corvee was being used for the holy task of building the temple it was resented and contributed, eventually, to the disintegration of Solomon's dynasty.

V. THE CHANGE FROM TENT TO TEMPLE

The purpose of the Lord, the peace through David, and the economic strength from Solomon came together in Solomon's reign in such a way as to permit the erection of a permanent sanctuary for Yahweh. Using both materials and craftsmen from neighboring nations Solomon constructed a fantastically beautiful and expensive building. In spite of the foreign influence the Temple had the same basic floor plan and articles of furniture as the Tabernacle. And the most important item, the Ark of the Testimony, was the original, hand crafted in the wilderness.

The sacrifices, the priesthood, the regulations remained the same. Israel's religion had not changed, her God had not changed, even though the central sanctuary had a new appearance.

What is the impact of all these changes on the mission of Israel and the church?

At the dedication of the Temple Solomon prayed for the *foreigner who has come* from a distant land because of the name of the Lord. Solomon also asked for the Lord to answer the foreigner's prayer in order that *all the peoples* of the earth might know His name (I Kgs. 8:41-43). Solomon wanted the whole world to know Yahweh, but he expected it to come about because of the way God treated the foreigners, not necessarily because of anything that Israel did. Logic would lead one to believe that Solomon believed Israel should accept any foreigner who came to worship Israel's God, but there was no thought of Israel taking the message of God to others. Solomon's concept of religion was centripetal not centrifugal. This is reinforced by the

123

fact that he spoke of *one* foreigner coming to the Temple, and all the nations knowing God as a result of the experience of the one man. The missionary here was not an Israelite but a converted foreigner.

Solomon repeated his concept that Israel was the means through which the whole world would learn of the Lord,

> may . . . he uphold the cause of his servant and the cause of his people Israel according to each day's need, *so that all the peoples of the earth may know that the LORD is God* and there is no other (I Kgs. 8:59-60 emphasis mine).

Again we see the familiar pattern: benefit/blessing. Israel was given the privilege of having a king, a kingdom, and a Temple, not for their own benefit, but for the purpose of bringing a blessing to the world in the knowledge of the true God.

At no time in this period of Israel's history do we see Israel with a sense of evangelism to bring other people into the covenant with Yahweh. The Gentiles were either obliterated, or incorporated into the political nation as ethnic groups without any effort to bring them to the same religious faith. The kings even solidified their alliances with forbidden marriages with pagan women.

Apparently they saw themselves as having received the promise to Abraham in that they fully occupied the land promised to him. There is no evidence, however, that they thought of themselves as a channel of blessing to the other nations. Israel was very self-centered and concerned with what God had done for them and had no apparent concern with what God wanted to do for others. The closer they came to the physical goals for Israel, the further they were from the purpose of God.

The most that could be said of Israel's outreach is that David said that through the victories that Yahweh gave David's armies the foreigners will see that Israel's God was stronger than their own (II Sam. 22:38-51). David declares he will praise Yahweh for these victories (v. 50) but there is no idea that the nations will praise Yahweh as a result of their defeat by the armies of Israel.

There are at least two lessons here. One, David did not see the nations as peoples to be brought into a covenant relation with Yahweh, but peoples to be conquered. And, two, evangelism by force, though often tried in the Christian era, is not a biblical, or effective, way to win the loyalty of a people.

The establishment of the kingdom of David became a prophecy for the future Messianic kingdom. The Messiah was to be a son of David. That Jesus filled this role was established in the Gospels and in the preaching of apostles, a fact that we shall examine later.

In this view God's promise to bless the Gentiles was not a physical promise and was not to be fulfilled in David. It was a spiritual promise to be fulfilled only with the coming of the Christ, the forgiveness of sin, and the promise of eternal life. Abraham's promise had two sides: the physical promise to Israel which included a large number of descendants of Abraham and the occupation of the Promised Land; and the spiritual promise which pointed to Jesus who reconciled all men, Jews and Gentiles, to God.

The nature of the kingdom under David has raised the question as to the nature of the Messianic kingdom. David's kingdom *was* of this world, Jesus said, "my kingdom *is not* of this world." And indeed, the kingdom established on Pentecost was spiritual in nature. But the kingdom was not completed then. It is yet to come. Some see the consummation of the kingdom as being ultimately fulfilled in heaven. Others believe that it will be necessary for Jesus to return to earth and establish a kingdom on earth with the capital in Jerusalem and a rule on earth much like David's. The basis of this kind of eschatology comes, not from the New Testament, but from a certain kind of interpretation of the Old Testament. One's theology of the kingdom directly affects one's theology of mission and, subsequently, one's mission practice. But more of this when we examine the Gospels and Acts.

The kingdom of Israel at no time perceived themselves to be emissaries of Yahweh to the world. But they provided the physical structure through which the Messiah would come, and through which the ambassadors of the kingdom of Christ could go "to the ends of the earth."

SUMMARY

The period of history we have just covered in this chapter is the climax of the history of Israel. At the same time, it is the anticipation of the Kingdom of Christ in a fuller way than we have seen heretofore.

This period has seen the fulfillment, finally, of the physical side of the promise of Abraham for a promised land.

This period has been a transition period characterized by many changes: from rule by judge to rule by king, from an amphictyony to a national state, from being a small group of invaders of a limited territory to the controllers of a vast area, from being an enclave of slaves to being exercisers of great economic power, and in religion from worshipping at a portable tent to having a temple of enormous value.

In this transition period Israel laid a foundation for world wide influence that later Christian missionaries would find as containing effective avenues for their message.

Although the Israelites were not fully cognizant of the implications, Solomon's Temple broke down the Jewish wall of exclusivism and opened the door for the Gentiles to become a part of the people of God.

And David's kingdom became the foundation of the Messiah's kingdom that was to be inaugurated with the enthronement of David's Descendant.

5

THE POETRY OF THE KINGS

THE PSALMS

The psalms comprise the hymnbook of the religion of Israel. They were meant to be sung. Although it is not always clear which psalm was to be sung on what occasion it is clear that many of them were to be used on public occasions of worship. Many, for example, are "for the director of music." In a few instances the tune to which they were to be sung is given.

These hymns constantly reminded the people of God of God's actions in their lives. "There is scarcely a single event of importance in sacred history which does not find some expression in the Psalter."[1]

---

1. Delitzsch, "Exposition of the Psalter," Keil and Delitzsch, *Old Testament Commentaries*. (Grand Rapids: Associated Publishers and Authors, Inc., n.d.), III:878.

The Psalms are also an important source for the understanding of Israel's salvation-history.

> And it is also a source of information for the history of the revelation of redemption, in as much as it flowed not from the Spirit of faith merely, but mainly also from the Spirit of prophecy: but preeminently, it is the most important memorial of the progressive recognition of the plan of salvation, since it shews how, between the giving of the Law from Sinai and the proclamation of the Gospel from Sion, the final, great salvation was heralded in the consciousness and life of the Jewish church.[2]

The hymns of any religion serve two important functions in their effect upon the worshippers. One, the singing reinforces the ideals of the faith as expressed in the lyrics. Two, the singing aids the memorization of the ideals by embedding them in the mind.

Therefore, insofar as cross-cultural evangelism is mentioned in the psalms, every time those psalms are sung the idea of missions is held up before the people as an ideal advocated by God.

Thus Israel was not allowed to forget that the ultimate purpose of God included the incorporation of the Gentiles into the people of God. That the Jews of the day of Jesus had become exclusive, some going so far as to say that God had created the Gentiles to be the kindling for the fires of hell, does not set aside the fact that God from the beginning had planned for the Gentiles to be saved.

> . . . [A]nd the Psalms shew us how this seed-corn of words and acts of divine love has expanded this vital energy in the believing hearts of Israel. They bear the impress of the period, during which the preparation of the way of salvation was centered in Israel and the hope of salvation was a national hope. For after mankind was separated into different nations, salvation was confined within the limits of a chosen nation, that it might mature there, and then

---

2. Ibid.

bursting its bounds become the property of the human race. At this period the promise of the future Messiah was in its third stage. The hope of overcoming the tendency in mankind to be led astray into evil was attached to the seed of woman, and the hope of a blessing for all peoples, to the seed of Abraham; but, at this period, when David became the creator of psalm-poesy for the sanctuary service the promise had assumed a Messianic character and pointed the hope of the believing ones toward the king of Israel, and in fact to David and his seed; the salvation and glory of Israel first, and indirectly of the nations, was looked for from the mediatorship of Jahve's Anointed.[3]

Fifteen of the Psalms have something specific to say about mission. They are Psalms 2, 22, 24, 33, 47, 50, 66, 67, 72, 96, 97, 98, 117, 145, and 146. Seven lesons about mission can be learned from a study of these Psalms.

I. THE PURPOSE OF GOD

God's ultimate desire is for man, all men, to praise Him. According to the Psalms that praise is to take place here on earth. There is nothing in the Psalms about praise in heaven. The Psalms were written by men living in the world to be sung by men living on earth.

Sing joyfully to the LORD, you righteous;
   it is fitting for the upright to praise him (Psa. 33:1)

It is the duty and the joy of the righteous to praise God.

These alone know God, whose true nature finds in them a clear mirror; so on their part they are joyfully to confess what they possess in Him. For it is their duty, at the same time their honour, to praise Him, to make their boast in Him.[4]

---

3. Ibid., pp. 898-899.
4. Ibid., p. 1139.

Let all the earth fear the LORD;
  let all the people of the world revere him (Psa. 3:8).

The inhabitants have cause to fear Jehovah for by a mere word He can bring into being that which before was nothing.

For he spoke, and it came to be;
  he commanded, and it stood firm.
The LORD foils the plans of the nations;
  he thwarts the purposes of the peoples.
But the plans of the LORD stand firm forever,
  the purposes of his heart through all generations.

Blessed is the nation whose God is the LORD,
  the people he chose for his inheritance.
From heaven the LORD looks down
  and sees all mankind;
from his dwelling place he watches
  all who live on earth —
he who forms the hearts of all,
  who considers everything they do (Psa. 33:9-15).

The righteous are directed to sing "joyfully to the Lord." The Israelites might have interpreted this to mean that only they could praise God in this way. The psalmist, however, makes it clear that God's purpose from the creation was that all men should sing praise, not artificially, not mechanically, not lethargically, not slavishly, but joyfully.

This is not too much to expect since "the earth" itself "is full of his unfailing love." That is, each plant, each tree, each animal, each fish, each insect, each rock, etc. is an expression of His love in creation.

Because of this creation the author writes, "let all the people of the world revere him."

The psalmist was not a man blinded by national prejudice, he did not desire to restrict the worship of Jehovah to the seed of

Abraham. He looks for homage even to far off nations.[5]

This is more than a personal feeling on the part of the writer. "What is here placed as a wish may also be read as a prophecy; yet the adoration of God will yet be universal."[6]

The Creator who made all men made every man equal in His sight.

> he who forms the hearts of *all*,
>   who considers everything they do.

> But the eyes of the LORD are on those who fear him,
>   on those whose hope is in his unfailing love (Psa. 33:15,18 emphasis mine).

Jew or Gentile, king or beggar, man or woman, each may choose the LORD and have the privilege of singing joyously to Him. This was God's intention from the beginning.

II. THE MESSIAH MAKES THE PURPOSE POSSIBLE

As the first Psalm is about man, the second is about The Man. It is one of the few Messianic psalms.

> Why do the nations rage
>   and the peoples plot in vain?
> The kings of the earth take their stand
>   and the rulers gather together
> against the LORD
>   and against his Anointed One (Psa. 2:1-2).

This prophecy was fulfilled initially in David. (Delitzsch prefers

---

5. C.H. Spurgeon, *The Treasury of David*, 5 vols., (Byron Center: Associated Publishers and Authors, Inc., 1970), I:117.
6. Ibid., p. 118.

Uzziah or Hezekiah.) But it was fulfilled ultimately in Jesus. We have an inspired statement of the fulfillment. The congregation in Jerusalem during their persecution quoted Psalm 2:1-2, and gave this interpretation:

> Indeed Herod and Pontius Pilate met together with the Gentiles and the people of Israel in this city to conspire against your holy servant Jesus, whom you anointed. They did what your power and will had decided beforehand should happen (Acts 4:27-28).

> The One enthroned in heaven laughs;
>   the LORD scoffs at them.
> Then he rebukes them in his anger
>   and terrifies them in his wrath, saying
> "I have installed my King
>   on Zion, my holy hill" (Psa. 2:4-6).

This enthronement occurred when Jesus ascended to heaven and was seated at the right hand of God (Acts 2:29-36).

> He said to me, "You are my Son;
>   today I have become your Father" (Psa. 2:7).

The writer of Hebrews quotes this strophe as proof of the superiority of the Son over the angels (Heb. 1:5). And Paul in his sermon in the synagogue at Pisidian Antioch refers to the verse as being fulfilled in the resurrection of Jesus (Acts 13:33). As he wrote in Rom. 1:4, "a descendant of David . . . was declared with power to the the *Son of God* by his resurrection from the dead: Jesus Christ our Lord" (emphasis mine). In anticipation of this enthronement Jesus is declared to be the Son of God at His baptism by the voice from heaven (Matt. 3:17).

> Ask of me,
>   and I will make the nations your inheritance,
>   the ends of the earth your possession.
> You will rule them with an *iron scepter*;

you will dash them to pieces like pottery (Psa. 2:7-9 emphasis mine).

John sees the woman giving birth to a boy "who will rule all the nations with an *iron scepter*" (Rev. 12:5 emphasis mine). He also sees the King of Kings and Lord of Lords riding on a white horse judging and making war with an *iron scepter* (Rev. 19:11-16).

> Therefore, you kings, be wise;
>   be warned you rulers of the earth.
> Serve the LORD with fear
>   and rejoice with trembling.
> Kiss the Son, lest he be angry
>   and you be destroyed in your way,
> for his wrath can flare up in a moment.
>   Blessed are all who take refuge in him (Psa. 2:10-12).

"I will make the nations your inheritance," informs us that this conquest of the world will come "not by might, not by power but by my spirit" (Zech. 4:6). God works through human beings who are committed to Him but the change of human allegiance does not occur by human effort or military force but by the power of God.

David (see Acts 4:25) in this early Psalm anticipated that the nations (*goyim*) as well as Israel would come under the rule of the King of Kings.

The nations are urged to "kiss the son," an expression of homage. For example, when Samuel anointed Saul he "kissed him, saying, 'Has not the LORD anointed you leader over his inheritance?' " (I Sam. 10:1). Thus to "kiss the son" is a figure of voluntarily surrendering to the reign of Christ. In contrast, Judas used an insincere kiss to betray his master.

Psalm 27, another Messianic Psalm, describes the extent of the Messianic rule.

In many places in the Third World 95% of the land is owned by 5% of the people. The result is a few rich people control the lives of the great majority of very poor people. The poor are crying out for justice. Half of the children of these impoverished people die before the age of five. Starvation and preventable diseases are taking their young lives.

No modern missionary can ignore the plight of the poor. It is not enough just to preach the gospel.

> Let grain abound throughout the land;
>   on the tops of the hills may it sway.
> Let its fruit flourish like Lebanon;
>   let it thrive like the grass of the field (Psa. 72:16).

No longer can we interpret this verse as a figure of the growth of the kingdom. It must be understood as addressing the needs of the poor.

Psalm 146:7 anticipates that the Messiah will do this very thing.

> He upholds the cause of the oppressed
>   and gives food to the hungry.

Jesus fulfilled this prophecy in feeding the multitudes. And in so doing set an example for His disciples to meet human needs. The Psalmist, like Isaiah, predicts the nature of the ministry of Jesus, and so sets a model for the Twentieth Century missionary.

> The LORD sets the prisoners free,
>   the LORD gives sight to the blind,
> the LORD lifts up those who are bowed down,
>   the LORD loves the righteous.
> The LORD watches over the alien
>   and sustains the fatherless and the widow,
>   but he frustrates the ways of the wicked (Psa. 146:7c-9).

He will rule from sea to sea
   and from the (Euphrates) River to the ends of the earth (Psa.
72:8).

As Solomon's reign encompassed all the land of promise, the Messiah's Rule will extend over all the earth. His rule is complete.

The kings of Tarshish and of distant shores
   will bring tribute to him;
the kings of Sheba and Seba
   will present him gifts.
All kings will bow down to him
   and all nations will serve him (Psa. 72:10-11).

The Psalmist had a clear vision of the universal extent of the coming Messianic kingdom. The Messiah Himself said that the "gospel of the kingdom will be preached in the whole world as a testimony to all nations" (Matt. 24:14).

Kings and commoners will do obeisance before Him. "The desert tribes will bow before him" (Psa. 72:9a). Although they may have been wild and lawless they will willingly submit to His yoke.[7] "And his enemies will lick the dust" (Psa. 72:9b). Not only was the serpent compelled to crawl in the dust, his progeny will follow. The oriental custom required the most humiliating form of homage. And so "his enemies will lick the dust."

The Messianic rule will be concerned with the poor. Unlike so many kings who accumulated great wealth for themselves, the Messiah's concern is help for the helpless.

For he will deliver the needy who cry out,
   the afflicted who have no one to help.
He will take pity on the weak and the needy
   and save the needy from death.
He will rescue them from oppression and violence,
   for precious is their blood in his sight (Psa. 72:12-14).

---

7. Spurgeon, II:319.

III. THE SACRIFICIAL DEATH OF THE MESSIAH WAS NECESSARY TO ACHIEVE GOD'S PURPOSE

The twenty-second Psalm is ascribed to David. Some scholars have challenged this. Ewald dates it to the period prior to the destruction of Jerusalem. Bauer put it in the exile. Hitzig proposes Jeremiah wrote the first portion while in prison and the second section later under milder restraint. Olhousen places the writing at the time of the Macabees. But Delitzsch argues convincingly for the Davidic authorship.[8]

Although David may be writing of his own experience, "[h]is Spirit moulds even the utterances of David concerning himself the type of the Future One."[9] All conservative scholars see Psalm 22 as Messianic.

This is peculiarly a psalm of missions because

> starting with a disconsolate cry of anguish, it passes on to a trustful cry for help, and ends in vows of thanksgiving and a vision of world-wide results. . . . The first portion exactly coincides with the suffering of Jesus Christ, and the second with the results that have sprung from the resurrection.[10]

> From you comes my praise in the great assembly;
>   before those who fear you will I fulfill my vows.
> The poor will eat and be satisfied;
>   they who seek the LORD will praise him —
> may your hearts live forever (Psa. 22:25-26).

The reference to the poor eating may be a reference to the thank offering. After the sprinkling of the blood and the laying of the fat on the altar, the worshipper used the remaining flesh to make a joyous meal which often extended into the night and sometimes into the next day (Lev. 7:15ff.).

---

8. Delitzsch, pp. 1060-62.
9. Ibid., p. 1063.
10. Ibid., pp. 1060, 1062.

The Hebrew (*anavim*) refers both to the materially and spiritually poor. There was no requirement that the poor be invited but this in fact frequently happened. They in turn praised Yahweh for this blessing.

"May your hearts live forever" suggests that the participants were getting a meal that would impart enduring refeshment. This, then, speaks of the eternal spiritual blessing that came from partaking of the Messiah's spiritual banquet.

> All the ends of the earth
>   will remember and turn to the LORD,
> and all the families of the nations
>   will bow down before him,
> for dominion belongs to the LORD
>   and he rules over the nations (Psa. 22:27-28).

The writer expects the ultimate conversion of all peoples. Those heathen who have forgotten Yahweh will remember Him. Those peoples who have been stiffnecked and rebellious will bow in submission to His Lordship.

> All the rich of the earth will feast and worship (Psa. 22:29a).

The food they eat at the Messiah's table is the food that satisfies the soul. Isaiah refers to the feast,

> On this mountain the LORD Almighty will prepare
>   a feast of rich food for all peoples,
> a banquet of aged wine —
>   the best of meats and finest of wines (Isa. 25:6).

> All the rich of the earth will feast and worship;
>   all who go down to the dust will kneel before him —
>   those who cannot keep themselves alive (Psa. 22:29).

"Dust" commonly refers to the dust of the grave. According to the scripture the body of man returns to dust. There is nothing that man can do to prevent this death.

"All . . . will kneel before him." This worldwide conversion is based upon the right of Yahweh to be king. "The conversion of the heathen by that sermon will, therefore, be the realization of the kingdom of God."[11]

> Posterity will serve him;
>> future generations will be told about the Lord (Psa. 22:30).

This refers to the descendants of the early believers. As Psalm 71:18 says,

> Even when I am old and gray,
>> do not forsake me, O God,
> till I declare your power to the next generation,
>> your might to all who are to come.

The last verse of Psalm 22 reads,

> They will proclaim his righteousness
>> to a people yet unborn —
> for he has done it (22:31).

The establishment of the kingdom is not completed in a day. Each generation of believers is expected to evangelize not only their own but the next generation.

IV. PRAYER FOR THE NATIONS

In Psalm 67 the Psalmist prays,

> May God be gracious to us and bless us
>> and make his face shine upon us (v. 1).

---

11. Ibid., 1077.

What blessing does he seek? Spurgeon suggests, "Forgiveness of sin is always the first link in the chain of mercy experienced by us."[12]

The prayer for blessing is not a selfish prayer although it may seem so at first glance. Here the worshippers are to be blessed in order to bless others. God's light is to shine on them so that they in turn may transmit that light to others: "may your ways be known on earth, your salvation among all nations" (Psa. 67:2).

"May your ways be known." "Ignorance of God is a great enemy of mankind."[13]

"Your salvation among all nations." "This all nations need, but many of them do not know it, desire it, or seek it."[14]

> May the peoples bless you, O God;
>   may all the peoples praise you.
> May the *nations* be glad and sing for joy,
>   for you rule the peoples justly
>   and guide the *nations* of the earth.
> May the peoples praise you, O God;
>   may all the peoples praise you (Psa. 67:3-5 emphasis mine).

The Jews commonly referred to the Gentiles as "nations." If they were thinking about the words, or listening to what they were singing, such a hymn of petition must have had an impact on their attitude and behavior.

"You rule the people justly" is a better translation than the older "Thou wilt judge peoples in uprightness." As Delitzsch remarks,

> His judging (shaphat) in this instance is not meant as a juridical punishment, but as a righteous and mild government, just as in the christological parallels lxxiii.12 sq., Isa. 11:3 sq.[15]

---

12. Spurgeon, III:205.
13. Ibid., p. 206.
14. Ibid.
15. Delitzsch, p. 1343.

Psalm 67 needs to be sung in the churches today as well. The self-centered songs used in many Christian worship services need to be replaced with musical petitions for the salvation of the people of other cultures. Missionary hymns need to replace the songs that focus on our happiness if our churches are going to become missionary-sending and missionary-supporting congregations.

> Then the land will yield its harvest,
>   and God, our God, will bless us.
> God will bless us,
>   and all the ends of the earth will fear him (Psa. 67:6-7).

This Psalm, sung joyously just after the earth has yielded its harvest, anticipates the time when the sowing of the seed of the gospel will return its fruit in the hundredfold response from "all the ends of the earth" as they "praise our God."

The author recognizes that blessings will come to the people of God *after* they have taken the message of salvation to the nations.

Those individuals and churches that have made missions a priority have learned that they have been blessed in many unexpected ways when they have given generously to missions. In spite of this biblical principle many individuals are still saying, "I can't afford to give more." And churches are declaring, "We have to take care of our needs at home first."

V. ALL NATIONS ARE INVITED TO PRAISE GOD

Five of the Psalms specifically invite the nations to praise God. The first we will consider is Psalm 47.

Initially the Psalm may have been written against the background of Jehoshaphat's warless victory over the allied neighboring nations. The text describes the defeat, "the LORD had fought against the enemies of Israel" (II Chron. 28:29).

140

Since Israel celebrated victory over her enemies, is the church to celebrate the defeat of her enemies who stand in the way of the advancement of Christianity and the progress of the salvation of the peoples of the world?

Further we note that the victory in Jehoshaphat's reign was of limited duration, but the permanent victory shall come when the "kingdom of the world shall become the kingdom of our Lord and his Christ."

Clap your hands, all you nations;
shout to God with cries of joy (Psa. 47:1).

Clapping is a nearly universal expression of appreciation, thanks, and praise. It is used here figuratively for praise.

How awesome is the LORD Most High,
the great King over all the earth (Psa. 47:1)

God is not a local deity. The Hindus, for instance, have thousands of deities. Each tribe may have its own god which will be unknown to a group two tribes away. Jehovah is not so confined. He is the King over all the earth. The largest city is subject to Him. The smallest hamlet is under His rule.

He subdued nations under us,
peoples under our feet (Psa. 47:3).

What could this possibly mean? There are two possible explanations.

Taking his cue from the term "subdue," Spurgeon writes,

Idolatry, infidelity, superstition, we shall yet tread upon, as men tread down the stones of the street. . . . How changed will be the position of affairs in coming ages! The people of God have been under the feet of men in long and cruel persecutions, and in daily contempt; but God will reverse the position, and the best in character shall be first in honor.[16]

On the other hand Thomas Willcocks explains, "under our feet,"

[b]y this manner of speech is meant, that the Gentiles shall be *scholars*, and the Jews *schoolmasters*, as it were, to them; for *to sit under the feet*, or *at the feet*, is used in Scripture for being a scholar, or learning, as Acts xxii.3[17]

In either case the point is that the time is coming when the people of God will be responsible for taking the good news of salvation to the whole world and they will voluntarily accept the rule of the King of Kings.

He chose our inheritance for us,
    the pride of Jacob, whom he loved (Psa. 47:4).

The inheritance God promised Jacob sounds a lot like the promise to his ancestor, Abraham:

I will give you and your descendants the land on which you are lying. Your descendants will be like the dust of the earth, and you will spread out to the west and to the east, to the north and to the south. All peoples on earth will be blessed through you and your offspring (Gen. 28:13-14).

Had Jacob had the opportunity to choose his inheritance he probably would not have chosen as many or as great gifts as the Lord provided. In addition to the large number of future descendants in this earthly life he obtained the wife of his choice, a large family, and great wealth.

God has also a great inheritance in store for those who work

---

16. Spurgeon, II:394.
17. Thomas Wilcocks, quoted by Spurgeon, p. 398.

in His vineyard. And as with Jacob, God's gifts to us are beyond our imagination.

God has ascended amid shouts of joy,
    the LORD amid the sounding of trumpets.
Sing praises to God, sing praises;
    sing praises to our King, sing praises (Psa. 47:5-6).

The reference to the sounding of trumpets was the reason Psalm 47 was used on New Year's Day in the synagogue where, according to the Talmud, God rises from the seat of judgment and sits on the throne of mercy.

In Western Christianity Psalm 47 was used to celebrate the ascension of Christ to heaven since verse 5 says, "God has ascended."

For God is the King of all the earth;
    sing to him a psalm of praise (Psa. 47:7).

The Jews of Jesus' day resented the fact that Jehovah was King of all the earth. "They would have kept God to themselves, and not even have allowed the Gentile dogs to eat the crumbs from under his table."[18]

Is it not true that the majority of Christians today selfishly keep the good news to themselves and do not tell the other nations? This selfishness probably does not stem from a belief that the gospel is not for other people, or that God does not love others. It probably comes primarily from self-interest. We want to spend our time in pursuit of our own interests, we prefer to spend our money on the things that we want.

God reigns over the nations;
    God is seated on his holy throne.

---

18. Ibid., p. 395.

The nobles of the nations assemble
　　as the people of the God of Abraham,
for the kings of the earth belong to God;
　　he is greatly exalted (Psa. 47:8-9)

"In the mirror of the present, even the poet reads the great fact of the conversion of all peoples to Jahve which closes the history of the world."[19]

It is no small thing that the nobles in their ornate robes bow to God, and the kings lay their crowns before them. They come, entrance is granted, not because of their royalty, but because they are the people of the God of Abraham. It, therefore, is faith, not position, that allows them to enter into the presence of the Supreme Ruler of the universe.

The next Psalm calling the Gentiles to praise God is 66.

Shout with joy to God, all the earth!
　　Sing to the glory of his name;
　　offer him glory and praise! (66:1-2).

"All the earth" refers to

heathen nations, who have not known Jehovah hitherto, with one consent let the whole earth rejoice before God! The languages of the lands are many, but their praises should be one, addressed to [the] one [and] only God.[20]

Say to God, "How awesome are your deeds!
　　So great is your power
　　that your enemies cringe before you (Psa. 66:3).

The God of the Bible is the God who acts. The gospel is a recitation of what God did. Men are motivated to surrender to

___

19. Delitzsch, p. 1236.
20. Spurgeon, III:182.

Him because of what He does. And, here, men are praising Him
for His deeds. The God of the Scriptures is not remote; He is active in the world He created.

All the earth bows down to you;
   they sing praise to you,
   they sing praise to your name (Psa. 66:4).

The men of Athens worshipped an unknown God. God will
not be unknown. He is a person and as a person He has a name.
His praise, then, is directed to His named person.

One conclusion that must be drawn from this is, that if God is
to be worshipped He must be made known to all who know Him
not. The faceless entity of supreme power takes on personality
and character when His name is made known. It is not enough
that men "worship what they know not."

Come and see what God has done,
   how awesome his works in man's behalf!
He turned the sea into dry land,
   they passed through the river on foot —
   come, let us rejoice in him (Psa. 66:5-6).

As Israel pointed the nations to the mighty deeds of God in
the deliverance of oppressed Israel from Egypt, so the church today points the world to the mighty acts of God at the battle of the
cross and tomb, whereby He delivers all men from the bondage
of sin.

The divine directive, "you shall be my witnesses" (Acts 1:8),
was that the disciples were to bear testimony to the mighty acts of
God. Witnessing in the New Testament is not the relating of personal experiences but saying, "Come and see what God has
done."

We turn next to Psalm 96, which, like Psalm 98, instructs us
to sing a new song. Israel had been singing for centuries. What is
this new song they are given? Spurgeon answers, "the design of

the Holy Ghost in this psalm was to give forth a song for the Gentiles, a triumphant hymn wherewith to celebrate the conversion of the nations to Jehovah in Gospel times."[21]

> Sing to the LORD a new song;
>   sing to the LORD, all the earth.
> Sing to the LORD, praise his name;
>   proclaim his salvation day after day (Psa. 96:1-2).

The song is for Jehovah alone, the hymns which chanted the praises of Jupiter and Neptune, Vishnoo and Siva, are hushed forever; Baccanalian shouts are silenced, lascivious sonnets are no more.[22]

"All the earth."

National jealousies are dead; a Jew invites the Gentile to adore, and joins with them, so that all the earth may lift up one common psalm as with one heart and voice to Jehovah, who hath visited it with salvation. No corner of the world is to be discordant, no rose of heather to be dumb. All the earth Jehovah hath made, and all the earth must sing to him.[23]

> Declare his glory among the nations,
>   his marvelous deeds among all peoples (Psa. 96:3).

Evangelism requires declaration of the gospel. One must be present to evangelize, but presence evangelism does not adequately communicate the good news. Helping people in need is important, and may even be essential, but even though the unevangelized see the love of God in action, they cannot know the actions of God that motivated these actions unless someone tells them.

---

21. Ibid., p. 336.
22. Ibid., p. 337.
23. Ibid.

146

The United States has expended a great fortune promoting the glory of Old Glory in the world. At the Pan Am games in Indianapolis, in 1987, the opening ceremony was an expensive extravaganza telling the other American nations how great, how successful, how powerful the United States is. To say the least the program was in poor taste. The host country which has the largest population, the greatest wealth, and was destined to win the most medals, did not need to brag about herself. We would have done better to emphasize the things the Americas have in common, or to have praised and encouraged our smaller less wealthy neighbors.

As Christians we need to declare His glory not ours. As Christians we need to be more willing to spend our fortunes to promote the glory of God, more willing to send our sons and daughters to "declare his glory among the nations."

> For great is the LORD and most worthy of praise;
>   he is to be feared above all gods.
>
> For all the gods of the nations are idols,
>   but the LORD made the heavens (Psa. 96:4-5).

The Hebrew, *elohim*, used by the Psalmist and translated "gods" does not mean that the writer equates the gods of the nations with the God of creation. Not only does he in this passage use YHWH (translated LORD) in contrast with gods, he specifically contrasts "the LORD who made the heavens" with "the gods of the nations." And although the reader may get the impression occasionally from the Psalms that the God of the Hebrews is just one among many gods, a careful reading of the text indicates otherwise. For instance, when the article "the" is used with *elohim* the meaning is "the one true God." But the article is not necessary for *elohim* to have the meaning of one true God. *Elohim* is used frequently both in poetry and prose to refer to YHWH.

147

Thus, the gods are not to be construed as real gods, but "nothings, good-for-nothings, unreal, and useless."[24] Isaiah, who so severely condemns idolatry, uses *elohim* more frequently than the other Old Testament authors.

It is more than poetic irony that the idols of the nations are made by man, but that Yahweh made man. Isaiah is scathing in his remark that men make an idol from one end of a log and keep themselves warm by burning the other end.

Splendor and majesty are before him;
  strength and glory are in his sanctuary (Psa. 96:6).

Something of the nature of Yahweh that calls for the universal worship is given. "Strength and majesty" is the usual couplet for royal glory. He is therefore king.

Ascribe to the LORD, O families of nations,
  ascribe to the LORD glory and strength.
Ascribe to the LORD the glory due his name;
  bring an offering and come into his courts.
Worship the LORD in the splendor of his holiness;
  tremble before him, all the earth (Psa. 96:7-9).

"Give . . . give . . . bring (AV)." The triple repetition here and in Psalm 24 picture the peoples coming with their gifts as in Isaiah 60. In this procession are people of every color, race, and ethnic group. Each of them is appropriately clad in "holy" attire. One is reminded of the wedding garments in Jesus' parable (Matt. 22:11-14). The holy attire may be understood to be deeds of righteousness.

Say among the nations, "The LORD reigns."
  The world is firmly established, it cannot be moved;
  he will judge the peoples with equity (Psa. 96:10).

---

24. Delitzsch, p. 112.

Yahweh not only radiates royal glory as in verse six but performs the very practical function of providing stability and foundation for a world racked by sin, war, and anarchy. He is the foundation that cannot be shaken. This brings joy that pervades the whole creation:

Let the heavens rejoice, let the earth be glad;
   let the sea resound, and all that is in it;
   let the fields be jubilant, and everything in them.
Then all the trees of the forest will sing for joy (Psa. 96:11-12).

The ultimate motive for accepting Yahweh as king is that He is also Judge and one day will judge the world according to His standard of righteousness.

[T]hey will sing before the LORD, for he comes,
   he comes to judge the earth.
He will judge the world in righteousness
   and the peoples in this truth (Psa. 96:13).

Psalm 98 reads,

Sing to the LORD a new song,
   for he has done marvelous things;
his right hand and his holy arm
   have worked salvation for him (Psa. 98:1).

It was God who effected salvation. He did it without the aid of others. In fact, God alone could save man.

More than that, it was by His "right hand." That is to say, with His unweaponed hand. Sin, death, and hell were defeated by seemingly powerless means. The spiritual power of a sinless life, death on a criminal's cross, and the resurrection of the dead, one provided the victory of salvation.

The LORD has made his salvation known
   and revealed his righteousness to the nations (Psa. 98:2).

149

Yahweh is not only to be praised for providing salvation but also for making this salvation known to man. Mankind needs not flounder in seeking salvation. The Bible is not even a record of man's search for God. Rather, it is a revelation of God's will for man.

> All Scripture is God-breathed and is useful for teaching, rebuking, correcting and training in righteousness, so that the man of God may be thoroughly equipped for *every* good work (II Tim. 3:16).

Now that Jehovah has given His revelation to His church it is encumbent upon us to make His salvation known to those who are unreached.

The word translated "made known," *yada*, comes from a root that means to lay up what is preserved. Thus it

> denotes not only a *publication* and promulgation, but also a clear and certain demonstration which produces conviction and causes the matter to be *laid up* in the mind and memory and preserved. The word (*galah*) is added, which properly means *to uncover, to be uncovered*, hence *be revealed* or *uncovered*, that it might be both naked and clear, for the purpose of more fully illustrating the character of the manifestations of the Gospel, opposed to what is obscure.[25]

> He has remembered his love
>   and his faithfulness to the house of Israel;
> all the ends of the earth have seen
>   the salvation of our God (Psa. 98:3).

Salvation begins with Israel, but whether or not Israel accepts the Messiah, it continues until it reaches the ends of the earth. Luke picks up this idea in his account of the commission, "you will be my witnesses in Jerusalem, and in all Judea and Samaria,

---

25. Venema quoted by Spurgeon, p. 378.

and to the ends of the earth" (Acts 1:8).

Psalm 117 is the shortest Psalm. But whereas it is little in letter, it is large in spirit. It bursts beyond all constraints of race or nationality. Paul quotes verse 1 as a prophecy of the conversion of the gentiles in Rom. 15:11.

> Praise the LORD, all you nations;
>   extol him, all you peoples.
> For great is his love toward us,
>   and the faithfulness of the LORD endures forever (Psa. 117:1-2).

Spurgeon again helps us to see that this brief poem is clear proof that the Old Testament differed greatly in spirit from the narrow bigotry of the Jewish leaders of the Lord's day. The nations are invited to praise Jehovah, but they could not have expected to join in the praise unless they were already partakers of the benefits of salvation. Delitzsch tells us that this peculiar *goy* refers to all nations without exception.

In the language of Moses' song, "Rejoice, O nations, with his people" (Deut. 32:43). People from every tongue are represented in this chorus of praise. John describes the ultimate scene from Patmos,

> You are worthy to take the scroll and to open its seals, because you were slain, and with your blood you purchased men for God from every tribe and language and people and nation (Rev. 5:9-10).

VI. ALL NATIONS ARE SUMMONED TO JUDGMENT

We have a choice whether to accept the invitation to praise God. But we have no option as to whether we appear before the Judge. We have only the choice whether we will appear as forgiven or unforgiven sinners.

Psalm 97, like Psalm 96 and Psalm 98, has Yahweh as King as its theme. It is less explicitly addressed to the nations of the world. But its universal application is clear: the earth is to be glad, let the distant shore rejoice, His lightning lightens the world, the earth sees and trembles, He is Lord of the whole earth, all people see His glory, all the gods worship Him, and He is Most High over all the earth.

The reason given for this universal recognition of Yahweh is "because of your judgments." Thus the whole world is warned that they will appear in judgment before Yahweh.

> The LORD reigns, let the earth be glad;
>   let the distant shores rejoice.
> Clouds and thick darkness surround him;
>   righteousness and justice are the foundation of his throne.
> Fire goes before him
>   and consumes his foes on every side (Psa. 97:1-3).

The Psalmist begins with the present rule of Yahweh which anticipates His coming judgment on mankind. Those who live on "distant shores," the Gentiles, have occasion to rejoice, but they are also warned that God "consumes his foes on every side." The basis of His judgment is righteousness and justice, pictured here as the foundation of His throne.

> His lightning lights up the world;
>   the earth sees and trembles.
> The mountains melt like wax before the LORD,
>   before the LORD of the earth.
> The heavens proclaim his righteousness,
>   and all the peoples see his glory.
> All who worship images are put to shame,
>   those who boast in idols —
>   worship him, all you gods! (Psa. 97:4-7).

Light both illuminates, dispels darkness, and destroys evil. As the rays of the sun start a consuming fire, so the intense light of

God's presence can "melt mountains." The metaphor is explained in the destruction of idols and their worship.

But the same light that destroys evil also brings joy to the righteous:

> Zion hears and rejoices
>> and the villages of Judah are glad
>> because of your judgments, O LORD (Psa. 97:8).

Psalms 96 and 98 which we examined in the last section also warn us of the impending judgment,

> He will judge the people with equity (Psa. 96:10c).
> . . . .
>> he comes to judge the earth.
> He will judge the world in righteousness
>> and the people in his truth (Psa. 96:13).

> He will judge the world in righteousness
>> and the peoples with equity (Psa. 98:9b; see also Psa. 9:7-8).

God is not capricious. The rules of the game will not be changed when we appear before His bench. He has given us the standards by which we will be judged: righteousness, truth, and equity.

Again this is another motivation for Christian missions. We have the message that will make men righteous and enable them to stand innocent in the day of judgment.

That He will judge in equity, means among other things that those who have not told will be held in greater judgment than those who have not been told.

Psalm 50 reads,

> The Mighty One, God, the Lord,
>> speaks and summons the earth
>> from the rising of the sun to the place where it sets (Psa. 50:1).

There is an interesting and suggestive grammatical construction in this sentence. Three names of God comprise the subject of the sentence: El, Elohim, and Yahweh. Structurally there are three subjects. But the verb, "speaks," is singular! Three things are implied by this unique construction. One, El, Elohim, and Yahweh are not three different gods as suggested by some critical scholars, but three names for the same God. Two, as John Gill suggests, this may help us to understand the doctrine of the Trinity. And, three, under whichever name or names, or person or persons God speaks, He speaks as one. His message is unified.

"From the rising of the sun to the place where it sets" tells us that "the dominion of Jehovah extends over the whole earth, and therefore to all mankind is his decree directed."[26]

And to what does He summon His people? Judgment!

> He summons the heavens above,
>   and the earth that he may judge his people:
> Gather to me my consecrated ones,
>   who made a covenant with me by sacrifice.
> And the heavens declare his righteousness,
>   for God himself is judge (Psa. 50:4-5).

Knowledge of the coming judgment should be a great motive for the nations to turn from their pride.

> Arise, O LORD, let not man triumph;
>   let the nations be judged in your presence.
> Strike them with terror, O LORD;
>   let the nations know they are but men (Psa. 9:19-20).

The Christian, however, need not fear the judgment for "there is now no condemnation for those who are in Christ Jesus" (Rom. 8:1).

---

26. Spurgeon, II:429.

VII. JEHOVAH IS NEAR TO ALL NATIONS

Verse 18 is the key to Psalm 145:

The LORD is near to all who call on him,
    to all who call on him in truth.

The dominant motif in this Psalm is that God loves all people and that all people have access to Him.

David begins by telling the fact that the love of God is expressed in His acts which are then promulgated to all:

One generation will commend your works to another
    they will tell of your mighty acts.
They will speak of the glorious splendor of your majesty,
    and I will meditate on your wonderful works.
They will tell of the power of your awesome works,
    and I will proclaim your great deeds (Psa. 145:4-6).

The reason is:

The LORD is gracious and compassionate,
    slow to anger and rich in love.
The LORD is good to all
    he has compassion on all he has made (Psa. 145:8-9).

There is nothing in Psalm 145 of narrow Judaism or of ethnocentrism of any sort. In reading or singing this poem one can not help but be impressed with the universal nature of the biblical religion.

The basis of this universal love of God is the fact that God created the whole world, and hence everyone and everything in it is His possession as expressed in Psalm 24.

At the time of the second temple each day of the week had a specific Psalm for the day. Psalm 24 was to be sung on

Sundays.[27] What better way to start the week than by praising God with these inspired words:

> The earth is the LORD's and everything in it,
>> the world, and all who live in it;
> for he founded it upon the seas
>> and established it upon the waters (Psa. 24:1-2).

Only Yahweh may be said to have created everything and, therefore, He possesses everything and everyone. The heathen deities can claim only limited sovereignty.

> Who may ascend the hill of the LORD?
> Who may stand in his holy place? (Psa. 24:3).

Is it only the Jew who may enter the holy place? The Anglo-Saxon? The American? David answers:

> He who has clean hands and a pure heart,
>> who does not lift up his soul to an idol
> or swear by what is false (Psa. 24:4)

Fellowship with God is not dependent upon birth or station in this world. The Psalmist lists four conditions for this fellowship: innocent actions, purity of mind, a soul that has not sought vain things, and one who has not deceived others.

> He will receive blessing from the LORD
>> and vindication from God his Savior.
> Such is the generation of those who seek him,
>> who seek your face, O God of Jacob (Psa. 24:5-6).

The blessing that is given is a right relation to Yahweh. Note that it is not earned by the worshipper, but is given by God. The

---

27. Delitzsch, p. 1852.

Psalmist anticipates the righteousness described by Paul in Romans.

> Lift up your heads, O you gates;
>> be lifted up, you ancient doors,
>> that the King of glory may come in.
> Who is this King of glory?
>> The LORD strong and mighty,
>> the LORD mighty in battle.
> Lift up your heads, O you gates;
>> lift then up, you ancient doors,
>> that the King of glory may come in.
> Who is he, this King of glory?
>> The LORD Almighty —
>> he is the King of glory (Psa. 24:7-10).

This Psalm was composed to celebrate the moving of the Ark to the tabernacle on Zion. This may have been when David moved the Ark from Kiriath Jearim to Jerusalem (II Sam. 6:17; 11:11; I Kgs. 1:39). Or, more appropriately, according to Delitzsch, at a later date when the Ark was returned to Mount Zion after accompanying the army into battle (II Sam. 11:11; Psa. 68).[28]

The ultimate fulfillment of the entrance of the King is the ascension of Jesus to the eternal realms.

> Is it too much to imagine that the heavenly hosts come out to meet the conquering King and escort His triumphal way — up the steps of light, through the pearly gates, down the golden streets, singing as they went?[29]

SUMMARY

Think of the impact on the members of a congregation that

---

28. Delitzsch, p. 1084.
29. Kane, p. 214.

sings Psalms like these Sabbath after Sabbath. As the congregation voices the words the concepts thus expressed enter the thought processes of the mind. Men who sing, "let all the people of the world revere him"; "I will make the nations your inheritance"; "may your ways be known on earth, your salvation among the nations"; "Sing to the LORD a new song; sing to the LORD, all the earth"; "he will judge the peoples with equity"; "The LORD is righteous in all his ways and loving toward all he has made"; "The LORD is near to all who call on him, to all who call on him in truth," cannot but have their ethnocentrism destroyed, and sense an obligation to proclaim the message of Jehovah to all nations.

Since corporate singing is as effective today as in Old Testament times, would it not be appropriate to sing at least one of these Psalms every Lord's day?

6

THE PROPHETS SPEAK

ISAIAH - MALACHI

The finest jewels are mined from the hardest rock. We will have to work hard to extract the great missionary lessons from the Old Testament prophets. Most of us find understanding the prophets difficult because they are addressing historical situations we don't really understand, they write of places and people that have names that are difficult to pronounce, and even more difficult to identify, and at times, especially in the poetic sections, they use terminology that is unfamiliar.

These men were prophets of God to Judah and Israel. They wrote in the languages of these people, Hebrew and Aramaic. They were prophets primarily to the People of God. However, they had a lot to say about the relation of Yahweh and the People of the Covenant to the *goyim*. They especially had something to say about the Messiah's kingdom which was yet to come. And it is from these messages that we learn some more lessons about mission.

The writing prophets were contemporary with the kings of Judah and Israel after the division of the kingdom. So chronologically this chapter follows Chapter Four, "The Kingdom of Israel and the People of God."

I. THE PRE-EXILIC PROPHETS

1. Elijah

Elijah is neither a writing prophet nor does he have anything to say about a Gentile population. But he clamors for our attention because of a major event in his ministry — the contest with the prophets of Baal on Mount Carmel (I Kgs. 18).

Today this kind of confrontation is called a "power encounter." Today's Baals are idols and evil spirits, believed by their adherents to exercise real control over human lives. Many of the devotees of these supernatural beings must see a demonstration that the Christian God is more powerful than their gods, before they will become Christians. Thus missionaries today employ power encounters as a missionary method.[1] These may take any one of six forms.

a. Challenge[2]

A few have advocated a duplication today of Elijah's experience. They have suggested that the Christian missionary deliberately set up a similar encounter. This, it seems to me, is not justified for three reasons: one, we have no such examples in the ministry of the apostles.[3] Two, no one today has the gift of dis-

---

1. See Alan R. Tippett, *Introduction to Missiology* (Pasadena: William Carey Library, 1987), Chapter Twenty-five.

2. I use "challenge" with a different meaning than Tippett. See Tippett, p. 318.

3. The one possible exception is the girl with the gift of ventriloquism in Philippi. Paul used the gift of exorcism to command the spirit to leave her. And, here, his purpose was not to demonstrate the superior power of God as an evangelistic method, but to get rid of a nuisance (Acts 16:16-18).

cerning of spirits so as to know the nature of these opposing forces. And, three, there are no prophets today who have the insight or gift of Elijah.

b. Preaching the Gospel

For Paul, who possessed more spiritual gifts than most (I Cor. 14:18), it was the gospel that was the "power of God" (Rom. 12:16; I Cor. 1:1). No other influence has been so effective in changing spirit-possessed men to Spirit-filled men, idol worshippers to slaves of the living God, drunkards to sober men, dope addicts to free men, than the Gospel. And this power is in the possession of *every* Christian. It is not a special spiritual gift, but a power that *every* believer can exercise.

> the word of the cross is the divine wisdom as opposed to all worldly wisdom (1 Cor. 1:18 ff). Therefore the powers of this world are overcome by the preaching and spreading of the Gospel, and Paul is leading as a missionary in a triumphal march through the country, propagating the *euodia christou* ("the savor of Christ," 2 Cor. 2:14ff).[4]

c. Prayer Power

In those cases where it is perceived that evil spirits so control men's lives that they cannot respond to the Gospel, Christian missionaries invoke the power of God to intervene. This is rarely mentioned in mission literature and hardly believed in U.S. churches.

d. Medical Healing

A major activity of evil spirits is causing disease and death. The belief in the influence of spirits and in the power of the witchdoctor is so strong that Christians frequently go to the witchdoctor instead of a medical doctor, even when one is available. And, unless the individual is a mature Christian of many years, most missionary physicians find that their patients have all already

---

4. Ferdinand Hahn, *Mission in the New Testament* (Naperville: Alec R. Allenson, Inc., 1965), p. 99.

gone to the witchdoctor before coming to them for treatment.

An epidemic of pinkeye swept through the Motilones. The witchdoctor sang her incantations over them but none were cured. So many suffered from this painful infection though the witchdoctor worked twenty hours a day trying to help. But none of her potions or chants helped. Bruce Olson suggested she try some Terramycin he had. She refused, saying it was white man's medicine and would not work on the Motilones. Bruce tried an experiment. He took pus from the eye of an infected man and put it in the corner of his own eye. In five days he had pinkeye. He then asked the witchdoctor to put some of his Terramycin in his eye. She did it and within three days he was cured. Since the epidemic was not decreasing, while her energy was as she worked such long hours without success, he offered again to let her use his ointment. This time she accepted and within a few days the pinkeye epidemic disappeared from the village. This opened the door for further teaching about both physical and spiritual health care.[5]

e. Changed Lives

Perhaps the most powerful encounter occurs when lives are changed by the Gospel.[6] Opium addiction, for instance, cannot be stopped by mere will power. The Morse family works in the Golden Triangle where most of the world's supply of opium is grown. They have had remarkable success breaking the opium habit of addicts of the area. They do it "cold turkey," in a two week program of Bible study, prayer, rest, and good food. Tribal neighbors of the addicts have been so impressed with the power of Christ to halt the opium habit that many have become Christian.

f. Destruction of Paraphernalia

The practice of animism is characterized by the existence of,

5. Bruce E. Olson., *Bruchko* (Carol Stream: Creation House, 1973) pp. 130-132.

6. For illustrations of this experience see Tippett, pp. 315-18.

and use of, a variety of physical objects that represent spiritual powers. These include such things as spirit shelves, charms, amulets, relics, sacred objects, etc. In the view of the adherents these contain real power. It is of no use to argue that they have no power. The adherents, and some Christians, "know" these objects possess spiritual power. Therefore one of the things the new convert must do is to destroy these paraphernalia.[7] If the new convert retains these sacred items, he may be under frequent temptation to use them. However, to destroy them is to make a real break with the past.

Those people who still believe in the power of the spirits usually expect some catastrophe or punishment to come to the convert who so challenges the spiritual forces. The rite of destruction is seen as a real power encounter. The fact that no harm comes to the one destroying the items frequently leads to the conversion of other animists.

It is important that the right person and the correct method of destruction be employed in the act. Otherwise, the adherents will not recognize that a power encounter has occurred. For even the most ardent believers in mana and taboo recognize that the spiritual power resident in a piece of paraphernalia is limited to certain people and to specific things.

2. Amos

Amos, a shepherd of Tekoah, was called to be a prophet to Israel when Uzziah was king of Judah and Jeroboam II ruler of Israel. Under the leadership of these two monarchs the two kingdoms had risen to the height of their economic prosperity. However, Amos does not commend them for their success but announces judgment and destruction.

a. Judgment is universal

Amos begins by announcing judgment on Israel's neighbors: Damascus, Gaza, Edom, Ammon, Moab, and Judah. The style

---

7. For illustrations of these events see Tippett, pp. 318-22.

of the pronouncement is uniform, "for three sins . . . even for four, I will not turn back my wrath." The pronunciations of judgment are brief. We get the distinct impression that these six prophecies are introductory to the major announcement of Amos, judgment on Israel. However, Amos writes them here in brief to point out the enormity of Israel's sin and the magnitude of her judgment.

As we see in Amos, Yahweh shows no favoritism in judgment. All will be judged. As Keil has written,

> The six heathen nations mentioned, three of which are related to the covenant nation, represent all the Gentile nations, which rise up in hostility to the people of the kingdom of God.
> . . . .
> Whilst, on the other hand, the extension of the prediction of judgment to the Gentiles indicates the necessity and universality of judgment, which is sent to promote the interests of the kingdom of God, and preaches the truth that every one will be judged according to his attitude towards the living God; on the other hand, the place assigned to the Gentile nations, viz. before the covenant nation, not only sharpened the conscience, but taught this lesson, that if even the nations which had only sinned indirectly against the living God were visited with severe punishment, those to whom God had so gloriously revealed Himself (ch. ii.9-11,iii.1) would be punished still more surely for their apostasy (ch. iii.2).[8]

The most important contribution Amos makes to our understanding of mission is that:

b. Israel will be restored in the establishment of the church.

Israel was to be destroyed but not utterly annihilated. God could not destroy the Covenant People or change His purpose. "All the sinners among my people will die by the sword" (Amos 9:10). There were those who were not sinners and, therefore, who did not deserve death. Out of that remnant,

---

8. Ibid.

In that day I will restore David's fallen tent. I will restore its broken places, restore its ruins, and build it as it used to be (Amos 9:11).

In the day of destruction Yahweh will set up a new kingdom. "David's fallen tent" is in contrast with the palace he built in Jerusalem (II Sam. 5:11). The reference, of course, is not to the actual structure, but to the disintegration of the house of David, the dynasty he founded. The beginning of the destruction took place with the division of the nation into two kingdoms. It was furthered by the conquest of Israel by Assyria, and the captivity of Judah by Babylon. The restoration did not occur until 800 years later in the inauguration of the new kingdom in Jerusalem.

Three phases of this restoration are described by Amos. One, "I will repair its broken places" (which Keil and Delitzsch translates as "I will wall up its rents"). The figure of the tent is continued. It is from the remnants of this damage the new kingdom is to be formed. Two, "to restore its ruins" is a reference to David's reign. Three, "to build it" does not mean to build but to finish building. "As it used to be" looks back to the promise in II Sam. 7:11-12,16 according to which David's house, throne, and kingdom were to last forever. Jesus, who was in David's lineage, fulfilled that promise with his enthronement on the heavenly throne and the beginning of His rule on Pentecost.

[S]o that they may possess the remnant of Edom and all the nations that bear my name, declares the LORD, who will do all things (Amos 9:12).

Again, the purpose of the existence of the kingdom of David, and the purpose of the kingdom of the Messiah, is stated: "that all the nations" may come into the kingdom. Edom is mentioned specifically of all the nations. This is probably because Edom, of all nations, not only was related to David's family, but also was the most hostile toward David's kingdom. Thus the new kingdom not only welcomed but aggressively courted the most truculent

165

foe of Yahweh. The Edomites had passed out of existence by the First Century A.D. but we read of their genealogical counterparts, the Samaritans, who were welcomed into the church in the first expansion beyond Jerusalem (Acts 8:4-8).

"Nations" here is *goyim*, a word we studied earlier. The nations are to become citizens of the Messiah's kingdom. This event did not occur when David conquered the nations of the promised land, nor did it happen earlier under the conquest of Joshua and his successors. It was fulfilled only with the beginning of the Kingdom of Christ.

If there are any doubts about the fulfillment of Amos' prophecy, James lays them to rest permanently. In the dispute about receiving Gentiles into the church without circumcision, James quotes this passage from Amos (Acts 15:16-17). His purpose is to prove from this divinely inspired prophecy that the Gentiles are to be accepted in the kingdom without circumcision. But in so doing he also identifies the church with the kingdom. For James, the church fulfills Amos' prophecy of the restoration of the kingdom. As the kingdom of Israel was the locus of God's reign in that day, the church is composed of the people who accept God's reign in the new age. Although both the Old and New Testament writers recognize the sovereignty of God in the world, none of them speak of His reign over men who do not submit to His rule (although they proclaim that all men will ultimately submit to His judgment). Neither the prophets nor apostles subscribe to a dual fulfillment of prophecy that calls for the kingdom of Christ to be set up on earth twice, first at Pentecost, and secondly at the return of Christ. The dual fulfillment of prophecy is a hermeneutic device created by some theologians to find proof for their preconceived eschatological theories.

3. Isaiah

Thirteen times Isaiah calls Israel the servant of Yahweh (Isa. 41:8-9; 42:1-9,19; 43:10; 44:1-2,21,26; 45:4; 48:20; 49:3,6; 50:10). But what is Israel's role as a servant? Peters points out that the frequently recurring phrases "ye are my witnesses" (Isa.

43:10,12; 44:8), and "my messenger" (Isa. 42:19; 44:26) indicate that Israel's primary function is to declare the message of Yahweh to the nations.[9]

Unfortunately, the nation of Israel was a failure as a witness. Worse than that, not only did they fail to communicate the Lord's will to the nations, they copied the practices of their pagan neighbors (II Kgs. 17:7-23). As a consequence the ten northern tribes were carried away into Assyrian captivity, never to return.

At least one lesson is evident. When God's people, who have the responsibility of evangelizing the world, fail to do so, God may allow His own people to be wiped from the face of the earth.

A second lesson is also obvious. God will not allow His purpose to be thwarted. Out of His failed people He will raise a remnant that shall succeed. In this instance, the remnant came, not from Israel, but from Judah after her captivity in Babylon.

Israel, the servant of Yahweh, was to have its prophetic fulfillment in the Messianic Servant (Isa. 52:13-53:12) who was to be a light to the gentiles (Isa. 42:6; 49:6), and who was to give a new name to His people when "[t]he nations will see your righteousness, and all kings your glory" (Isa. 62:2) This prophecy had its fulfillment in Antioch as we shall see in chapter 12.

This promise of "all nations" streaming into the Lord's temple to be taught His ways in order to walk in His paths was to be fulfilled "in the last days" (Isa. 2:1-4). The New Testament writers understood that the last days began with the first advent of Jesus (Heb. 1:2; Acts 2:17; I John 2:18).

The promise is that ultimately "the earth will be full of the knowledge of the LORD as the waters cover the sea" (Isa. 11:1-11). In the face of persecution, opposition, closed doors, and decline, this promise of ultimate victory provides confidence and hope based, not on human strength or achievement, but on the promise of a faithful God. "Surely this is our God; we trusted in him, and he saved us" (Isa. 25:1-9).

---

9. P. 124.

4. Micah

Micah's messianic prophecy in 4:1-5 is essentially the same as Isa. 2:1-4.

5. Zephaniah

Zephaniah, the great-great-grandson of good king Hezekiah, prophesied during the reign of Josiah (Zeph. 1:1). Since the temple had been restored (Zeph. 3:4) it is assumed in spite of Josiah's reform (II Kgs. 22:1-23:30; I Chron. 34:1-35:19) that not all of Israel, including the priesthood, had been reformed.

The book appears as one prophecy with three parts: warning of judgment to come, exhortation to repentance, and promise of salvation. Since no occasion, or set of occasions, is given for the proclamation of these prophecies, we conclude this short treatise is a digest of the messages of Zephaniah during his prophetic career.

a. Judgment is universal.

Although Zephaniah addresses Judah primarily, the coming destruction that he predicts is coming to all men, not just citizens of Judah. More than that, it, like the flood of Noah's day, will destroy the animals and birds. It will be even more destructive in that even the fish will be destroyed (Zeph. 1:1-3,18). Yahweh will destroy the gods of the world in order that the nations may in turn worship Yahweh (Zeph. 2:11).

God, the Judge of the whole world, will bring all men to account, but especially Judah, the kingdom of God, will be brought into punishment in order to purge the dross from her silver. We are not to understand that this judgment is total or final. It is a judgment with the purpose of refining the People of God.

b. Repentance is required.

All the nations of the earth are called to change their behavior. "Gather together . . . seek the LORD . . . seek righteousness . . . seek humility, perhaps you will be sheltered" (Zeph. 2:1-3). Zephaniah specifically mentions the punishment coming to the near nations (Philistia and Moab), the distant nations, north and south (Assyria and Cush), and to the east and west countries (Moab, Ammon, and Philistia). And closest to home the punishment will come to their own capital, Jerusalem.

c. Salvation is for all peoples.

Then I will purify the lips of the *peoples*,
that *all* of them may call on the name of the LORD
and serve him shoulder to shoulder.
From beyond the rivers of Cush
my worshipers, my scattered people (Zeph. 3:9-10).

The lips of man had been defiled by invoking the names of the false gods they worshipped. Yahweh now forgives them and makes it posible for them to use these same lips to praise Him. This salvation is for all people, even the most remote "beyond the rivers of Cush."

The purpose of the punishment is now clear.

The end and goal at which they [the prophets] aim are rather the establishment of divine righteousness in the earth, and the judgment is simply the means and the way by which this, the aim of all the development of the world's history is to be realized.[10]

The promise that the Gentiles will participate in salvation looks forward to the coming of Christ and His kingdom. It is an event Paul describes in Romans 9: "The Gentiles, who did not pursue righteousness, have obtained it" (Rom. 9:30). The evangelism which was implicit in the prophets became explicit in the church.

6. Jonah and Nahum

The two prophets, Jonah and Nahum, not only present a contrast but a contradiction in proclamation and results. They do, however, have the same audience. Both address Nineveh. Jonah went to Nineveh and "proclaimed: Forty more days and Nineveh will be overturned" (Jonah 3:4). The text does not say that Jonah

---

10. Keil and Delitzsch, VI:1279.

169

preached repentance. And there is nothing in Jonah's attitude to suggest that he would have included repentance as a part of his message.

Nevertheless, the king repented, fasted, and prayed. And he issued a proclamation for the entire population to do the same (Jon. 3:6-9).

> When God saw what they did and how they turned from their evil ways, he had compassion and did not bring upon them the destruction he had threatened (Jonah 3:10)

The serious Bible student is immediately confronted with questions about the nature of God. Is God capricious? Does He send out contradictory messages? Does He change His mind? Does He change His plans? Others may see the problem not in the nature of God, but in the human authors of the texts. In that view Jonah and Nahum are not penning the revelation from God but writing their own views of the situation.[11]

The apparent theological contradiction can be solved in the context of the whole of Hebrew Scriptures. We have now examined most of the Old Testament. From the beginning we have seen that God's purpose has been the inclusion of all peoples into the kingdom of God. The entire history of the People of God has been to prepare them for the coming of Christ and the evangelization of the world. However, at no point in this period are the People of God instructed to evangelize their neighbors. Jonah, in spite of the missionary sermons based upon his experience, did not attempt to convert the Ninevites. The facts, however, that they repented and that subsequently God cancelled their destruction, do not make God capricious. It only reinforces the Bible's presentation of the purpose of God which is to reconcile all men

---

11. The assumption of the author of this book does not allow the Scriptures to be the record of man's search after God, but an inspired account of God's search for man.

to Himself. God is more interested in saving than in condemning, more concerned with reconciliation than with destruction.

But why Nineveh? And why now? Keil and Delitzsch help us to understand the historical situation.[12] Israel was about to go into captivity as punishment for her sins. In her ethnocentricity it would be easy to develop pride that she was better than her captors even while captive. And as the People of God she could develop hatred for the Gentiles whom she might regard as the enemies of God. But Israel was to become the vehicle of salvation for the whole world. Thus she needed a visible demonstration of the fact that God loved, forgave, and accepted Gentiles. No better example could be given than the conversion of the capital of Assyria, the impending captors of the ten tribes.

The mission of Jonah also served as a type of the future relation of Israel to the Gentiles.[13] That time was coming in the Messianic Age. Jonah's incarceration in the fish's belly became a type of Jesus' death, burial, and resurrection (Matt. 12:46). Jonah, the Jewish evangel, became a type of the early Jewish/Christian missionaries. And the conversion of Nineveh became a picture of the conversion of the Gentiles.

The text does not tell us how Nahum delivered his message, whether in person or writing. "The *book* of the vision of Nahum the Elkoshite" (Nahum 1:1) suggests that Nahum's prophecy, unlike most other prophets, was written first, and not preached and then later collected and assembled in one volume.[14] Perhaps this "oracle concerning Nineveh" (Nahum 1:1) was not delivered to them all, but related to Judah for Judah's benefit (Nahum 1:13,15), because Judah needed to hear that her enemy nation, Assyria, would be destroyed. Jonah, on the other hand, was sent to Nineveh to preach his message in the city streets.

---

12. VI:1083.
13. Ibid., pp. 1083-86.
14. E.B. Pusey, *The Minor Prophets* (New York: Funk & Wagnalls, Publishers, 1885), II:130.

Nahum was a message of unmitigated woe. Subsequent to Nineveh's repentance as a result of Jonah's preaching, she has returned to her former ways and has become an enemy of God and His people. Nineveh is not told to repent. Nineveh is to be destroyed. There is no hope for her salvation. "Nothing can heal your wound; your injury is fatal" (Nahum 3:19).

7. Habakkuk

There are four universals in Habakkuk.

a. The Universal Use of the Nations by God.

From Judah's perspective Babylon was remote. Babylon was an enemy. Babylon had no association with Yahweh. Yahweh could not use Babylon. Yahweh would not use Babylon. But, *look*, Judah!

> Look at the nations and watch — and be utterly amazed.
> For I am going to do something in your days
>> that you would not believe,
>> even if you were told.
> I am raising up *Babylonians*,
>> that ruthless and impetuous people,
>> who sweep across the whole earth
>>> to seize dwelling places not their own (Hab. 1:5-6).

Just as Yahweh earlier had used Egypt to preserve and discipline His people by captivity, He now was going to capture and discipline His people in Judah. These nations did not recognize Yahweh as the true god, but their usefulness was not totally destroyed. They had rejected Yahweh's reign. But God had not rejected them.

Habakkuk named Judah's captor, Babylon. He even told the time of their departure, "in your days." Still, the event was to be so great, so sudden, they would be "utterly amazed," and "would not believe."

b. The Universal Justification by Faith.

Judah tried to live by law and failed (Hab. 1:4). "Clearly no one is justified before God by the law" (Gal. 3:11). In fact, observance of the law brings a curse (Gal. 3:10), the consciousness of sin (Rom. 3:20), and death (Rom. 8:2).

Babylon lived by conquest and theft (Hab. 2:5-14). This kind of life would have its retribution. "Because you have plundered many nations, the peoples who are left will plunder you (Hab. 2:8).

Both Babylon and Judah were going to be destroyed. How, then, can one live? "The righteous will live by his faith" (Hab. 2:4). Paul makes it clear, by quoting this text, that the faith is faith in Christ (Rom. 1:17; Gal. 3:11; Heb. 10:37-38). This faith is available to Jew and Gentile alike. Faith is universal.

    c. The Universal Reign of God.

> For the earth will be filled
> > with the knowledge of the glory of the LORD,
> > as the waters cover the sea (Hab. 2:14).

"Sea" is a geographical term and the lesson is optimistic. Just as surely as the seabed is covered with the water of the sea, just as certainly the whole earth will be covered with the knowledge of the glory of God. At the time of Habakkuk the greatest geographical extent of Israel had occurred during the reign of David. The limits of Habakkuk's world were the Tigris and Euphrates Rivers, the Red Sea, and the Mediterranean Sea. It was inconceivable to Judah that the Reign of God would ultimately encompass that world, and it was beyond the wildest imagination that it would cover the world known to Twentieth Century man.

Isaiah had the same vision, except that he wrote of "the knowledge of the LORD" (Isa. 11:9) instead of "the knowledge of the glory of the LORD" as in Habakkuk. Keil and Delitzsch suggest that whereas Isaiah was writing from the perspective of the Messianic kingdom having been fully established, and therefore, wrote of the "knowledge of the LORD covering the earth," Habakkuk is anticipating that the pagan governments are yet to be overthrown by the power of Yahweh. When that occurs it is the *glory* of Yahweh that shall be known. In either case, the point is, that the Reign of God will ultimately triumph and all men will be brought under subjection to it.

d. The Universal Judgment of God.

> But the LORD is in his holy temple;
>   let all the earth be silent before him (Hab. 2:20).

The scene is in the temple. Yahweh is on His throne. The picture is of a living God ready to receive His worshippers, not of a dead idol who is insensitive to the petitions of his adorers.

But the earth is silent! Is this the silence of awe and reverence? Or is this the silence because of fear in men who have appeared before the Eternal Judge? Isa. 41:1 instructs the islands to be silent before the throne of justice. Further, the context seems to favor the concept of judgment in this case.

Habakkuk has the same concepts as Zephaniah has of a universal God, a universal faith, universal nations, and a universal judgment. Habakkuk goes somewhat further than Zephaniah in that he prophesies a future time when the knowledge of Yahweh will be universal.

EXILIC PROPHET

1. Daniel

Daniel's interpretation of Nebuchadnezzar's dream of "a large statue — an enormous, dazzling statue, awesome in appearance" is clear (Dan. 2:31). There is little room for misunderstanding the prophecy.

> In the time of those kings, the God of heaven will set up a kingdom that will never be destroyed, nor will it be left to another people. It will crush all those kingdoms and bring them to an end, but it will itself endure forever (Dan. 2:44).

174

Traditionally, the kingdom represented by the feet of iron and clay is identified with the Roman Empire. The stone cut without hands that struck the statue and crushed its feet is the kingdom of Christ inaugurated at Pentecost.

The kingdom of God is of a different order from the preceding four kingdoms because it was made without hands; that is, not of human origin, in contrast to the four preceding kingdoms erected by men, and shaped by men. The kingdoms though appearing strong as iron were defeated by a greater power — that of God. Appropriately, the new kingdom was of stone, an idea Jesus used of Himself when he told Peter, "on this rock I will build my church" (Matt. 16:18).

The stone struck the feet (not toes as some have interpolated) which would cause the giant image to topple and fall. The kingdom of God, in contrast, was eternal in nature, enduring forever. Further, it was to grow until it filled the whole earth.

In recent years there has been an effort by Dispensationalists to interpret the fourth kingdom as the Revived Roman Empire so that the stone that represents the kingdom of God can refer to a millennial kingdom established at the second advent of Christ. The text itself does not suggest or permit this interpretation. The Revived Roman Empire theory is a reading back into the text of a previously conceived eschatology rather than a development of eschatology from the text.

There are several lessons for mission. The kingdom of God was inaugurated with the coming of the King. The kingdom will be victorious over all other kingdoms. The kingdom will ultimately cover the earth. The work of the kingdom is made effective because it is being done in the power of God not man.

Daniel, himself, also had a dream of a future kingdom. There are several parallels between the king's dream in chapter two and Daniel's dream in chapter seven. In Daniel's dream of the four beasts, as was the case in Nebuchadnezzar's dream of the image, history is divided into four kingdoms. During the fourth kingdom, a fifth kingdom of a totally different nature is inaugurated. These dreams are tied together in another way. Although it is not apparent in English versions, both chapters are written in Aramaic rather than in Hebrew (as are chapters one, and two through twelve).

Space does not permit treatment of the entire dream or of the various interpretations that have been made.[15] However, a number of lessons about mission are gained from the dream and the interpretation given to Daniel.

One, this new kingdom will have its beginning with the beginning of the downfall of the kingdom of the fourth beast. This corresponds to the reign of Christ which began in the days of the Roman Empire, "The messianic interpretation of the one like a man is not demonstrable, but it is plausible and even probable."[16]

Two, the conflict between the tyrant and God is between the kingdom of *earth* and the intervention of God on *earth*. This new kingdom, then, is a kingdom made up of men on earth. It may be divine in its origin but its location is on earth.

Three, the new kingdom will embrace "all peoples, nations and men of every language" (Dan. 7:14). As we have seen so many times already, the kingdom of God was not limited to the Israelites but ultimately was to include all the peoples of the earth.

Four, this new rule was to be essentially spiritual in nature. Although it was in the world it was not of the world. The peoples (Dan. 7:14) and kings (Dan. 7:27) were to "worship" him. After centuries of departure from the theocracy instituted at Sinai, the theocracy was to be restored at Zion.

Five, the kingdom "is an everlasting dominion that will not pass away, and his kingdom one that will never be destroyed" (Dan. 7:14,27). It is easy to believe that the forces of righteousness will ultimately prevail when everything is going smoothly, the church is growing, and there is no persecution. But

---

15. For a scholarly discussion of chapter seven and its diverse interpretations see Beasley-Murray, Chapter Four.

16. Beasley-Murray, p. 35.

in those areas and in those times where the Christians constitute a tiny minority, the churches are losing members, evil is in the ascendancy, it is difficult to be optimistic about the future of God's kingdom or the effectiveness of His rule. It is at these times, especially, that the words of confidence in the future from Daniel and others give us the encouragement to persevere, knowing we are members of a victorious kingdom.

III. POST-EXILIC PROPHET

1. Joel

Joel holds out no hope for the contemporary nations. His message is that the only hope lies in the Messianic age. Joel promises the Holy Spirit, deliverance, and salvation (Joel 2:28-32).

We do not have to guess about the fulfillment. Peter quotes the passage in his sermon on Pentecost and applies it to the events of that day. "The great and dreadful day of the LORD" becomes "the great and glorious day." "And afterward" is "in the last days." The principal feature of this prophecy is the pouring out of the Holy Spirit. The presence of the Holy Spirit was not new. Israel had men and women on whom the Spirit had come. But these earlier experiences were limited to the people who were her leaders. The new dimension is that the Holy Spirit will be given to all of the People of God. The Messianic Age can very well be called the Age of the Holy Spirit because everyone who calls on the Lord will receive this spirit — whether male or female, young or old. The Holy Spirit is to be poured out on *all people*. Although Joel said that the Spirit was to be poured *on* the People of God in the new age, the Spirit *on* the people is not to be interpreted as a superficial or temporary experience. Paul tells us that the Spirit resides *in* the Christians and controls their lives (Rom. 8:9-11). Once Moses had wished that the Lord would put His Spirit on all His people (Num. 11:29). That wish is going to become reality in the New Age. It is this presence of the Spirit that

177

incorporates all believers into the new body (I Cor. 12:13) and makes the Christian era the glorious new age (II Cor. 3:8).

There is something else here. "All people" in Hebrew is *kol basar*, all flesh. We cannot restrict this pouring out of the Holy Spirit to Israel; language forbids it. The promised gift of the Spirit was to the *goyim* as well as to the sons of the covenant. Further, in Genesis 6:3 we are told that the Spirit of God would not contend with man because he was *basar*, flesh. What sin had done to alienate man from God, God is now planning to reverse because He is going to give His Spirit again to man in the flesh. The coming of the Spirit is not just because Israel has repented as Joel had asked. The pouring out of the Spirit is a part of the grand scheme of redemption that will ultimately reconcile man to God. To be sure, on Pentecost only people of Jewish ancestry received the Spirit. But that changes early in the history of the church as we shall see in Chapter 11.

Additionally, we note, that the Spirit-filled life is life in the *flesh*. Nowhere in the Scriptures is it taught that spirituality can exist only in a disembodied state. Similarly, sainthood is a state of the Christian in this world, and is not limited to the world to come.

The "pouring out" (*shaphak*) was not a small thing, like pouring cream in a cup of coffee. It signified abundance as in a waterfall. The Creator was not stingy but generous with His gifts.

The Messianic Age is new in another respect. No slave in the Old Testament ever received the Holy Spirit. The promise of the Holy Spirit is to slaves, both male and female.

Peter promised the gift of the Spirit in very specific conditions, "Repent and be baptized, every one of you, in the name of Jesus Christ for the forgiveness of your sins. And you will receive the gift of the Holy Spirit (Acts 2:38).

SUMMARY

If the message of the prophets for mission can be summed up

in one word, that word is "universal." Judgment is universal —
on all nations. Repentance is universal — all nations are called to
repent. The Messiah is universal — for men of all nations who call
on the name of the Lord. The Kingdom of God is universal — all
people will be included. Faith is universal — all are to live by faith.
The Holy Spirit is universal — He is given to all nations.

We have traced the history of the preparation for the coming
of the Messiah and His Reign. God's purpose for man will be
fulfilled in that new age. Now we turn to the development of the
mission of God as recorded in the New Testament.

7

JESUS, GOD'S PERSONAL MISSIONARY

THE GOSPELS

Jesus was the missionary *par excellence.* In the Introduction we examined the twelve components and the four essential ingredients of a biblical definition of mission. Jesus meets all the requirements of this definition. "He shines forth as the ideal missionary, the Apostle of God."[1] Therefore He is the perfect model for missionaries to emulate. And the lessons we learn from His life and ministry are especially important.

Of special interest, however, is the fact that He crossed the ultimate cultural barrier. He came from heaven to earth, from God to man, from perfection to imperfection, from a sinless society to a sinful people.

---

1. Peters, p. 36.

Jesus tells us He came for a missionary purpose. "For the Son of Man came to seek and to save what was lost" (Luke 19:10). Mark elaborates on this salvific mission: "For even the Son of Man did not come to be served, but to serve, and to give his life as a ransom for many" (Mark 10:45).

He did not come on His own authority. Although He came willingly, He was sent. "As the father sent me. . . ." And so He can say to His disciples, "All authority has been given unto me."

I. IN THE MIND OF GOD

The sending of Jesus to the world was not a last ditch effort to save the world, it was not an emergency measure, still less was it a matter of Jesus acting alone. The missionary effort of Jesus did not begin at the cross, or even in the manger. His missionary career was a part of the plan of God from the beginning.

Incredible as it seems, even before man had been created, God's plan for man was to send Jesus (Eph. 1:4). The motivation was love (John 3:16). Jesus' ministry was so closely identified with the Father that He said, "he who rejects me rejects him who sent me" (Luke 10:16). This advice, given to the seventy-two as they were sent out, was meant to be encouraging both to them and to all generations of missionaries. When they were rejected they were not to take it personally. The rejection was of Jesus, and ultimately of God Himself. On the other hand, those who would listen would be listening to the Lord. Thus success in the missionaries' preaching was victory for the kingdom of God.

II. HIS INCARNATION

There is no generic person, no universal man, no world-man. Everyone is born into a particular family, has a specific color, belongs to a definite people group, learns a peculiar language, and is a member of a certain political nation.[2] Jesus, too, had to be born of specific parents, at a definite date, and in an identifiable location.

In order for the Savior of the world to rescue man it was necessary for Him to become a man, face temptation, suffer, die, and be raised from the dead. In becoming incarnate He not only made this identification, He also provided a model for the cultural incarnation of the Christian missionary.[3]

The apostle John made it clear that in the action of Jesus' being born in a specific time and place to a specific family and race, He became the Universal Word, the Son of Man, and the Universal Man. This true light was to light *every man*, and although He made the world and was rejected by the world, yet *all in the world* who receive Him would become children of God (John 1:1-14).

1. Genealogy

Genealogy was important to the Hebrews. It provided their connection with the fathers of their nation, it delineated their roles in society, and it proved their purity. Both Matthew and Luke gave the genealogy of Jesus. His lineage was traced to David and Abraham proving His claims to the throne of David and to be the fulfillment of the promise to the patriarch. But of more interest to us is the existence of impurity in His line. Three foreigners, Tamar, Rahab, and Ruth, were included. Does not their inclusion suggest that He was not exclusively a Jewish Messiah, but that His Reign is for the whole world? Tamar and Rahab were prostitutes. Their sins would have resulted in their stoning had they been under the Mosaic law. Does not their acceptance mean that Jesus' kingdom is for sinners (Matt. 9:13)? Hezron and Ram were

---

2. An apparent exception may be Melchizedek who was "without father or mother, without genealogy, without beginning of days or end of life" (Heb. 7:3). However, he may be said to be without these specific identifying marks, not because he did not have them, but because they were unknown.

3. See Sherwood G. Lingenfelter and Marvin K. Mayers, *Ministering Cross-Culturally: An Incarnational Model for Personal Relationships* (Grand Rapids: Baker Book House, 1986).

individuals about which nothing is known. Does this not hold out hope for the "little" people of this world?

2. The Announcement by the Angels

The heavenly messengers who appeared to the shepherds had the perspective of the universal mission of the Child. It was "good news of great joy that will be *for all people*," and "*on earth peace to men* on whom the favor rests" (Luke 2:10-14). He was born *of* the Jews, but *to* the world.

3. Mary's Song

Mary's hymn of praise upon learning of her pregnancy reflects both her understanding of Scriptures and divinely inspired insight into the meaning of the birth of Jesus. She saw that His kingdom would be inverted from that normally perceived in Jewish thought:

> He has performed mighty deeds with his arm;
> he has scattered those who are proud in their inmost thoughts.
> He has brought down rulers from their thrones
> but has lifted up the humble
> He has filled the hungry with good things
> but has sent the rich away empty (Luke 1:51-53).

The "generations" to whom His mercy was extended and who will call Mary blessed, are to be understood as the generation of all the world and not just those of Jewish nationality. And her reference to Abraham (Luke 1:55) indicates that she understood that Jesus was the ultimate goal and fulfillment of the promise to Abraham and that through Him "all the peoples of the earth will be blessed" (Gen. 12:3).

4. Zechariah's Song

The father of John the Baptist also saw that Jesus was the fulfillment of the promise to Abraham. Under the inspiration of the Holy Spirit (Luke 1:67) Zechariah prophesied that John would prepare the way for the Most High who would complete the covenant made with Abraham (Luke 1:68-79).

5. The Visit of the Magi

The coming of the wise men from the East is an indication that what the Old Testament prophets had so many times foretold was beginning to be fulfilled — that the heathen should spontaneously come to an Israel that is glorified by God (Matt. 2:1-12).[4]

Later, in the context of healing the Centurion's servant Jesus underscored this idea, "I say to you that many will come from the east and west and will take their places at the feast with Abraham, Isaac and Jacob in the kingdom of heaven" (Matt. 8:11).

6. The Pronouncement by Simeon

Simeon, moved by the Spirit, was even more explicit in his statement about the ministry of Jesus who was to be: "a light for revelation to the Gentiles and for glory to your people Israel" (Luke 2:32).

7. The Declaration by John the Baptist

John understood that Jesus would bring salvation to all mankind (Luke 3:6) as prophesied by Isaiah (Isa. 40:3-5; 52:10) and by the Psalmist (Psa. 98:2). And when Jesus came to John to be baptized, John declared, "Look, the Lamb of God, who takes away the sin of the *world*" (John 1:29).

8. The Purpose of the Incarnation

Herbert Kane states three purposes for the incarnation: one, to reveal the Father (John 1:14,18; 14:6-7). Two, to destroy the evil (I John 3:8; Heb. 2:14-15; Col. 2:13-15). Three, to save the world (John 3:16-17; I John 4:14; II Cor. 5:14; John 12:32; Matt. 20:38; Col. 1:19).[5]

Sherwood G. Lingenfelter provides us with a fourth, and practical missiological purpose: Jesus is the model for cross-cultural missionaries.[6] Lingenfelter sees two significant facts about the incarnation of Jesus that relate to cross-cultural ministries. One, He was a helpless child, born to a humble family, in poor circumstances, in a subjugated land. Stephan Koralski points out

---

4. Bavinck, p. 32.
5. Kane, p. 36.
6. Pp. 16-17.

that cross-cultural missionaries start out in the same way, that is, without language, and in the position of an inferior, completely dependent on the host culture. He discovered, to his surprise that "[I]t was I who needed others and not others who needed me."[7]

Two, Jesus was a learner. Like every new arrival, Jesus needed to be enculturated. He who sat in the councils of eternity now sat at the feet of the teachers of the law, listening and questioning (Luke 2:46)! He who made the trees was now being taught to make furniture from the lumber! He who was equal with the heavenly Father was now being taught by Joseph!

> If we are to follow the example of Christ, we must aim at incarnation! Jesus said, "If anyone would come after me, he must deny himself" (Matt. 16:24). We must be willing to give up our American Christian lifestyle and begin as children, learning at the feet of those we have gone to serve.[8]

III. THE BAPTISM OF JESUS

Why was Jesus baptized? John's baptism was for repentance (Matt. 3:11) but Jesus had no reason to repent. Jesus said it was to "fulfill all righteousness" (Matt. 3:15) but His explanation only compounds the difficulty. He was already righteous, so Jesus' own words, taken by themselves, leave us as mystified as ever. Probably the most popular answer, "He was baptized as our example," may be partially true but does not really meet the requirements of the text. Oscar Cullmann's insight points us in the right direction.[9] He reminds us that the message of the voice from heaven, "This is my Son, whom I love; with him I am well pleased," is a quotation from Isaiah 42:1. This reference is a part

---

7. Dominique Lapierre, *City of Joy* (New York: Warner Books, 1985), p. 99.
8. Lingenfelter, p. 25.
9. Cullmann, Oscar, *Baptism in the New Testament* (Chicago: Alec R. Allenson Inc., 1950), Chapter I.

of the song of the Servant of Yahweh. This servant is the Suffering Servant who will ultimately suffer vicariously for His people.

Thus the application of the Suffering Servant prophecy to the baptism of Jesus was the divine recognition of the fact that in this action Jesus was taking the role of the Suffering Servant. In the words of Cullmann,

> [a]t the moment of his baptism he receives the commission to undertake the role of the suffering servant of God, who takes on himself the sins of his people.[10]

The others came to the Jordan because of their *own* sins. However, Jesus came to the Jordan because of *their* sins. Now we can understand why Jesus' baptism fulfills righteousness. This also gives meaning to Jesus' reply to James and John: "Can you . . . be baptized with the baptism I am baptized with? (Mark 10:38; Luke 12:50). His baptism in water was the acceptance of suffering on the cross, which was His baptism in suffering.

The baptism of Jesus gives new insight to the meaning of our baptism. As Jesus looked forward to the cross during His baptism, so we look back to the cross in our baptism. As Jesus accepted His cross and its righteousness in His baptism, so we accept His cross and its righteousness for us in our baptism.

> Or don't you know that all of us who were baptized into Christ Jesus were baptized into his death? We were therefore buried with him through baptism into death in order that, just as Christ was raised from the dead through the glory of the Father, we too may live a new life (Rom. 6:3-4).

The baptism of Jesus made mission possible and the baptism of new converts credible.

---

10. Ibid., p. 18.

IV. THE TEMPTATIONS OF JESUS

The devil tried to divert Jesus from His mission (Matt. 4:1-11; Mark 1:12-13; Luke 4:1-13).[11] "The triad of temptations posed real social detours to the true messianic mission."[12] It should not surprise us, then, that we are frequently tempted in ways that would derail us from our pursuit of the mission of Christ, or that would destroy our effectiveness.

Although the devil went away we are not to understand that Jesus faced no more temptations. Luke adds, "he left him until an opportune time" (Luke 4:13). The devil was persistent. Satan remembered Joash, who "did what was right in the eyes of the LORD" (II Chron. 24:2) in the early years of his kingship. But in the later years, after the death of the priest, Jehoida, found the temptation too great to resist. Similarly, there is no Christian servant who matures to the point that Satan will not attempt to lure him away from his task.

The first temptation to turn stones to bread was more than a temptation to perform a miracle to relieve his hunger pangs. "It was undoubtedly the urging to go back to Galilee and miraculously feed the masses."[13] It was a temptation to take the easy way — filling bellies, instead of changing lives; building a physical

---

11. There is an apparent contradiction between the accounts of Matthew and Luke. Matthew recorded,

"[a]fter fasting forty days and forty nights he was hungry.
The tempter came to him" (Matt. 4:2-3).

Luke said, "where for forty days he was tempted" (Luke 4:2). Matthew's chronology must be followed for two reasons: One, the adverbs Matthew uses, "then . . . afterward . . . then . . . again . . . then . . .then," indicate the order of events whereas Luke uses no indicators of sequence. Two, it is possible to translate the Greek of Luke, "and for forty days was led about by the Spirit in the wilderness, where he was being tempted by the devil." This translation harmonizes with Matthew's account.

12. Donald B. Kraybill, The Upside-Down Kingdom (Scottdale, Pennsylvania: Herald Press, 1978), p. 42.

13. Kraybill, p. 90.

kingdom on filling physical needs, rather than building a spiritual kingdom with spiritual means.

In so turning away from this temptation He did not turn away from human needs. He looked on the crowd's hunger with compassion (Mark 6:34; 8:2). On two occasions He miraculously fed the crowds (Mark 6:30-44; 8:1-13). But He was not deceived by His instant popularity. Later He told them the only reason they followed Him was because they were fed (John 6:26).

Missionaries in every generation have to struggle with the problem of showing compassion. Do such actions reveal the love of God and really help people, or do they create dependent folowers who are merely "rice Christians?" Gary Burlington built four church buildings for the people in Zambia. One of the men came to him and asked, "Have you been thanked?" Burlington replied, "No." The man told him that the people perceived the missionary to be very rich since he was able to build four church buildings. All of the Christians there together in their entire lifetimes could not earn enough money to build one building, much less four. And, if the missionary was rich enough to build four buildings, he could build eight. If he could build eight he could build sixteen. If he could build sixteen he could build thirty-two.[14]

The fundamental problem, as Burlington came to realize, was in two differing concepts of love. They saw love as getting. The Christian missionary understood love to mean giving. Consequently, as the missionary gave, he reinforced the pagan concept of love. It was not a simple thing to show love.

The temptation to jump off the temple was more than a temptation to play to the grandstand. The devil's appeal was for Jesus to embrace the Jewish religious system as it stood in order to avoid the hazardous cleansing of the temple and the scathing sermons against the religious leaders.

---

14. Gary Burlington, in an address at the National Missionary Convention, Sept. 28, 1988.

A miraculous appearance — as a sudden bolt out of heaven — would certainly convince even the most skeptical Sadducee or Pharisee. Why not ask God to accredit or certify his mission from the very beginning?[15]

Jesus was concerned with replacing ritual with righteousness, law with love, sacrifices with service, formalism with faith, and performance with personal relationship with God. In rejecting traditionalism He did not reject all traditions. He attended the synagogue, and told the cleansed leper to show himself to the priest.

Every missionary going to a new field is confronted with the fact that a traditional religion has the population in its grasp. Which, if any, of its beliefs, practices, and structures can be retained by the new Christians? The more of the old system that is retained the easier it is to make converts. Each missionary is tempted to jump from the pinnacle to obtain quick results.

Dr. Tom Dooley working in Vietnamese villages found that when he was called to deliver babies, the traditional village midwife was also called. She would throw earth on the abdomen and pubic area of the mother-to-be, believing that the casting of the earth with the attendant religious rituals would guarantee that the spirit would enter the fetus, and the child would be born alive and well. Dooley instructed the midwife to perform her magic first because it was "more important." Then Dooley would wash the expectant mother and deliver the child in as clean an environment as possible.

The third temptation was more than the opportunity to sit on the throne of all the world powers. It was the temptation to define the kingdom of heaven in the traditional Jewish way — as a kingdom of this world. This kingdom would be political in nature, and its control to be exercised by military force.

___

15. Kraybill, p. 65.

190

Of all three aspects of the temptation, the Zealot option of cut-throat violence was the most difficult to shove aside because in so many ways He agreed with their diagnosis of the oppressive social situation.[16]

One of the disciples Jesus chose was a zealot who advocated the violent overthrow of the Roman government. And Peter, who was not a zealot, nevertheless used a sword in the garden to defend Jesus against arrest. Jesus constantly had to remind the disciples, "my kingdom is not of this world" (John 18:36).

The temptation has not left us. It comes today in two subtle forms. Some liberation theologians, overwhelmed by the oppressive governments and enslaving landlords, and seeing the inability or unwillingness of the church to do anything, advocate the violent overthrow of political power.

Others, satisfied that the kingdom is spiritual in nature proclaim that Jesus will set up an earthly kingdom when, as they believe, He returns to rule for a thousand years from Jerusalem.

V. JESUS' STATEMENT OF PURPOSE

Early in His public ministry Jesus was visiting the synagogue services in His hometown. As the celebrated guest He was honored by being invited to read the Scriptures. He chose to read from Isaiah 61:1-2). If He had not commented on the text, the event probably would not have been recorded. But He said, "Today this scripture is fulfilled in your hearing" (Luke 4:21). In so doing He not only proclaimed Himself to be the Messiah, He defined His role as Messiah.

Since He is the model missionary, all missionaries must wrestle with the issues of this text and evaluate their mission in the light of the stated purpose of Jesus' mission.

---

16. Ibid., p. 63.

The first problem is an exegetical one: is the language to be taken literally or figuratively? How are we to understand the "poor," "prisoners," "blind," and the "oppressed"? The answer must be found in two sources; one, the meaning in the Old Testament context; and, two, the fulfillment in Jesus' ministry.

> The poor received, are receiving, are going to receive good news (Luke 6:20; 12:32); captives (to sin and Satan), release (Luke 13:16; John 8:31f.); the blind, recovery of sight (Luke 7:21,22); the oppressed, freedom (Matt. 11:28f.; John 7:37); while for all true believers "the acceptable year of the Lord" arrives (Luke 7:2; 10:24).[17]

The missionary ministry of Jesus was, therefore, twofold. It met both the physical and spiritual needs of mankind. Jesus established the pattern for a wholistic ministry. The old debate of whether we should preach the gospel or practice the social gospel is both out of date and out of harmony with the Scriptures. Arthur Glasser has written, "Christians believe and the Scriptures teach it is God's purpose in salvation that the whole individual be benefited."[18] And Donald McGavran, founder of the contemporary church growth movement, and often perceived as being opposed to any social action in mission, has said,

> A theology of mission does well to include feeding the hungry and looking after refugees as duties which Christians ought to perform under today's conditions. It does not do well to substitute the performance of these duties for proclaiming the gospel and pleading with all men and women to be reconciled to God. Any responsible theology of mission must make a sharp distinction between the great underlying essentials which apply in all cultures and all ages,

---

17. William Hendriksen, *New Testament Commentary: Exposition of the Gospel According to Luke* (Grand Rapids: Baker Book House, 1978), p. 254.
18. Arthur F. Glasser and Donald A. McGavran, *Contemporary Theologies of Mission* (Grand Rapids: Baker Book House, 1983), p. 110.

and the emphasis which here and there, in this time and that, must be stressed.[19]

VII. TEACHINGS OF JESUS

Jesus pictured Himself, or was portrayed by others, in several roles, but these functions were always in relation to the *world*.He said, "I am the light of the *world*" (John 8:12), "the true light" of the *world* (John 1:9), "the Lamb of God, who takes away the sin of the *world*" (John 1:29), "the Savior of the *world*" (John 4:24), and "the bread and life" of the *world* (John 6:33).

Jesus said His disciples were "the salt of the *earth*" (Matt. 5:13), and "the light of the *world*" (Matt. 5:14).

Even more specifically, He said that He "will draw *all* men to myself" (John 12:32), and that He came "to save the *world*" (John 12:47). He prayed that the disciples would be united "so that the *world* may believe" (John 17:21). He told the Twelve that the Holy Spirit would convict the *world* (John 16:8). Further He said that He had "other sheep" (John 10:16), people from East and West, who would take their places in the kingdom. And to the self-righteous He said that the kingdom would be taken from them and given to others (Matt. 21:43). He promised that the gospel would be preached "throughout the *world*" (Mark 14:9).

Jesus also used "man" in a universal sense. On several occasions when He used this term it cannot be understood in any narrow sense of a particular man or of a group of men, but of any man and all men everywhere. For instance, "Man . . . lives on every word that comes from the mouth of God" (Matt. 4:4). "No man can serve two masters . . ." (Matt. 6:24). "The Sabbath was made for man" (Mark 2:27). "Or what can a man give in exchange for his soul" (Mark 8:37).

---

19. Ibid., p. 184.

The purpose of Jesus, the evangelization of the world, so permeates the gospel accounts, that even if the Great Commission had never been recorded, the task of the church would be clear from these "incidental" allusions to the purpose of Christ.

VII. THE SELECTING, TRAINING, AND SENDING OF MISSIONARIES

1. The Model
Jesus had a whole world to convert. He could not do it alone. He selected and trained twelve men to continue His ministry. Afterward He left them to do His work. An apocryphal story of His return to heaven has been told. He was explaining to some of the angels that He had turned over His mission to the disciples. One angel asked, "But if they fail, what is your alternate plan?" Jesus replied, "I have no other plan." Jesus' plan was work through men — selected, trained, commissioned men.

Perhaps no activity of Jesus has been studied more and practiced less than His method of selecting, training, and sending missionaries. It worked then, it will work today. And it will meet our greatest need today — which is for more missionaries. That need can be met if we apply Jesus' methods. Among the existing missionaries the greatest need is for effectiveness. That need can be met if we use Jesus' techniques.

Let us look at the principles of the method of Jesus.

a. The process was person-oriented. Jesus did not approach disciple selection and training with a rigid plan. He was dealing with people, so He was flexible not wooden in His methods. For instance, Andrew, a disciple of John the Baptist, came to Jesus without an invitation (John 1:35-42). Later he received a formal call to be one of the Twelve (Matt. 4:18-20). But Matthew was called directly from the office of tax collector (Mark 2:13-15).

b. The qualifications were limited in number but severe in their demands. We do not find a long list of qualities Jesus was looking for as we see later in Paul's itemization of leadership qualifications (I Tim. 3:1-13; Titus 1:5-9). In fact, Jesus' choices of men to carry on His spiritual ministry leave us shaking our head in wonder. In spite of their diversity the chosen men seem to have four things in common.

One, they accepted His Messiahship. Two, they were committed to Him as shown in their alacrity in following when He called them. Three, they were open to teaching. To be sure, they were sometimes slow in learning. And, four, they were willing to put Christ first in their lives, sacrificing all else to serve Him.

c. The training process was event-oriented. Jesus did not bring to the training program a formal syllabus of subjects to be covered. He did not set up a school. Rather He took His disciples with Him, and as they were confronted with situations and questions (John 9:1-12), Jesus gave His explanations.

d. It was a true apprenticeship. You will recall from our word study in the Introduction that the "disciple" in the Greek world was an apprentice. Jesus used the same "hands on" teaching method. The disciples observed what Jesus did, were given a few words of instruction, and then sent out to "practice" what they had been taught. When they returned they went through a de-briefing and were given corrective instruction.

Why did not Jesus set up a Bible College in Jerusalem, or Capernaum? It was not because He did not know how. There were various kinds of schools in His day. It seems evident that He chose the apprentice method because it would give the results He wanted.

Is it not a viable method in the Twentieth Century as well? Perhaps there are subjects that are better taught in the classroom, such as Greek and hermeneutics. But following such formal instruction, would not an apprenticeship be in order? Many have observed that the new missionary spends most of the first term on the field learning how to function in a cross-cultural situation, and usually accomplishes little else. Would it not be appropriate to call the first term worker an apprentice, or intern, and deliberately

195

structure the first term to be an apprenticeship?

e. The Commission

They had been called. They had been trained. However, they could not yet be sent out. The major event in the life of Jesus had not yet occurred. The news they had to deliver was not yet the good news. Jesus had to die for the sins of the world, and be raised from the dead to provide hope of eternal life. When that was done it was time to commission the Twelve.

2. The Call

The call of Jesus to the first disciples was clear and unmistakable: "Follow me." The disciples knew that Jesus was speaking directly to them. They might refuse to follow, but there was no way that they could excuse their refusal by saying, "I didn't know you meant me."

Out of the thousands who became His followers only a handful were selected to be missionaries. Similarly, the command to "make disciples of all nations" is given to all Christians, we believe. But not everyone can, or should, actually go. Who, then, should respond? Who should say, "Here am I, send me"?

The qualifications are the same as in Jesus' day. Those who recognize the Lordship of Christ, are committed to Christ, are teachable, and are willing to sacrifice all to serve. Robert Glover gives a helpful illustration.

> This country when at war declares a draft of man power, in terms of which every man of military age and fitness is conscripted for active service. The norm is to go, not to stay.[20]

3. The Success

The command of Jesus was to "go into all the world" (Mark 16:15). The prophecy was that the "gospel of the kingdom will be preached in the whole world as a testimony to all nations" (Matt. 24:14).

---

20. Glover, p. 139.

We are on a winning team! We may have set backs. We may become discouraged. Victory is not yet ours. But we believe the words of Jesus. We have every confidence that the Kingdom of Christ will spread to all the nations. That faith enables us to go forward in spite of the obstacles. That faith gives us assurance of victory when everyone seems to be against us.

VIII. JESUS AND THE NON-JEWS

Any consideration of Jesus' ministry to the Gentiles presents us with a series of paradoxes. He said He came to the world, but He also said He came only to the people of Israel. He limited His healing ministry to the Jews, but He also healed several Gentiles. He first told His disciples to go only to the children of Israel, then He sent them to the world. He was a Jew, but during most of His ministry He lived and worked where there was a fairly large concentration of Gentiles. How are these apparent contradictions resolved?

1. Jesus' choice of residences.

a. Egypt

Because of the threat to the life of the infant Jesus by Herod, Joseph at the direction of an angel took Jesus to Egypt (Matt. 2:13-18). However, the residence in Egypt must have been brief.[21]

b. Nazareth

When Joseph, with his family, returned to Israel, they settled in Nazareth located in "Galilee of the Gentiles" (Matt. 4:15) which had a mixed population of Greeks, Romans, and Jews.

c. Capernaum

Although there was a large Jewish population and a synagogue (built by a Roman army officer [Luke 7:5]), Caper-

---

21. Alfred Edersheim, *The Life and Times of Jesus the Messiah*, 2 vols. (Grand Rapids: William B. Eerdmans Publishing Company, 1947), I:217.

naum was a city of mixed population.

Early in His ministry Jesus moved to Capernaum (Matt.
4:14). Thus it became the center from which He conducted much
of His ministry. Important messages were given there (John 6;
Luke 9:47-50). Many miracles were performed there (Matt. 8:5;
John 4:46; Mark 1:31; Matt. 9:1; Mark 1:23; Mark 5:22; Matt.
11:23; Mark 1:34). Nearby the Sermon on the Mount was
preached (Matt. 5-7) and some of the disciples called (Mark 1:16;
Matt. 9:1).

2. Jesus' restricted ministry to the Jews

When Jesus sent the Twelve on one of their training missions
He specifically forbade them to go to the Gentiles or Samaritans
but limited their ministry to the "lost sheep of Israel" (Matt.
10:5-6). At the same time He told them that some Jewish homes
and towns would not welcome them. Of them He said, "it will be
more bearable for Sodom and Gomorrah on the day of judgment
than that town" (Matt. 1:15). Why, then, did He not send His
trainees to the more receptive Gentiles?

Jesus' analysis of His own ministry was that He would have
been more effective if He had performed miracles in Tyre and
Sidon rather than in Capernaum, Korazin, and Bethsaida (Matt.
11:20-24). Why, then, is He so insistent in concentrating on the
Jews in His own ministry? However, the responsiveness of these
particular Gentiles must not be assumed to be greater than it really was. The residents of Tyre and Sidon were considered to be
money-mad, proud and cruel. And in Amos' day they were the
people who sold the Israelites into slavery (Amos 1:9; Joel 3:6).
The real point Jesus is making is not the responsiveness of the
Phoenicians so much as the heavy responsibility borne by those
who were privileged.

Paul interprets the ministry of Jesus to the Jews as having the
purpose "that the Gentiles may glorify God" (Rom. 15:9).

3. Jesus' Ministry to the Gentiles

Six incidents are recorded where Jesus ministered to a Gentile: the Samaritan woman (John 4:1-42), the servant of the Cen-

turion (Matt. 8:5-13; Luke 7:1-10), the son of the nobleman (John 4:43-54), the Gadarene demoniac (Matt. 8:28-34; Mark 5:1-29; Luke 8:26-37), and the deaf man of Decapolis (Matt. 15:29-31; Mark 7:31-37), the Syrophoenician woman (Matt. 15:21-28; Mark 7:24-30). When the Greek woman begged Jesus to cast the demon out of her daughter, His reply, "first let the children eat all they want" (Mark 7:22), implied that the Gospel was to be taken to the Gentiles in due time, but not yet.

The cleansing of the Temple directly benefited the Gentiles because it was the Court of the Gentiles that Jesus returned from a pavement of commerce to a place of prayer (John 2:13-17). And Jesus was very specific in teaching that the gospel was for the *whole* world (Matt. 26:13; 24:14).

In spite of Jesus' intent to include the Gentiles in the Kingdom of Heaven, He made some uncomplimentary statements about the Gentiles (Matt. 6:7,32; 18:17; 5:26; Mark 7:27; 10:42). On two occasions He at first refused to help a Gentile because, as He explained, His ministry was to the Jews (Matt. 15:24; Mark 7:27).

How are the above paradoxes to be resolved? There are three factors to be considered.

One, the gospel was not complete until after the death and resurrection of Christ. Until those events occurred there really was no good news to take to the Gentile world.

Two, this was a training period for the Twelve. Their full ministry, which included the whole world, would not begin until Pentecost. Bavinck wrote, the "moment in time to spread the gospel over the whole world had not yet come."[22]

Three, there were both short and long term goals of Jesus. Kane explained it well:

He had to begin *somewhere*, and the most natural place to begin was with His own people. . . . Not all the centers of Jewish life

---

22. Bavinck, p. 33.

could be covered. . . . To send the disciples *at that time* on a world wide preaching mission would have served no purpose.[23]

In the long term the "gospel of the Kingdom will be preached in the whole world as a testimony to all nations" (Matt. 24:14; Mark 13:10). Incidentally, this verse gives us virtually the only clue as to the timing of the return of Christ and the end of the world: "then will the end come." Until this purpose is achieved He cannot return.

Four, Ferdinand Hahn suggests that Jesus did not go to the Gentiles, but that they came to Him as His fame spread throughout Galilee (Mark 1:28), over the Jordan, and to Tyre and Sidon (Mark 3:7).[24]

IX. THE DEATH AND RESURRECTION OF JESUS

Central to the Christian faith was the death and resurrection.
1. These events were the plan of God. When Paul and John were released from prison they offered a prayer filled with history and theology.

Indeed Herod and Pontius Pilate met together with the Gentiles and the people of Israel in this city to conspire against your holy servant Jesus, whom you anointed. They did what *your power and will had decided beforehand should happen* (Acts 4:27-28 italics mine).

"Both events were part of God's original plan — not simply an incident, much less an accident, of human history."[25] Jesus was fully aware that this was the ultimate purpose of His life on earth (John 1:29; 2:4; 7:30; 8:20; 12:23; 13:1; 17:1; Mark 10:45).

---

23. Kane, p. 41.
24. Hahn, pp. 39, 112.
25. Ibid., p. 43.

2. The death of Jesus made possible the forgiveness of sin of the world.

Drawing on the typology of the sacrifices in the Old Testament, the writer to the Hebrews tells us that Jesus as the high priest takes His own blood in the presence of God and obtains eternal redemption and clean consciences for all men (Heb. 9:12-14).

3. The resurrection of Jesus makes possible our resurrection from the dead.

The resurrection was far more difficult to accept than the death for sin. It was a stumbling block for Jew and Gentile alike. It also gave rise to some strange doctrines about the future of man. But if there was no resurrection, there is no message, and no hope (I Cor. 15).

4. The Good News was for the Gentiles.

Paul wrote to the Roman church that it was by the resurrection that Jesus was declared to be the Son of God with power. And because of that sonship, and through that authority Paul "received grace and apostleship to call people *from among all the Gentiles* to the obedience that comes from faith" (Rom. 1:1-6).

5. The resurrection provided the confirmation and motivation for mission of the disciples.

When the women came to the tomb and found it empty they were met by an angel who invited them to *come and see* the empty tomb, and then *go and tell* the disciples. So they hurried "afraid yet filled with joy" (Matt. 28:5-8). To accept the benefits of the resurrection brings an immediate opportunity to spread the incredible message. Kane makes a significant comment on this experience, "to accept the challenge but refuse the command is a contradiction."[26]

Jesus had made it clear throughout His career that He came not to reign, but to serve (Matt. 20:28), not to live, but to die

---

26. Ibid., p. 200.

(Matt. 16:21). Nevertheless, the disciples had expected the Messiah to be an earthly king (Matt. 16:22; Luke 19:11; Acts 1:6; Luke 24:21; Matt. 11:3). It was not until after the resurrection that the disciples understood either His role as the Suffering Servant (Luke 24:26-27), or as King (Acts 2:29-36).

X. THE ASCENSION OF CHRIST

The ascension is probably today's most neglected Christian doctrine. The apostles thought it important, however. For instance, being present for the ascension was one of the necessary qualifications for the person who was to succeed Judas (Acts 1:22).

Jesus came to this earth for a specific, limited, historical purpose. He never intended to stay on earth permanently. "The ascension was the natural, inevitable, and altogether fitting conclusion to the life of the Son of God on earth."[27]

Jesus went to heaven to prepare a place for His followers (John 14:1-3). He went in a body.

One of the great mysteries of the incarnation is that Jesus did not shed the mantle of His humanity when He returned to heaven. He took it with Him when, as forerunner of redeemed humanity, He entered heaven's gates. He is there today as our High Priest, able to sympathize with our weaknesses.[28]

His departure was also necessary in order that the Holy Spirit could be sent in His place and to allow Him to have a ubiquitous and universal presence and power in the lives of His followers (John 7:39; 16:7). Only in this way could the disciples perform the "greater works" He had promised they would be able to do

27. Ibid., p. 211.
28. Ibid., p. 215.

202

(John 14:12).

Further, Jesus had said, "I will build my church" (Matt. 16:18). The church is a spiritual entity. Therefore it requires a Lord who is physically absent. The center of the church is in heaven. Had Jesus remained on earth, the center would have been in Jerusalem, or such other place where Jesus was present. In which case it would have "found itself bound hand and foot by the grave clothes of Judaism."[29] "Thus the Christian religion would have been localized, secularized, and paganized."[30]

The ascension made it possible for Christ to be exalted to the right hand of God and to be seated on His throne. In that position He is our mediator (Heb. 5:14-16), and head of the church (Eph. 1:20-23; Col. 1:18).

XI. THE SECOND COMING OF CHRIST

Jesus promised to return to earth (Acts 1:9-11). Many self-styled prophets have speculated and predicted the date of His return. They claim greater knowledge of this future event than even Jesus Himself (Acts 1:7). Although the New Testament writers mention His return, they never speculate as to the time of the return. They do, however, write much about what the Christians should be doing in the interim: preaching (Mark 13:10; Matt. 24:14), and living the Christian lifestyle (Phil. 1:10).

Here we see closely and significantly joined together two vital matters: first, the risen Lord's marching orders to the Church to take the Gospel to the whole world; and second, the announcement by heavenly messengers that He would come back, personally and visibly as they had just seen Him go. That these two things — the world-wide mission of the Church and the "blessed hope" of the Lord's return — are thus intimately related the one

---

29. Ibid., p. 217.
30. Ibid., p. 218.

to the other is surely altogether obvious. The departing Lord left a distinctive program, and engrossing task, for His Church to carry out during His absence, and the promise of His return was added, the natural inference being that He would come when that program was fulfilled, that task complete.

XII. JUDGMENT OF CHRIST

Another great event that is yet to come, but should be a controlling influence in our behavior is the judgment. Jesus Himself will sit in judgment (John 5:22-23), and will judge people from all nations. Those who are judged righteous will receive eternal life, those who are unrighteous will receive eternal punishment (Matt. 25:31-46).

"God prefers salvation to judgment. Herein lies the missionary element. God's wrath makes the gospel necessary: His love makes it possible."[31]

SUMMARY

This chapter began with the fact that the Father sent His only Son to be a missionary to the alienated population of the world. His purpose was to launch the Kingdom. With only three years of apprenticeship the disciples were commissioned with the task of "making disciples of all nations." Jesus gave them, and us, a model for carrying out this ministry.

Now He is saying to us, "so send I you."

---

31. Ibid., p. 20.

8

THE PARABLES OF JESUS

"Once upon a time. . . ."[1] And our attention is captured. We anxiously await the "rest of the story." The story that follows is a parable — one of the favorite teaching tools of Jesus. The parables are interesting. They are memorable. But the principal reason Jesus uses them is, at the same time, to reveal and to conceal the mysteries of the kingdom (Matt. 13:11).

The opponents of Jesus had deliberately rejected the clear teachings of the Master. And they had become increasingly hostile to His ministry (Matt. 9:11,34; 12:2,14; 11:20-24). So, Jesus, in His public teaching chose to speak in parables, the

---

1. William Hendriksen says that *idou* is a little word that is used to get attention. A number of dynamic equivalents are available including "once upon a time." William Hendriksen, *New Testament Commentary: Exposition of the Gospel According to Matthew* (Grand Rapids: Baker Book House, 1973), pp. 131, 551.

meaning of which "cannot be perceived by unaided human reasoning."[2] Thus the enemies of Jesus would not even have the opportunity of understanding His teaching. Since they had not used their opportunity to learn from Jesus, they were going to lose.

> Whoever has will be given more, and he will have an abundance. Whoever does not have, even what he has will be taken from him (Matt. 13:12).

Jesus quotes Isaiah's message to Israel prior to their exile. This exile, which was a punishment for its hardness of heart, is a type of what was happening to those who rejected the message of Jesus.

Jesus introduces the quotation not with the words "might be fulfilled," but with "is being fulfilled," thus indicating that the punishment of Israel, only partly completed in the exile, was now being completed in the lives of those who rejected Jesus.

> You will be ever hearing but never understanding; you will be ever seeing but never perceiving. For this people's heart has become calloused; they hardly hear with their ears, and they have closed their eyes. Otherwise they might see with their eyes, hear with their ears, understand with their hearts and turn, and I would heal them (Matt. 13:14-15).

The verbal forms He uses are interesting. Aorist indicatives have been substituted for the Hebrew imperatives indicating that the things Isaiah had predicted have now become realities. The word translated "calloused" literally means to make thick or heavy. A form of this word is found in pachyderm, which refers to a thick-skinned animal as an elephant or rhinoceros. "Hardly hear" has a form of the word we use in barometer, an instrument which measures the heaviness of the atmosphere. And to "close"

---

2. Hendriksen, p. 553.

the eyes means to shut down.

On the other hand, the purpose of the parables was to reveal to the disciples the Messianic message. "Many prophets and righteous men longed to see what you see . . . and to hear what you hear" (Matt. 13:17). Jesus does not leave the disciples mystified by the mysteries of the parables. He explains the stories to them. And they are capable of understanding. They have accepted Jesus as their Master. They believe Him. True, their understanding is not complete for the death and resurrection of Jesus has not occurred, and they have not yet received the Spirit. "No one can see the kingdom of God unless he is born again" (John 3:3). But they are in a position to be instructed. "Blessed are your eyes because they see, and your ears because they hear" (Matt. 13:16).

I. A PARABLE OF RECEPTIVITY — THE PARABLE OF THE SOIL — MATT. 13:1-9,18-23; MARK 4:1-9; LUKE 8:4-8

Jesus called it "the parable of the sower" (Matt. 13.18). But the emphasis is on the soils. Taylor wrote, "the main thought of the parable is in its literal sense: *the growth of the seed depends always on the quality of the soil.*"[3] Because of this emphasis, it has a great deal to teach us about mission.

Although Jesus spoke this parable to the crowd on the lakeshore near Capernaum, its message was intended for His disciples — His missionaries to the unreached world (Matt. 13:11). There are at least nine specific lessons here for the cross-cultural worker.

1. We are to go to the responsive populations.

The intent of the farmer was to grow a crop, not to waste

---

3. William M. Taylor, *The Parables of the Savior* (New York: A.C. Armstrong & Sons, 1886), p. 21.

seed. The sower was broadcasting the seed on ground that he perceived to be fertile and moist. The fact that some seed fell on the well-trodden path was accidental. Perhaps the reason he threw some seed on shallow soil, or on soil filled with weed seeds, reflected that he had not studied the soils carefully enough. Modern illustrations of this principle in the area of mission work are easily found.

The Conservative Baptists have had missionaries in Thies, Senegal, for twenty-five years. The population is composed principally of the Wolof tribe, who are strongly Islamic. Presently there are eight missionaries in Thies. But in a quarter of a century they have only been able to establish a church of twenty-five members. In contrast, the Finnish Lutherans have had a mission at Fatik, Senegal, for nearly as long. And they have one thousand nine hundred believers. What is the difference? The Lutherans are working with the Serer tribe, who rejected Islam and remained animistic.[4]

In southern India the Toddy Tapper caste became Christian a generation ago. Their next door neighbors, the Maravar caste, remained Hindu, worshipping the local god, Sudalaimadamswami. However, about ten years ago the Maravars also became receptive to the gospel. There were two observable reasons. One, they saw the upward social movement of the Toddy Tappers after they became Christians. And, two, an epidemic of cholera was decimating the population when a Christian doctor came and treated the people. As a result of his demonstration of care, they allowed a Christian preacher to come to their village. Today there are thousands of Christians among the Maravars and it is believed virtually the entire caste will become Christian in the next decade.[5]

Jesus intends for there to be a great harvest — thirty, sixty, one hundred-fold. The danger to the missionary is that he will not

---

4. From a survey done in Senegal by the author in February 1987.
5. From an interview with Arthur Morris in India in August 1979.

look for the most promising soil and, as a consequence, have a far smaller crop for his efforts than he might have had.

Does this not teach us that we should look for responsive populations for our missionary efforts? There are many criteria for selecting a mission field: human needs, ease of entrance, minimal language barriers, size of population, geographical location, appeal to the potential missionary, etc. The first parable of Jesus suggests the first priority should be attention to the receptivity to the gospel.

How do we measure receptivity? Men who work with metal use a Rockwell hardness tester to determine the hardness of the metal so that they will use the appropriate material for the project they are building. Would it not be convenient if we had an equivalent tester for the hardness of the souls of people? I believe there are some guidelines we can use. They are not as precise, or fast, or easy to use, but they are helpful. We will look at these briefly in Capter Eleven.

2. We are to preach the gospel in such a way that they can hear.

Notice the stipulation, "when anyone *hears* the mooooge" (Matt, 13:19,20,22,23). The difference between the man who, like an asphalted roadway, rejects the message, and the other three who receive it, is understanding. In the parable it is clear that the first man did not understand because of the hardness of his heart. It was a defect in his character, not the fault of the sower or the seed.

But in cross-cultural evangelism it is possible that the failure to understand is the fault of the sower. This can happen for at least three reasons.

One, the preacher does not know the local language. In 1965 I was preaching an evangelistic crusade on the street in Takoradi, Ghana. Since I did not know the language I was dependent upon a translator. Since he took much longer to say in the local language what I was saying in English I was suspicious. Finally I recognized some of what he was saying which was a distortion of my message.

Neither is it enough to know the language just well enough to get by. Every language is complex. And there are nuances of words and grammar that are important to communication and take years to learn.

Missionaries in West Africa asked the local people for a word that would be the equivalent of "grace." Believing they had the right word they continued to use it for years, although they observed that the native Christians rarely used the term, and then only in hushed tones. Finally they learned the word they had been using for grace was used only in black magic to cast spells on people.[6]

Two, the message must be culturally appropriate.

When the missionaries among the Higi in Nigeria described Jesus as the Shepherd, they were asked, "What is wrong with Jesus?" Mystified, the missionaries pursued the question and learned that in Higi society only demented men are assigned the task of shepherding sheep.[7]

Three, the method of communication must be culturally appropriate.

The missionaries among the Higi noticed that there were no older men coming for the preaching. They knew that conversion of the older men was essential to reaching the tribe. Charles Kraft then asked the men why they did not come to the services. They replied, "The preachers do all the talking." Kraft had the wisdom to ask, "How would you preach the gospel?" The local man pointed out the Higi way was to sit with the men and ask the oldest man, "What do you know about God?" After he replies then the missionary can tell what he believes about God.[8]

---

6. Eugene A. Nida, *Customs and Cultures* (New York: Harper & Brothers, 1954), p. 16.

7. Charles H. Kraft, "Receptor's Perception of Culture" a lecture given to the School of World Mission, Fuller Theological Seminary, 1978.

8. Ibid.

3. We must sow the right seed.

This parable is about soils, nevertheless it identifies the seed as the "message about the kingdom" (Matt. 13:19), which is also called simply "the word" (Matt. 13:21-23). When missionaries go from a western culture to a Third World society it is easy to confuse American or European church life for biblical Christianity and to preach western theology in place of the gospel. For instance, we may insist the natives wear clothes, sing western hymns, build Gothic church buildings, marry for romantic love, worship on Sunday morning at 11:00, etc., when none of these things is culturally appropriate.

G. Campbell Morgan insists that the seed to be sown is Christ. He bases his argument on the Greek pronoun, *autos*, which he insists must be translated "he."[9] The heart of the "message of the kingdom," of course, is Christ. But Morgan's exegesis is incorrect. It is true that *autos* can be translated "he," but it can also be translated "it," as the English translations of the text do. The translation depends on the context. And in this case the text demands "it" and not "he."

We must *sow*. The gardener who drools over the pictures in the seed catalog, but never plants a seed will have no harvest. Likewise, the Christian who dreams, or writes glowingly of what he is going to do, but never plants any seed will have no harvest.

4. We can not use this parable as an excuse for inappropriate or ineffective ministries.

If the growth of the kingdom depends upon the quality of the soil, as this parable indicates; and since I can not do anything about the nature of the soil, am I then still responsible if no fruit results from my labor? Indeed, I may be able to do nothing about the condition of the soil, but I can do something about my

---

9. G.Campbell Morgan, *The Parables of the Kingdom* (London: Hodder and Stoughton, 1907) p. 48.

211

ministry.

If I am in the wrong place, I can move.

If I am using the wrong method, I can find the right one.

If I am sowing the wrong seed, I can get the right one.

If I am doing nothing, I can start to work.

5. We can not force growth.

We not only must have the right seed in the right soil, we must allow enough time. It requires sixty years for a walnut to grow into a tree large enough to be harvested for lumber. Some plants, of course, produce fruit quickly. Mushrooms pop up overnight.

The gospel is a seed which, when planted in the human mind, takes time to produce faith, obedience, and a Christian life. This spiritual maturity can not be accelerated. I remember Estal Taylor, long-time preacher at Fortville, Indiana, tell of his experience in trying to speed up the blossoming process of some flowers. Taylor's hobby was growing roses. Usually the roses were in bloom by Mother's Day. So he planned to decorate the church with his roses on that day. But the weather had not cooperated. The roses were not going to be ready. Seeking to hasten their development, he cut the tips off the buds, hoping it would help. Unfortunately, it did not.

The Church, historically, has tried to force the growth of the kingdom. During the Crusades armed campaigners sought to bring the Moslems into obedience to Christ. They succeeded only in gaining the lasting hatred of the Muslim people. During the Inquisition the Roman church sought to force "heretics" into the church. They succeeded only in developing a terrible reputation for themselves. During the Evangelical Awakening and in many evangelistic campaigns many "converts" were arm-twisted down the sawdust trail, only to become plants in rocky soil. And food was used to entice people to become Christians on many mission fields. "If you will become a Christian, we will give you food." And the result was "rice Christians."

6. We can gain encouragement from this parable.

In all probability part of the reason for Jesus telling this parable was to give encouragement to the Twelve when things were not going well. At those times when we are making much effort, but getting little results from our labor, this is a parable to turn to. Preaching to some people is like talking to a brick wall. They are the beaten path. Others become Christians with great enthusiasm, and appear to set the world on fire. But at the first appearance of difficulty, they disappear. They are the rocky ground with only a thin layer of soil on top. Still others make an outward commitment to Christ. They are baptized but they are more interested in making money, in going to the ball game, and in going on vacation. They are like Demas who "loved this world, and has deserted" (II Tim. 4:10). They are the soil that is filled with thorns.

But, in spite of all these failures, there is good soil. And the seed does take root and produces fruit. If we are pessimistic by nature we will see only the failures. If we are optimistic by nature we will count only the successes. It seems to me that Jesus is saying, "look objectively at the results." Learn from failed growth in poor soil. Take heart in the success of the seed in good soil.

7, We must be prepared to take risks.

Some seed will be lost. Some missionary lives will be sacrificed. Some money will go to unfruitful labors. Some mistakes will be made. But unless we are willing to sow seed, nothing will grow.

My father was a building contractor. Often on a cloudy morning when it threatened to rain, the carpenters, masons, and laborers would say, "it is no use to go to the job, it is going to rain." Dad would always reply, "Make it rain." They then would pile in the trucks and head for the construction site. I noticed more times than not it did not rain. It was not until years later that I learned the source of Dad's philosophy:

Whoever watches the wind will not plant; whoever looks at the clouds will not reap (Eccl. 11:4).

213

II. TWO PARABLES OF GROWTH — THE PARABLE OF THE MUSTARD SEED AND THE PARABLE OF THE LEAVEN — MATT. 13:31-35; MARK 4:30-32; LUKE 13:18-21

Perhaps no parables have created more controversy over their meanings than the parables of the mustard seed and of the leaven. Both are parables of the growth of the kingdom.

That subject is the progress of the kingdom of heaven upon the earth; but the one gives prominence to the external contrast between its small beginning and its ultimate magnitude, while the other emphasizes the method of its internal operation, and the universality of its diffusion at the last.[10]

The interpretations fall into two categories. The millenarians who separate the church and the kingdom into two separate entities, and who believe the kingdom will not be established until Jesus returns and sets up His rule in Jerusalem, generally see the growth of the mustard seed as the abnormal growth of the church, and the spread of leaven as the pervasive influence of evil.

Virtually all other commentators, including the amillennialists, understand both the growth of the mustard seed and of the leaven as representing healthy growth of the kingdom here and now. That growth occurs both in the individual believer and the church. Space prohibits a thorough discussion of the conflicting views. These can be found elsewhere.[11]

We can, however, make some cursory observations as we look at the seven lessons for mission from these parables.

---

10. Taylor, p. 54.
11. A summary of the arguments from a premillennial point of view can be found in Herbert Lockyer, *All the Parables of the Bible* (Grand Rapids: Zondervan Publishing House, 1963), pp. 184-196. A summary from the amillennial point of view can be found in James H. Snowden, *The Coming of the Lord* (New York: The Macmillan Company, 1919), pp. 72-85.

1. The first, and most important, point is that the kingdom will grow. Trench wrote:

> nor can we consider these words, 'till the whole is leavened,' as less than a prophecy of a final complete triumph of the Gospel — that it will diffuse itself through all nations, and purify and ennoble all life.[12]

Twelve disciples is an inauspicious beginning for a world-wide and world-conquering kingdom. But the church has grown. And in spite of the explosive population growth in the last generation, twenty-five percent of the people in the world consider themselves to be Christian. And the promise is that the Gospel will be preached to the whole world (Matt. 24:14) and that the kingdom of this world will submit to the Lordship of Christ (Rev. 11:15).

What an encouragement this pair of parables must have been to the Twelve. Faced with rejection by the Jews, persecution by the Pharisees, incarceration and execution by the Romans, and the seemingly impossible task of evangelizing the world with a handful of preachers, the Twelve could visualize the growth of the tiny seed into a giant tree, and the penetration of the leaven throughout the lump of dough, and take heart.

Today's missionary also has reasons for discouragement. Work permits are not renewed, new missionaries cannot obtain visas, and the growth of Communism and Islam seem to thwart the progress of the Gospel. Pessimists abound. We believe that when Christ returns in judgment all wrongs will be made right and the Christian will have great victory in heaven. But we need a message of hope for the here and now. We need to see the mustard growing and the leaven expanding. The central message of the mustard and leaven, the kingdom is growing, is

---

12. Richard Chevenix Trench, *Notes on the Parables of Our Lord* (New York: N. Tibbals & Sons, 1879), p. 99.

for times like these.

There is little difference between the pessimist and the atheist. The atheist says, "there is no god." The pessimist says, "there is no god who can do anything." Jesus says, "there is a God and He *is* doing something: the kingdom *is* growing."

These are parables of *growth*. The growth of a plant may be almost imperceptible but it is real and it is powerful. When we moved into our present location there was a small tulip poplar sapling about a foot from the sidewalk. I said then that the tree would have to be removed or it would break up the concrete walk. However, I did not move it. And now, twelve years later the tree has pushed over one inch a three feet by six feet piece of concrete.

> The point of all these . . . parables is that the kingdom of heaven is growth and not a cataclysm; it is an unfolding seed and not exploding dynamite.[13]

An English newspaper reported that an admirer of the Prince of Wales picked up a grain of wheat that had fallen from the hand of the royal son. The single grain was planted. The following year all the grains from that single stalk of wheat were planted. The process was continue for five more years. By the sixth year, the grains from the original single seed planted sixteen acres of land.[14]

2. There are two dimensions of growth.

Commentators have seen the parables of mustard and leaven as a complementary pair. Both teach the growth of the kingdom, but in differing ways:

---

13. Snowden, p. 74.
14. Taylor, p. 68.

216

Mustard — Leaven

External — Internal

Extensive — Intensive

Visible — Invisible

The mustard seed stays in the garden where it is planted. Its tree adheres to the roots. The growth consists of developing its full potential in producing its fruit. The kingdom grows in this way. The church is expected to stay where it is planted and to develop its full potential in its locale.

But at the same time, as the parable of the leaven indicates, it has a cross-cultural responsibility. The mass of meal in which the leaven is working can mean nothing less than the world. And just as each molecule of fermentation develops its own potential, it is infecting neighboring molecules until the outer reaches of the meal is transformed into a new form. So the kingdom is expected to expand "until the whole was leavened" (Matt. 13:33 AV).

The external growth is the growth in number of believers. The book of Acts portrays the growth from one hundred twenty to myriads.

The internal growth involves the spiritual growth of the church. Paul writes, "that the body of Christ may be built up . . . mature . . . attaining to the whole measure of the fulness of Christ" (Eph. 4:13).[15] Jesus said it this way, "the kingdom of God is within you" (Luke 17:21).

3. The significance of small beginnings.

The mustard seed was among the smallest of seeds, and the molecules of leaven cannot be seen by the unaided eye. But there is tremendous power within each that is released when the seed is planted and when the leaven is "hid" in the meal. The same idea

---

15. For an important report on this dual growth of the church see Ralph D. Winter, *The 25 Unbelievable Years, 1945-1969*, (South Pasadena: William Carey Library, 1970).

is found in other similies of Jesus. A few grains of salt change the flavor of a whole pot of soup. A small ray of light dispels an enormous amount of darkness. The mustard seed was a proverbial expression for anything that was small. Jesus used it on other occasions (Luke 17:6).

On the one hundredth anniversary of Abraham Lincoln's birth, John T. McCutcheon drew a famous cartoon. He showed two Kentucky backwoodsmen standing at the edge of a wood in the winter. The snow was on the ground and the trees were bare. One asked the other, "Anything new?" The other man replies, "Nothing much. Oh, there's a new baby over at Tom Lincoln's. . . . Nothing ever happens around here." So, many years ago, someone might have asked in Bethlehem, "Anything new?" And the answer might have been, "No, nothing new. Oh, they say a woman named Mary had a baby in a stable last night. But nothing ever happens around here." So many of God's greatest happenings begin so unobtrusively that they seem no more important than planting a mustard seed.[16]

The lone missionary in a pagan world may feel that the power is in the massive amount of meal, not in the solitary witness to Christ. The single Christian, working in a factory or office filled with hedonistic materialists, may feel that he is a tiny, insignificant, and ineffective seed buried in hard impenetrable clay. We know that Luther understood us when he said the Christian is a solitary bird warbling his song on a rooftop.

Christians are in a minority. But the outcome is not going to be determined by a democratic election. If it were, the forces of righteousness would lose. But we will win because of the power inherent in the seed, and in the leaven. We are tempted to keep the seed in the packet, the salt in the shaker, the leaven in the bin, and the light under the bushel.

16. Gerald Kennedy, *The Parables* (New York: Harper & Brothers, 1960), p. 82.

What we need instead is to let God give us the godly nerve and the stouthearted audacity to venture out into the soup and the darkness of the world.[17]

4. The confidence in ultimate acheivement.
Taylor tells us the subject of this pair of parables.

That subject is the progress of the kingdom of heaven upon the earth; but the one gives prominence to the external contrast between its small beginning and its ultimate magnitude, while the other emphasizes the method of its internal operation, and the universality of its diffusion at the last.[18]

The mustard seed "becomes a tree." Lockyear informs us that this plant belongs to the species *khardal* which, in warm climates, may grow to a height of twenty feet.[19] Great flocks of birds have been seen in its branches, men on horseback have ridden under its limbs. The mustard tree was chosen, not because it is the largest tree, but because of the great contrast in the size of the seed in comparison to the size of the herb. The prophets used a similar picture as "a symbol of a great empire offering political protection to its subject states" (Dan. 4:12; Ezek. 31:6; 17:23).[20]

The leaven portrays the kingdom of heaven which is "endowed with a subtle power of spreading itself through society and transforming it."[21]

Helmut Thielicke told of the time he conducted his first Bible study as a pastor. The only people present were two very old ladies and an even older organist. He was a good man, but his

---

17. Helmut Thielicke, trans. John W. Doberstein, *The Waiting Father: Sermons on the Parables of Jesus* (New York: Harper & Brothers, 1959), p. 64.
18. Taylor, p. 54.
19. Lockyear, p. 186.
20. C.H. Dodd, *Apostolic Preaching And Its Development* (London: Hodder & Stoughton, 1936), p. 190.
21. Henry Barclay Swete, *The Parables of the Kingdom* (London: Macmillan and Co., Limited, 1921), p. 42.

fingers were so palsied that his playing was something of an embarrassment. Outside the church building battalions of youth of Hitler's Third Reich marched by. It appeared that the kingdom of the Lord was dead, or at least dying. The forces of evil were winning. Right was on the scaffold and wrong was on the throne. Thielicke concluded,

> We have a Saviour to whom the world belongs and before whom every knee shall bow. And because we are marching on to his day with power we are not shortwinded and shortsighted. And therefore even the smallest need not be too small for us.[22]

5. The Requirement of Patience

Growth is slow. A giant redwood may reach the spectacular height of three hundred feet. But it takes three thousand years for the tree to accomplish this.

There have been spurts of growth in the history of the church but there have also been setbacks. Overall, the growth of the kingdom has been gradual. And now, two thousand years after Pentecost, only twenty-five percent of the world's population accepts Jesus as Lord. And, unfortunately, many of these are only nominal Christians.

These parables teach patience. As Americans we want immediate results. We do not like to stand in queues at the checkout stands in the local market. We want our pain killers to destroy our headaches within minutes. We complain more about the airplanes being late than we do about a poor safety record. And similarly, we expect our missionaries to convert an entire tribe during their first term of service.

Impatience can result in the use of the wrong methods to achieve the growth of the kingdom.

One inappropriate method is coercion. I was preaching on the street in an Indian village. During the invitation I was startled

---

22. Thielicke, pp. 62, 70.

to see some of the non-Christian men pushing young boys forward to make a commitment to Jesus. The missionary, a man of several years experience, was wise enough to stop the invitation and refuse to take the confessions.

Another poor method is compromise. We can be so anxious to win converts that we overlook some critical pagan practices. Keeping a spirit shelf in the house may not seem so evil, especially if we do not believe in the actual existence of those spirits, so we do not require the destruction of the spirit shelves as a part of repentance. The result is syncretism — a blend of Christian and pagan practices. Haiti is a nearby example. While ninety percent of the Haitians are Roman Catholics, eighty percent of the population practice Voodoo.

A third unfortunate method is corn. That is, buying the membership of people by paying them in food, medicine, housing, jobs, or other physical benefits. I visited a Christian medical clinic in Haiti that required patients to come to the clinic one hour before the clinic opened. During that time the physician in charge preached to the waiting sick people. After the service each attendee was given a ticket. Possession of a ticket was required before the doctor would see the patient. If someone came late, he was required to wait until the next morning to hear the sermon and get a ticket. The only exception was made for emergency cases. One hundred people were baptized each month during this program. The method was effective, but was it right?

The signs of the times result in mixed interpretations. Half a century ago the end of the world was not in sight. In every thing, in every way, everything was getting better. Nearly everyone was optimistic about the future. It was easy to believe the kingdom of God was growing and that within a few years, even within that generation, the whole world would be won to Christ.

Such optimism does not come easy today. The ozone layer that protects human life from the ultra violet rays of the sun is disintegrating as a result of man's misuse of nature. Several countries, many of them unstable, have the capability of destroying the entire world population with atomic bombs. AIDS threatens to wipe out most of the population of Africa. Many interpret these signs to mean the end is near. Time is running out. The Church, using the techniques of the past, cannot hope to bring about the Reign of Christ on earth.

The parables of the mustard seed and leaven were written for such a time as this. In spite of appearances, the mustard seed is growing! The leaven is working! God's will will be done. Christ will reign.

6. Growth is God's Gift.

Joyce Kilmer was right. Only God can make a tree. Men can make things that look like seeds, have the same chemical composition as seeds, but they do not behave like seeds. But only God can put the germ of life in them. And these seeds have remarkable ability to retain their growing ability. In 1965 I visited Cairo Museum. Included in the items exhumed from King Tut's tomb was a box of seeds. Scientists had planted a few of them. Remarkably, after thousands of years, they germinated, sprouted, and grew.

However, we sometimes use the concept that only God can cause the kingdom to grow as an excuse to do nothing. William Robinson provides the lyrical parody for those people who so avoid their responsibility:

> Sit down, O men of God,
> His Kingdom he will bring,
> Whenever it may please his will;
> *You cannot do a thing!*[23]

7. There is something for man to do.

Jesus chose scenes from the daily life of His contemporaries to make His point. The farmer was sowing seed in his field

---

23. William Robinson, *The Devil and God* (New York: Abingdon-Cokesbury Press, 1945), p. 98.

(mustard was a field plant, not a garden herb, as its size required), and a woman was kneading bread for her family. God causes the seed to grow, the leaven to expand — but only if they are "hid" in the hearts of men. These parables

> call for human effort. The harvest waits for reapers, and it is in this light that Jesus sets His own work and that to which He calls His disciples.[24]

One of the interesting characteristics of leaven is that if it is not used it will decay. Leaven has to be fed sugar. It normally obtains the required sugar as it is working in the dough. Although Jesus did not make this point from the parable, it is true that the church that does not evangelize will perish. In fact every church is only one generation away from extinction.

Thielicke describes the Christian "who is only quiet, a Christian who keeps his mouth shut about what has been bestowed upon him" as "nothing but a dud. He is dynamite that fails to go off."[25]

II. THREE PARABLES OF INCLUSION OF THE GENTILES

The Great Banquet, the King's Wedding Feast, and the Wicked Husbandmen all open the door of the kingdom to the Gentiles. However, there is a progression in the development of opportunities offered the Gentiles.

The Great Banquet (Luke 14:15-24)

Jesus was a guest in the home of a Pharisee early in His ministry before the hostility of the Pharisees toward Jesus had become so intense. Jesus instructed His host to invite the poor, the crippled, the lame, and the blind when he hosted a feast (Luke 14:14). The immediate response of one of the guests was,

---

24. Dodd, p. 194.
25. Thielicke, p. 67.

"Blessed is the man who will eat at the feast in the kingdom of God" (Luke 14:15). It was natural that he would identify feasting with the kingdom of God. That idea had been around since Isaiah (Isa. 25:6). But he had missed the point, giving Jesus the opportunity to tell the parable of the Great Banquet.

The account of the feast in the parable followed the traditions of the East and would need no explanations to the original hearers. In the parable the announcement of the banquet was followed by invitations to the guests. "But they all alike began to make excuses" (Luke 14:18). Whereupon the host sent the servant out to invite "the poor, the crippled, the blind and the lame" — people who otherwise would not have had the opportunity to attend the party. In the book of Acts we see the kingdom opened to the lame man (Acts 3:1-10), the Samaritans (Acts 8:4-8), the Sorcerer (Acts 8:5-24), the mutilated man Acts 8:26-40), and a killer (Acts 9:1-19). Most commentators understand this invitation is directed to sinners of the Jewish race.

But when the banquet hall is not filled the servant is sent out to "roads and country lanes" to compel the potential guests to come to the banquet. Virtually all commentators see this invitation as an invitation to the Gentiles to enter the kingdom. The history book of the early church records this development in the conversion of Cornelius (Acts 10), the acceptance of the Greeks at Antioch (Acts 11:20), the formal approval of acceptance of Gentiles without circumcision (Acts 15), and Paul's missionary trip to Europe (Acts 16:6-10).

Jesus gives the reason, "my house will be full." The rejection of the kingdom by the Jews opened the door for the entrance of the Gentiles. Those who rejected the invitation "will not get a taste of my banquet." This explanation for extending the invitation to the Gentiles is not to be construed in such a way that the Gentiles could come only if the Jews rejected the opportunity. For we have seen in our study that it was God's plan from the beginning that the Gentiles were to be included. What we do see here is the horrible consequences for the Jews as a result of their rejection.

The second phase in the development of the Gentile participation in the kingdom is given in the parable of the Marriage Feast (Matt. 22:1-14). Although the parables are similar in many ways they are not to be considered as the same parable recorded differently by different writers. The setting is different, the time is different, and the lessons to be learned are different. The guests who were invited to the wedding acted in a defiant and offensive manner. They did not even have the courtesy to give excuses. They just went about their business as if there had been no invitation. Worse, some of them seized, mistreated, and killed the servant who came with the invitation. Barclay has pointed out that if one rejects Jesus, there is no further appeal. Such a rejection has an irreversible finality about it.[26] Christian missionaries have, on many occasions, been treated with the same kind of reception experienced by the servant of the host of the wedding banquet.

In this parable, as in the first, the people who came in off the streets are the Gentiles. But when the king came in he noticed one man without a wedding garment. No doubt, he had said to himself, "I am what I am, I do not need to change. What I have is good enough." He had no excuse for not changing. When the king entered he asked the man, "Friend, how did you get in here without wedding clothes?" The man was speechless. The Greek word means his mouth was stopped, he was gagged. He stood self-condemned. Most commentators observe that the king at the Oriental wedding feasts of that time provided wedding garments. This man could have had a proper garment, but he simply refused to put it on. The invitation to enter the kingdom is to all men. But that does not mean that we can come as we are. Our acts of self-righteousness are as filthy rags. We must "put on Christ." "For all of you who were baptized into Christ have clothed yourselves with Christ" (Gal. 3:27).

---

26. William Barclay, *And Jesus Said: A Handbook on the Parables* (Philadelphia: The Westminster Press, 1970), p. 144.

So his banquet did not fall through. When the geniuses fail, God turns to the nobodies. When the bearers of the Christian traditions, the church Christians, walk out and descend into dogmatic hairsplitting or church politics, he turns to the neopagans and rejoices in the freshness of their new-found Christianity. For God has no prejudices. A man can come as he is, even an utterly poor, utterly sinful, and utterly unlovable person, who can not understand what God can see in him. The fact is he cannot see anything in him, but he makes something of him; he makes him his beloved child.

So there they all were, all seated around the table; the beggars and the prostitutes, surviving bankrupts and broken down geniuses, poor wretches whom nobody takes seriously, and artful dodgers — all in all a nice gang of people.

And then the king appeared.[27]

The third parable of this set is quite different. It is the parable of the Wicked Husbandmen (Matt. 21:33-45; Mark 12:1-12; Luke 20:9-19). The principle lesson here is not that the kingdom is extended to the Gentiles, but that the work of the kingdom is given to the Gentiles to do.

The Jewish people and especially the religious leaders had been a recalcitrant lot. They are pictured in this parable as farmers who are to take care of the Lord's vineyard. The servants he sent to collect his rent were the prophets who were killed by the Israelites. This literally happened to the Hebrew prophets. Isaiah was sawn in two by Manasseh, Jeremiah was stoned while in exile in Egypt, Amos was murdered with a club, John the Baptist was beheaded, and, in the Christian era, Stephen was stoned to death. The son of God was not treated any better. He was crucified.

The verdict is:

Therefore I tell you that the kingdom of God will be taken away from you and given to a people *who will produce fruit* (Matt. 21:43).

---

27. Thielicke, p. 189.

THE PARABLES OF JESUS

This is an advancement in thought. The Gentiles are not just being invited into the kingdon; they are given the task of producing fruit. The responsibility of evangelizing the world was taken from the Jews and given to the Gentiles. After the death of the Twelve virtually all the evangelists of the Church were Gentiles.

This is more than an historical event; this is a universal principle which can be seen applied repeatedly throughout history. Every church, every Christian nation, has had its opportunity to evangelize the world. But when their evangelistic zeal lagged, or they refused to send missionaries, the opportunity was taken away from them and given to another. Worse still, the church declined or died. Europe once was considered Christian. And as long as the European countries were sending out missionaries, even though they were agents of the colonial governments, the church remained strong. Their efforts flagged, however, the churches are now dead, and the area is known as "post-Christian" Europe. The churches in the United States took up the mantle dropped by Europe and most of the Christian missionaries during the last century were sent from America. Higher Criticism from Germany invaded the mainline churches in the U.S. and infected them with liberalism. As a result the number of missionaries declined, the churches started dying, and today the center of Christian influence is moving to sub-Saharan Africa which many believe will become the next Christian continent.

V. A PARABLE OF MEETING HUMAN
NEED — LUKE 10:25-37

The parable of the Good Samaritan is an account of a redefinition of terms. We encounter three sets of people in this story. Each gives a new meaning to an old word.

The first person we encounter is the man in the ditch. Jesus here redefines "neighbor." Neighbor can no longer be used for someone of the same religious persuasion. That was the Jewish view. In fact, the Pharisees reserved "neighbor" to refer to other Pharisees. Neither can we use neighbor for someone who lives nearby. That is the popular American use. Neighbor for the Christian now must refer to the man in need, wherever he lives. The man and his family living under a bridge in Goiania, Brazil; the child who is starving in Maranda, Zimbabwe, because there has been no rain for five years; the ten year old girl with the broken leg in the Ituri Forest in Zaire; and the Karen opium addict in the Golden Triangle who just sold his children in order to buy more opium now are all neighbors.

The second set of people we meet in the parable are the religious leaders. Jesus redefines religion. Religion no longer can mean the performance of ritual, but the practice of righteousness. The priest and the Levite had their excuses for not helping the man in the ditch. Jesus fortunately spares us the sorry excuses they made. We can, however, imagine what some of them might have been. The text tells us he was left "half dead." He must have appeared dead to the passerby. And if he were dead the religious leaders dare not touch him. They could do him no good, and it would make them unclean so that they could not perform their rituals in the Temple. On the other hand, the text tells us they were going "down from Jerusalem to Jericho." Perhaps they had completed their rotation at the Temple and were hurrying home to their families. Dinner was waiting. The children were waiting. Their wives were waiting. They just did not have time to help the injured man. G. Campbell Morgan somewhere wrote that their sin was in not going toward the man. I had always assumed that they were walking down the side of the road where the man lay, and walked away from him. Morgan suggests that the sin may have been more subtle: they may have been on the other side of the road and chose not to go toward the man in need.

The most frequently heard excuse among American Christians for not supporting missions is "we have not converted all the people in our town. We have enough to do here, without taking on the responsibility of converting the rest of the world." Those who say this frequently quote Acts 1:8 as justification for their view: "you will be my witnesses in Jerusalem, *then* in all Judea and *then* Samaria, and *then* to the ends of the earth." Read this way, somehow our own hometown always is Jerusalem, and we do not have to go anywhere else until our hometown is won to Christ. We need to read the text more accurately. What it really says is, "you will be my witnesses in Jerusalem, *and* in all Judea *and* Samaria, *and* to the ends of the earth." Our responsibility is both/and not either/or. At *the same time* we are evangelizing at home we have the responsibility of sending missionaries to all other parts of the world.

I sometimes play a historical game. I call it "What If?" What if the first church in Jerusalem had accepted our philosophy of converting the hometown before launching out to the rest of the world? What would have happened? The fact is that Jerusalem never became a Christian city. Had they waited until it had, they would never have left town. And there would be no Christians in my hometown, or your home community.

The third person in this revolutionary parable is the Samaritan. And his behaviour is so exemplary that we call him the "Good Samaritan." Jesus here redefines the religious man. The religious man can no longer mean the man who believes the right thing, but the man who does the right thing. John said it well, "he who does what is right is righteous" (I John 3:7). This does not excuse false doctrine, or wrong belief. But it does say that we can believe the right things and still go to hell. Faith in the Scriptures is always coupled with action (Matt. 25:31-46; James 2:14-17; Eph. 2:8-10). Faith in Jesus, who gave us the commission to go into all the world, requires our obedience to that commission.

The parable of the Good Samaritan should settle once-for-all the debate whether we should preach the gospel, or practice the social gospel. The gospel is not good news unless it is told. But it is not understood unless it is demonstrated in helpful actions toward the needy.

SUMMARY

The most memorable teaching of Jesus was couched in the graphic parables. Those we have examined in this chapter have taught us several lessons about the kingdom of heaven, and consequently about the mission of the Church. We have learned that there are both receptive and unreceptive populations, which helps us form a strategy for sowing the gospel. We have learned that the seed is potent and that it will grow, albeit slowly, which gives us encouragement. We have learned that not only have the Gentiles been invited to enter the kingdom, but they now have the responsibility of extending the kingdom, which should impress upon us the duty of spreading the gospel lest that privilege be taken from us. We have learned that the good news is good news for the here and now, as well as for the there and then, which enables us to include a ministry of service for human needs in our ministry of expressing the love of God for the world.

9

"HE TOUCHED HIM"

THE MIRACLES OF JESUS

More than half of the miracles of Jesus are miracles of healing. Not only did Jesus heal the sick, He apparently expected His disciples to continue a healing ministry. Although the command to heal is not specifically mentioned in the Great Commission, He did command (*therapeute* is imperative) the seventy-two to "heal the sick" (Luke 10:9). And the apostles carried on a healing ministry after Pentecost as we shall see in Chapter Eleven. These miracles impact on the theory and practice of mission. Space does not permit a study of each of these miracles so I have chosen one, the healing of the leper recorded in Mark 1:40-45, to represent all of them. From this miracle, I believe, we can gleen most of the lessons for mission found in the parables.

His fingers were missing. Most of his toes were gone. He was a leper! I met him in Christian Hospital, Madrapakkam, India.

Madrapakkam is a small town with a big leprosy problem. In 1975 there were six hundred twenty-three students in the local school. One hundred twenty-eight of them were suffering from leprosy. Roughly one person in five has leprosy. Madrapakkam may be worse than most but nearly every village in this area of India has its share of leprosy patients.

The Fellowship of Associates of Medical Evangelism built a general hospital there in 1976. Because of the nature of its location seventy-five percent of the case load has been leprosy patients. I visited the hospital after it was built. I saw the leprosy patients. I smiled with them. I talked to them. I took pictures of them.

But I must confess my sin — I did not touch one of them. It was not out of fear of catching leprosy. I knew that most adults have a natural immunity to leprosy. I knew I could not get leprosy by shaking hands. I knew that it takes prolonged, direct, personal contact to contract leprosy. Still I did not touch one. Why? There is something repulsive about leprosy.

Mentally, I excused my behavior by thinking, "I am being friendly. I am talking with them. I am smiling. I am taking pictures of them. I raised most of the money to build this hospital: that is all they should expect of me." Leprosy, like AIDS, makes people lonely. It isolates them. The greatest need of leprosy patients is to be touched. The one thing they needed most I did not give. As far as the lepers were concerned it would have been better had I never come. I fear the Judge will say to me, "Depart from me, you are cursed, into the eternal fire prepared for the devil and his angels . . . . I was sick . . . and you did not look after me" (Matt. 25:41,43).

A man with leprosy came to him and begged him on his knees, "If you are willing, you can make me clean." Filled with compassion, Jesus reached out his hand and *touched* the man. "I am willing," he said. "Be clean!" Immediately the leprosy left him and he was cured.

Jesus sent him away at once with a strong warning: "See that you don't tell this to anyone. But go, show yourself to the priest and offer the sacrifices that Moses commanded for your cleansing, as a testimony to them." Instead he went out and began to talk freely, spreading the news. As a result, Jesus could no longer enter a town openly but stayed outside in the lonely places. Yet the people still came to him from everywhere (Mark 1:40-45, emphasis mine).

This text raises several questions. I want to address six of them.

I. WHY IS A PERSON SICK?

More specifically, why did this man have leprosy? The answer will also give us the reason for all disease.

May I suggest that the answer must be a religious answer? Only a theological reason will meet the deeper needs of man. However, this does not mean that every religious explanation of sickness is right.

1. The most common religious reply is that sickness is the result of sin.

The Jewish rabbis traced all disease to sin. They said, "No death without sin, no pain without transgression." "The sick is not healed, till all his sins are forgiven him." In the matter of leprosy they listed eleven sins that could cause this dread disease. The disciples of Jesus were infected with this philosophy. In the case of the man born blind they asked, "Rabbi, who sinned, this man or his parents" (John 9:1)? Jesus rejected this as an adequate explanation when he replied, "Neither this man nor his parents sinned" (John 9:3).

2. Related to the first explanation is the theory that disease is sent as punishment for sin. Again Rabbinism advanced this idea. The rabbis said childlessness and leprosy were sent as chastisement for sin! Can you imagine the guilt such a theology places on innocent people?

Some modern preachers have not advanced beyond this

view. The other day I heard one of the media preachers proclaim that AIDS was God's punishment for homosexual conduct.

3. In the Third World, where animism is the principal religion, disease is viewed as being caused by the presence of evil spirits in one's body. I saw a Pokot man who came to the FAME clinic in Kiwawa, Kenya. He had three deep cuts about six inches long in his side and back. They had been made by the witchdoctor to let out the evil spirits which he said were causing the man's illness.

4. It seems to me that the biblical explanation of disease includes three factors: One, God created a world that was good, and free from disease and death. Two, God's world functions in an orderly manner. The observed rules of this orderliness are usually called "laws." Three, man's disregard of the principles that control the world often results in disease and death.

This world view allows for both what the Scriptures reveal about God and His world, and what science has discovered through research. This philosophy has two direct applications to life. One, the germ theory of disease causes us to be aware that if a well person has contact with a person with an infectious disease there is a high degree of the probability that the well person will also become ill. Coming in contact with germs cannot be regarded as sin. But doing nothing about the germs or the spread of germs is sin. Two, a few years ago I bought a bushwhacker. This tool has a steel sawblade that is capable of cutting through small trees. Consequently it is a very dangerous tool to use. There were labels and tags all over it warning, "Read the directions before using." The manufacturer, who knew the tool best, gave instructions with the tool. To ignore the instructions could result in severing a leg. I see a parallel. God gave us bodies that are both useful and dangerous. With the body He gave a set of instructions — we call it the Bible. If it is read and followed a happy and useful life may follow. But if ignored or disobeyed there can be disease and death. For example, sex is a potent force that can be both pleasurable and capable of reproduction. But if the basic principles that govern the operation of the human body are ignored then the result may be venereal disease and AIDS. In which case, then, God is not punishing man. And although such diseases may be the result of sin, sin must be seen as ignoring and violating the instructions that came with the body.

We have to get our theology straight before we can help the man with leprosy. Our view of God determines our definition of disease. And our concept of God determines what we will do with disease.

II. ARE ONLY BELIEVERS TO BE HELPED?

The leper came as a believer in the power of Jesus' healing ability. His only question was, "If you are willing?" He did not ask, "Are you able to heal me?" Our first question is, how did he become a believer? No doubt he was familiar with Jewish history. From that he would have known that there were only two cases of healing leprosy in the Old Testament. It would have taken great faith to believe that Jesus could cure leprosy.

"Faith comes by hearing." But what had he heard? Was he present for the Sermon on the Mount? Had he heard about the other miraculous healings of Jesus?

But the real question is, could Jesus heal only those who believed in Him? And concomitantly, should missionaries give medical help only to believers?

Perhaps a still more pertinent question might be, as missionaries give medicine to non-believers, should it be for the purpose of converting them?

Faith, either by the sick person, or on behalf of him by his friends, was the normal qualification for healing by Jesus. As He said, "According to your faith will it be done to you" (Matt. 9:29). There are only four recorded healings where faith is not stated or implied. But there are those four! Most notable of them is the healing of the soldier's severed ear (Luke 22:50-51).

Paul summarizes the philosophy of charity for the Christian,

"Therefore as we have opportunity, let us do good to all people, especially to those who belong to the family of believers" (Gal. 6:10).

Medical missions has been justified for several reasons: one, it allows Christians to enter countries that are closed to evangelistic missionaries. Two, it is a tool of evangelism. Three, it is a continuation of the ministry of Jesus. Four, it is an expression of a concern for the whole man, body and spirit. Most frequently two or more of the above reasons are given. Personally I think the highest motive is the wholistic approach that is concerned with taking the whole gospel to the whole man because I see it as a replication of the earthly ministry of Jesus who healed both the body and spirit.

Several times in the Gospels and Acts the people who were healed were said to have been "made whole." In nine of these occurrences the word "whole" could be translated "saved" (*sozo*, Matt. 9:12-22; Mark 5:28,35; Mark 6:56; 10:52; Luke 17:19; Acts 4:9). Cyril Simkins, in his doctoral dissertation, has pointed out that it is said they are "saved," or "made whole," only when both the body and spirit are mentioned.[1]

But how does one link health care with evangelism?

Dr. Paul White was a missionary doctor in Tanganyika. The local chief brought a twelve year old boy to him with the explanation,

"Bwana, a child, with a *du-du* (an insect) in his ear." Dr. White asked the boy, "Tell me, old man, what happened."
"I was asleep in my house, lying with my head in my blanket, on a cow-skin near the grain bin. A *du-du* crawled into my ear, and has been walking, walking, walking ever since. I shook my head and poke round with a bit of grass, but it would not come out. My relative tried blowing into the other ear. They stood me on my head, and gave me medicines to make me very sick, but the insect still walked. Then my father took me to the witch-

---

1. Cyril Simkins, *Salvation in the Early Church* (Lincoln, IL: Lincoln Christian College, 1979).

doctor. First he poke with a thorn — *Kumbe!* How it hurt! Then he poured boiling medicine into my ear. *Yah!* How I screamed and struggled, but it did no good. My ear was burnt outside and inside, but the insect still walked — and now — my head throbs and throbs. I cannot sleep. The pain and the throbbing nearly drive me mad. Oh Bwana, help me!"

After Dr. White removed the insect with crocodile forceps the dresser, Daudi, asked, "could you get rid of the insect yourself? Or could the witch-doctor — by your own efforts?

"*Hamba hadodo* (not a little bit). But Bwana could, with his crocodile forceps."

"Yah," said Daudi. "That *du-du* is like sin. You cannot get rid of it yourself, no matter how hard you try. Only Jesus Christ, the Son of God, who loved you and gave Himself for you, can do that."[2]

The Fellowship of Associates of Medical Evangelism (FAME) built five medical clinics in the Dominican Republic. Each one is an integral part of a local church building. So even in those cases where no verbal witnessing is done by the medical personnel, the patients are able to identify the care they receive with the local church and are aware that help is given because of the compassion of Christians.

To reject the kind of evangelism that pressures people to become Christians frequently leads to the practice of presence evangelism. Presence evangelism says that an evangelist does not need to preach. In fact, he probably should not preach. His task is simply to be present. As a result of seeing his lifestyle and the good deeds he performs his neighbors will ask him about his religion which then gives him the opportunity to witness. I like presence evangelism. It relieves me of the burden, awkwardness, and embarrassment of deliberately trying to make disciples. But it does not meet the biblical demand to "Go into all the world and preach the good news to all creation" (Mark 16:16).

---

2. Paul White, *Jungle Doctor* (London: The Paternoster Press, 1942), pp. 77-80.

III. HOW CAN WE PRACTICE HEALING TODAY?

I do not have the gift of healing. Although some claim to have that gift today, I personally do not know of anyone who can heal miraculously with a word or touch. Is then the Twentieth Century church excluded from a healing ministry? I do not think so. Beginning with Luke (Acts 28:9) the Church has continually carried on a medical ministry for two thousand years. Healing through western medicine is not a miracle in the same sense that Jesus' healing was. But the net result in curing disease, relieving suffering, and showing love is the same.

Missiologists today are advocating confrontation with pagan cultures. By this they are referring to the impact of prayer, the Holy Spirit, and other spiritual forces in contrast with evil forces in the world. I see missionary medicine as having a similar impact on non-Christian people. The contest between men of God and forces of evil opens the door to the good news. It was after a preaching and healing tour throughout Galilee that crowds of people came and listened to the Sermon on the Mount (Matt. 4:23-25).

One of the things that has troubled commentators is Jesus' "strong warning, 'See that you don't tell this to anyone' " (Mark 1:43-44). The word for "strong warning" is also used of the snorting of an angry horse. Why would Jesus be so upset with such good, unsolicited testimony from one He had helped? Today we want our healing ministries to be told. We desire the public relations to enhance our image. Jesus deserved the praise, why was He so reluctant to receive it?

Three plausible explanations have been advanced.

One, He did not want to be known as a miracle worker but as the harbinger of the Kingdom. It is easy to get a program out of balance, to reverse our priorities. Jesus is telling the Church it is essential to have humanitarian programs, but wrong to make humanitarianism primary.

Two, he wanted to prevent a premature crisis. The cross and

238

the tomb had to come in the fullness of time. Certain facets of His ministry needed to be completed first. In the instability of governments today a chief purpose of mission is to plant a church with effective trained leadership before the forced departure of the missionaries.

Three, beginning at this event there was the deliberately planted presence of hostile Scribes and Pharisees seeking ways to destroy Him. We know, too, in Muslim, Hindu, and other religious contexts, that there are hostile religious leaders who are trying to destroy the church. Persecution in such places is our promise. But we must behave in such a way that we are persecuted for Christ's sake not for our political or personal behavior.

IV. HOW CAN WE ENCULTURATE THE GOSPEL?

In popular terminology, we must ask ourselves, how can we make the gospel, and specifically medical missions, culturally appropriate?

Missionary medicine by its very nature is scientific medicine. But the science upon which this medical practice is based is western in origin, conceptualization, and development. It may, therefore, be called western medicine.

This immediately raises two problems relative to contextualization. First, is western medicine biblical, or, at least, consistent with biblical concepts of health, sickness, and healing? To those who are westerners in thought pattern, western medicine is not only right, it is the only way to provide healing and health. And, therefore, it must be the way God intended for illness to be cured. If, then, the biblical account does not correspond with our current practice the biblical record is explained away as reflecting the cultural practice of that ancient pre-scientific time.

For example, since the scientific explanation of epilepsy was unknown to the biblical writers, seizures could be explained as demon possession, an explanation no longer acceptable in the

239

western, scientific world view. Westerners, then, tend to measure the Bible by science rather than evaluating our scientific ideas and practices by the scriptures.

Second, medical missionaries do not enter a medical vacuum when they go to the Third World. An explanation of sickness and acceptable treatment already exists. In many, if not most, instances the traditional view will be in direct conflict with western medicine. The medical missionary is immediately faced with an issue of contextualization. Shall he ignore the traditional healer? Cooperate with him? Try to learn from him? Build on the medical concepts already present? Deny and contradict the traditional practice? Or "all of the above" as the occasion warrants.

Jesus set the model. He said, "go show yourself to the priest and offer the sacrifices that Moses commanded for your cleansing, as a testimony to them" (Mark 1:44). Jesus "was born under the law." In time He planned to replace it with a higher law. But in the meantime He demonstrated His obedience. Further, Jesus had another motive.

The rabbis had compiled a list of remedies for various diseases. But they had no cure for leprosy. Leprosy was a kind of moral death that only God could cure. Therefore, for the priests to recognize this cleansing was to acknowledge the divinity of Jesus. But their subsequent refusal to accept Him as the Messiah, based on the evidence they accepted in this case, results in their self-condemnation in the day of judgment. If, on the other hand, they attributed the cure to the power of evil they stood self-condemned for rejecting the evidence Jesus provided in performing the miracle.

V. IS IT NECESSARY TO TOUCH THE LEPER?

G. Campbell Morgan says that Jesus never touched the leper.[3]

---

3. G. Campbell Morgan, *The Great Physician: Series of Fifty Studies: The Method of Jesus with Individuals* (London: Marshall, Morgan and Scott, 1937), p. 97.

His theory is that the man was healed before Jesus' finger came in contact with his skin and therefore Jesus touched a clean man. I think this is semantic gymnastics, or legal sophistry. It is the kind of argument the Pharisees used. Jesus' whole life was an act of touching the unclean. "The Word became flesh and made his dwelling among us" (John 1:14). He ate with the publicans. He dwelt with the sinners. He ate and drank with the publicans. He entered the home of Zacchaeus. He died a criminal's death. The fact that He ignored the taboo about touching an unclean person is not only insignificant; it is in harmony with the rest of His life.

The rabbis thought of a leper as morally dead and prescribed that he was to have the appearance of a mourner. He was to wear garments that were rent, to have dishevelled hair, to cover the face from the upper lip down, and to cry mournfully, "unclean, unclean." Presumably Jesus could have healed him with a word, but He chose to use His hand. And how appropriate. Leprosy victims live the most lonely lives. And the sense most appreciated by the lonely is touch.

> Francis of Assisi came to the turning point of his life and found his vocation when he realized that little good was done by throwing a coin to a beggar. He had to dismount from his horse, get alongside the beggar, befriend him, reach out to him a brotherly hand. It was not enough to "send a subscription" to the local leper house, he had to go among the lepers. He faced the hardest of tests when the challenge came to him to overcome fear, squeamishness, disgust — to visit the leper house, go round to each of the sufferers, kiss the hand of each, then put a coin in it.[4]

Was it important for Jesus to touch the leper? It may have been essential! But we can touch condescendingly. We can touch mechanically. We can touch unconcernedly. It is not enough to

---

4. Robert McCracken, "The Human Touch," *Best Sermons, 1968*, G. Paul Butler, ed. (New York: Trident Press, 1968), p. 268.

say that we love, somehow the manner in which we touch must convey that love.

There are few with leprosy today. But there are millions who are lonely. One of the megatrends is urbanization.[5] And the move to the cities is greater and is having even more negative impact in the Third World than the First. One factor is that the closer we get to one another the more distant we become. Someone has said that in the city you have propinquity but not community. If there was ever a need for someone with a healing touch, it is now.

We also live in the age of high technology. And the Church is using it. Christian messages are being radioed into closed countries and inaccessible areas. Video messages are being sent by satellites. Solar powered tape players are being used where itinerant evangelists cannot visit. It is appropriate to use every technology available. But the world will never be won through technology that does not allow touching. Peter Wagner says the greatest growth taking place today is in Mainland China. But it is not coming from the radio messages that have been beamed there. It is occurring as a result of one Chinese telling another.

Touching has yet another ramification. We must put our love into deeds not just words. John said it well ,"He who does what is right is righteous" (I John 3:7). Approximately one thousand people are being baptized annually at Christian Hospital in Madrapakkam. Most of these are leprosy patients and their families. They are not won through preaching alone, but because some emissaries of the Great Physician have touched them.

VI. HOW DO WE OBTAIN POWER TO HEAL?

Immediately before the story of the healing of the leper, Mark records, "Very early in the morning, while it was still dark, Jesus got up, left the house and went to a solitary place, where he

---

5. John Naisbitt, *Megatrends* (New York: Warner Books, 1982).

prayed" (Mark 1:35). From chapter thirteen we learn that this was during the fourth watch of the night which was between 3:00 a.m. and 5:00 a.m. The source of power was the Father. And the means of communication was prayer. When Jesus prayed we can expect wonders. Is it possible that our ineffectiveness as evangelists, church planters, authors, or as leaders may have its roots in a poor prayer life? Leonard Ravenhill wrote a little book several years ago, *Why Revival Tarries*. His thesis was that all great revivals have been preceded by extended periods of intense prayer. Therefore, any future revivals will have to have significant prayer preparation.

Here we study the technical side of church growth. We study cultural anthropology. We study medicine. These are essential. God uses the knowledge and skills we gain. But the real changes that take place in human life are divine in origin. And it is the spiritual power obtained through prayer that is most desperately needed.

SUMMARY

Jesus, through His miracles of healing, provided the model for missionary medical practice today. We learned that sickness is not the punishment for sin, but the natural result of breaking the "laws" that govern life in this world. We learned that all the sick should be helped, with a special emphasis on those who are of the household of faith. We learned that western medicine can legitimately perform the same functions as the miraculous healings of Jesus. We learned that other cultures also have health systems. This requires western practitioners to evaluate the situation so they can provide the culturally appropriate treatment as well as the scientifically approved procedures. We learned that touching was not only essential for those with leprosy but also for all the lonely people in the world. And we learned that the source of real healing power is God, who is contacted through prayer.

243

10

THE PRINCIPLES OF MISSION PRACTICE

ACTS OF THE APOSTLES

Flip Wilson used to describe himself as the preacher of "The Church of What's Happening Now." If we can turn aside from the irreverence of his implications, we might retitle the fifth book of the New Testament, "The Church of What's Happening Now." Although Acts may be a history of the Church the book does not really end. It just stops. There is no formal ending, no benediction.

It simply breaks off abruptly with the picture of Paul at Rome, the great imperial metropolis of the world of that day, "preaching the kingdom of God, and teaching those things which concern the Lord Jesus Christ, with all confidence, no man forbidding him." This conclusion is altogether fitting, for the work was not finished but "the doings of the missionaries" were still to continue, and will yet continue until the end of the present age.[1]

It is as if Luke expected to write more. Is it possible he was contemplating a third volume to his work? In any case, the lessons learned in Acts help us to be effective missionaries today.
Acts is the *history* of the church.
Acts is the *divine* history of the church.
Acts is the divine history of the *mission* of the church.

Acts contains *more* divine history of the mission of the church than all the rest of the New Testament combined.

Therefore a careful study of the book of Acts is critical to the understanding and practice of mission today. Acts, however, is not a book of theology of mission; it is not a handbook for mission strategy. It is a record of *events* in the First Century Church. We can develop both a theology and a strategy of mission from this book if we 1) make a careful exegesis of the text, 2) understand the historical and cultural context of the events, 3) think critically about the text, and 4) prayerfully apply the principles learned to the current situation. This I will atempt to do. I am making certain assumptions about the text: 1) the text is accurate, 2) the apostles have both a theology and strategy even if it is not explicitly articulated, 3) their theology and strategy can be discovered, and 4) such a theology and strategy is both a model and a norm for our mission practice today.

The book of Acts naturally divides itself into two divisions: chapters 1-12, and chapters 13-28. It has often been noted that the first division follows the activities of Peter's ministry, whereas the second division follows Paul's mission. Rarely noted but equally significant is the fact that each of these periods of time was inaugurated by pivotal events, first in Pentecost[2] and then in An-

---

1. Glover, p. 28.
2. See Martin Boer, *Pentecost and Mission* (Grand Rapids: Wm. B. Eerdmans Publishing Co., 1981).

tioch.[3] These events are so significant that they deserve a special attention in a study of Acts, or of mission.

Further subdivision of Acts is suggested in the pregnant leitmotif, ". . . and you will be my witnesses in Jerusalem, and in all Judea and Samaria, and to the ends of the earth" (Acts 1:8).[4] This outline in embryo suggests that it is the intention of the author to show the expansion of the church. This expansion can be followed along three lines in Acts. There is numerical expansion, geographical expansion, and cultural expansion.

1. Numerical Expansion

It is hard to understand how Paul Loeffler could say, "God's purpose is the salvation of all, of the total cosmos, yet in order to achieve this, God elects, calls and converts a few."[5] This statement seems to contain an irreconcilable contradiction. It seems also to be in direct conflict with the numerical growth of the church recorded in Acts.

Luke's concern for counting converts is reflected in the frequency of the appearance of the number of believers. It started with 120 believers (Acts 1:15) and 3000 were added (Acts 2:41) the first day. The number increased as "the Lord added to their number daily" (Acts 2:47). The number of men grew to about 5000" (Acts 4:4). Then "more and more . . . were added to their number" (Acts 5:14). "The number of disciples in Jerusalem increased rapidly (multiplied)" (Acts 6:7). "And a large number of priests became obedient to the faith" (Acts 6:7). "The church throughout Judea, Galilee and Samaria . . . grew (multiplied) in numbers" (Acts 9:31). "All those who lived in Lydda and Sharon saw him and turned to the Lord" (Acts 9:35). "A great number of

---

3. See Chapter Twelve, "Antioch, the Model Missionary Church."
4. Peters calls Acts 1:8 the leitmotif of Acts. George W. Peters, A Theology of Church Growth (Grand Rapids: Zondervan, 1981), pp. 13, 15. He also uses Acts as the framework for his book.
5. Paul Loeffler, "The Biblical Concept of Conversion," Study Encounter, Vol. 1, No. 2, 1965. Quoted in Allen H. Howe, "The Church: Its Growth and Mission," in Shrenk, The Challenge of Church Growth, p. 56.

people were brought to the Lord" (Acts 11:24). "The word of God continued to *increase (multiply) and spread*" (Acts 12:24). "On the next Sabbath almost the *whole city* gathered to hear the word of the Lord" (Acts 13:44). "The word of the Lord *spread* through the *whole* region" (Acts 13:49). "A *great number* of Jews and Gentiles believed" (Acts 14:1). "They won a *large number* of disciples" (Acts 14:21). "So the churches . . . *grew daily* in numbers (Acts 14:21). "*Some* of the Jews . . . a *large number* of the God-fearing Greeks and *not a few* of the prominent women . . . joined Paul and Silas" (Acts 17:4). "*Many* of the Corinthians . . . believed and were baptized" (Acts 18:8). "*All* the Jews and Greeks who lived in the province of Asia heard the word of the Lord" (Acts 19:10). "*Thousands* (literally *'myriads, tens of thousands'*) of Jews have believed" (Acts 21:20, emphasis mine).

This early, and inspired, church historian did not regard the prohibition against counting the Israelites during the conquest as applying to the church, and consequently recorded some church growth statistics. Measuring success, then, is not just a phenomenon of American business. The early church measured its performance, too. McGavran wrote, "A chief and irreplaceable purpose of missions is church growth."[6] McGavran here was talking about numerical growth which could be objectively measured.

And measurement is necessary. Without accurate counting we may not know whether the church is growing. Otherwise we may very well have the delusion of growth. Without numerical evaluation it may be impossible to know if a program is successful or not.

I was once told by the elders of a local church that an evangelistic meeting with a "high powered" evangelist a few years earlier had resulted in few lasting Christians. Of the one hundred six additions to the church they knew of few who were still active.

---

6. Donald McGavran, *Understanding Church Growth* (Grand Rapids: William B. Eerdmans Co., 1970), p. 32.

THE PRINCIPLES OF MISSION PRACTICE

I obtained the names and discovered that eighty-five percent were either still active in some church or had gone to their reward. The leaders were about to abandon a successful evangelistic tool because of lack of accurate measurement.

However, statistical studies can get out of balance. When one reads Virgil Gerber's *God's Way to Keep a Church Going and Growing*, one gets the impression that making graphs and doing diagnostic research alone will produce church growth.[7]

It is evident that the Founder of the Church wanted the church to grow. He was not pleased with fishing without catchinf fish (Luke 5:4-11), an empty banquet table (Luke 14:15-23), sowing without reaping (Matt. 13:3-9), a fig tree without figs (Luke 13:6-9), sheep that are still lost (Matt. 18:11-14), a lost coin that is not found (Luke 15:8-10), a ripe harvest that is not reaped (Matt. 9:36-38), and a proclamation without a response (Matt. 10:14).

2. Geographical Expansion

Luke specifically names four geographical areas where the church was to expand. The final location, "to the ends of the earth," shows that from its inception the church was intended to be worldwide in scope and to encompass every city and province in the world. Acts 1:8 may be listed as follows: Jerusalem, Judea, Samaria, and Ends of the Earth.

However, as we read Acts we find that the four areas of Acts 1:8 are expanded in a much more detailed way: Jerusalem, Judea, Samaria, Ethiopia, Antioch in Syria, Cyprus, Asia Minor, Macedonia, Greece, Malta, Italy, and The Ends of the Earth.

3. Cultural Expansion

Even more important than the geographical expansion of the church was the cultural expansion hinted at in Acts 1:8 and elaborated throughout the book. The church started with almost a

---

7. Virgil Gerber, *God's Way to Keep a Church Going and Growing* (Glendale, California: Regal Books, 1973).

completely Jewish population in Jerusalem. However, from the very beginning an number of Gentile proselytes to Judaism were incorporated in the church (Acts 2:10-11; 6:5).[8]

When Philip went to Samaria a cultural barrier was crossed allowing these "mixed-breeds," whom the Jews hated, to enter the church.

The conversion of the Ethiopian eunuch is seen as the next step of cross-cultural evagelism.[9] But the Ethiopian eunuch is an enigma. Was he a Jew? Was he a proselyte? Was he Gentile? Many commentaries assume he was a black man and, hence, the first Gentile admitted into the church. Some liberal scholars suggest that Luke downplays the importance of his conversion in order to give credit to Peter, rather than to Philip, for the first Gentile convert. Others propose that the Ethiopian was a proselyte to Judaism, and that the proscription of Deuteronomy 23:1 had already been lifted as Isaiah prophesied.[10] Otherwise, as a eunuch he would not have been permitted to become a proselyte.[11] The unique situation of the Ethiopian treasurer that explains the incorporation of the record of his conversion in the divine history was that his body was mutilated, and according to Jewish law, he was forbidden entrance into the temple (Deut. 23:1). Further, his presence in Jerusalem is more easily explained if he is considered to belong to the Jewish race and to be seeking to worship Yahweh according to the faith of his ancestors. We also know that a large number of Jews were living in Ethiopia at that time. And it is possible that, like many of his na-

8. Although it is not specifically stated that the proselytes present at Pentecost became followers of Jesus, it may be reasonably assumed that some of them did.

9. See Ernst Haenchen, *Acts of the Apostles: A Commentary* (Philadelphia: The Westminster Press, 1971), p. 314, and I.Howard Marshall, *The Acts of the Apostles: An Introduction and Commentary* (Grand Rapids: William B. Eerdmans' Publishing Company, 1980), p. 162.

10. Isa. 56:3-5.

11. Marshall, ibid.

tionality who are gifted in financial matters, his ability allowed him to rise to the office of national treasurer. The point is that Christianity allowed him access to God that Judaism denied him. Haenchen summarizes it well,

> Luke here leaves his readers with the feeling that with this new convert the mission has taken a step beyond the conversion of Jews and Samaritans . . . as a stepping stone between those of the Samaritans and the Gentiles.[12]

The greatest cultural leap then is taken with the admission of Cornelius. The great amount of space given to, and the special visions required for, the conversion of Cornelius, and the great importance of his conversion stressed by its retelling, incline me to think Cornelius and his household, and not the Ethiopian eunuch, were the first Gentile converts. He is the first listed as a "God fearer" (Acts 10:2) rather than as a "convert" to Judaism (Acts 2:11; 6:5). Although this Gentile family was welcomed into the church they remained the rare exception, because, following their conversion, the church apparently did not actively seek Gentile converts in mass.

Substituting cultural terms for geographical language gives a new significance to the expanded list: Jews, Proselytes, Samaritans, Eunuch, Roman Army Officer, Gentiles, Displaced Greeks, and Europeans.

For the purposes of this book the lessons we learn from Acts will be divided into two chapters. In the remainder of this chapter we will examine the universally valid principles of mission. These are the essential features of mission practice. That is, they compose the divine dimension without which there may be results from our mission activity, but which can hardly be called a Christian church.

---

12. Ibid.

The next chapter, Chapter Eleven, will tackle the elements of the human dimension of mission, that is, the strategies and methods that men select to use in specific situations to do mission work. This division of topics is somewhat arbitrary and others may want to use different categories and place the subjects in different categories.

THE UNIVERSALLY ESSENTIAL PRINCIPLES

These principles are *universal*; that is, they are valid at all times and in all places. They are *essential*; that is, these are factors that are essential to making disciples and planting churches. To practice anything less will result in something less than the Church. They are *principles*; that is, they are integral to the church planting process. They are not just strategies but basic elements to the nature of the church. However, let it be noted that I am not here attempting to develop an ecclesiology. The New Testament has more to say on the church than is stated here. I am limiting the topics to be discussed to those items that directly relate to missions. What I am trying to establish is a biblical foundation on which a theology of missions can be built.

I. PURPOSE

Perhaps the best summary of the purpose of the church is found in II Cor. 5:17-19:

Wherefore if any man is in Christ, he is a new creature: the old things are passed away; behold, they are become new. But all things are of God, who reconciled us to himself through Christ, and *gave unto us the ministry of reconciliation* (emphasis mine): to wit, that God was in Christ reconciling the world unto himself, not reckoning unto them their trespasses, and having committed unto us the word of reconciliation.

252

The Church has a clear and singular purpose — the evangelization of the world. The church continues to grow and prosper as long as it retains its purpose. To the degree that it loses its purpose, to that degree it ceases to be the church. For that reason Satan strives valiantly to obscure or subvert the purpose of the church in the minds of her members.

False doctrine (Gal. 1:6-9), immorality (I Cor. 5), contention (I Cor. 6:1-11), and neglect of members (Acts 6:1-2) do enter the church from time to time and do impede the evangelistic work of the church.

More subtly, Christians are often caught up in worthwhile activities which divert them from their purpose and drain off their energies into good, but less than significant, endeavors.

Having a commitment to a clear purpose is essential to the life and growth of a church. Tim Coop says it well, "A church that is not controlled by purpose will be controlled by personality, power, or preservation."[13]

The story has been told of a seashore community located on a treacherous shore where many ships were wrecked. The members of the town, seamen all, volunteered to make it their business to save as many shipwrecked people as possible. When word of a shipwreck came they dragged their boats to the ocean and launched their lifesaving mission. One day one of them said, "We could save time, and more lives, if we left our boats on the beach." Sometime later another said, "It would be a good idea to build a boat house on the beach to protect our boats and ensure that they are seaworthy in times of emergency." Then someone suggested that they install some beds in order for a few men to be on duty twenty-four hours a day. But that required that meals be prepared at the boat house so a kitchen and dining room were added. With so many people around and with so much time on their hands activities were planned and new people given assignments of running the library, the classes, the craft activities,

---

13. Tim Coop, in a lecture at Cincinnati Bible Seminary, October, 1987.

and the games. The people at the boat house became so busy they did not have time to go out on rescue missions. So someone said, "Let us hire a few full-time life-savers who can go out on the rescue missions while we keep the program going at the boathouse."

A few people objected, "Life-saving is the task of all of us. We all should go to sea when a ship sinks." Since no one listened to them, they moved further down the beach and devoted themselves to the pure work of saving lives. One day one of them said, "It would save time, and lives, if we left our boats on the beach." Then one day someone else said, "It would be a good idea to build a boat house. . . ."

II. PRAYER

The two pivotal events of Acts occurred after a period of prayer. I choose "occurred" instead of "launched" because even though the disciples did something on those notable days, it was God who acted on Pentecost and at Antioch. Prior to Pentecost, the Twelve along with certain women, the mother of Jesus, and His brothers "joined together constantly in prayer" (Acts 1:14). Only after these ten days of sustained prayer "All of them were filled with the Holy Spirit and began to speak in other tongues as the Spirit enabled them" (Acts 2:4).

And at Antioch, only after the leaders of the church had worshipped and fasted, did the Holy Spirit say, "Set apart for me Barnabas and Saul for the work to which I have called them" (Acts 13:2).

Prayer is mentioned over thirty times in Acts. "They continued in prayer" (Acts 2:42) characterized the activity of the disciples.

The Church is a divine institution. Jesus said he will build *his* church. Luke records, "the *Lord* added" to the church. Presumably it is possible for God to establish and develop His church without human effort. But He chooses not to. The conversion of men and their incorporation into His church requires the combined and cooperative effort of men and God.

Of Gossner, who single-handed sent out 144 missionaries, it was said: "He prayed up the wall of a hospital, and the hearts of the nurses; he prayed mission stations into being, and missionaries into faith. . . . Prayer was his atmosphere: he could not live without it.[14]

Similarly, A.C. Dixon in a sermon preached years ago said,

When we rely upon organization, we get what organization can do; when we rely upon education, we get what education can do; when we rely upon eloquence, we get what eloquence can do. And so on. But when we rely upon prayer, *we get what God can do*.[15]

III. THE HOLY SPIRIT

The founding of the church on Pentecost was characterized more by the influence of the Holy Spirit than by any other feature. The human efforts expended on that occasion would have failed had it not been for the power of the Spirit. "The most important single event in the Acts of the Apostles is the coming of the Holy Spirit at Pentecost."[16] Harry Boer in his important book, *Pentecost and Mission*, made the point that it was the Holy Spirit within men, not the commission from without that gave the church the motive and the power for mission.

Jesus told the disciples, "Unless I go away, the Counselor will not come to you; but if I go, I will send him to you" (John 16:7). "It is impressive to observe the divine order: Christ went *up*, the

---

14. Glover, p. 180.
15. Ibid., p. 186.
16. Kane, p. 125.

Holy Spirit came *down*, the disciples went *out*."[17] Jesus gave no explanation why the Spirit would not come until He had gone to heaven. It led Kane to suggest there have been three ages in the history of redemption.

> The first age was that of the Father and covers the entire period of the Old Testament. The second age was that of the Son. It was the shortest of the three and lasted only some thirty years recorded in the four gospels. The third age is that of the Spirit. It began at Pentecost, has continued to the present, and will continue until the age ends with the Second Coming of Christ.[18]

The ministry of the Holy Spirit is mentioned fifty-five times in Acts. This frequency prompts many authors to suggest that the book should be called the Acts of the Holy Spirit rather than the Acts of the Apostles.

Whereas special functions of the Spirit were limited to a few people and for a short period of time the work of the Holy Spirit was not so limited. Peter promised on Pentecost that everyone who repented and was baptized would receive "the gift of the Holy Spirit" (Acts 2:38). It was this divine power in the lives of the Christians which was to change their lives and produce the "fruit of the Spirit" (Gal. 5:22).

Jesus tells His followers that the Holy Spirit "convicts the world of guilt in regard to sin and righteousness and judgment" (John 16:8). This raises a question. If the Holy Spirit is given to the Christians, how can He convict those who have not yet received Him? It is through the preaching of the Spirit-inspired word (II Tim. 3:16). The Christian, as he wields "the sword of the Spirit" (Eph. 6:17), brings the Holy Spirit into action in the thinking and behaviour of the sinner. The Christian, then, has the responsibility to communicate the Word of God. He does not

---

17. Glover, p. 58.
18. Kane, p. 227.

256

have the obligation to change men's lives; in fact, he cannot for that is the work of the Spirit.

> [F]rom the Scriptures we do know that in all soteriological opera-
> tions the Holy Spirit binds Himself to the persons and to *means* —
> the Word of God — to bring about His purposes.[19]

Thus in the tradition of the Reformers we use the "sword of the Spirit." When we use the divinely inspired Scriptures in an exegetically correct way and apply them appropriately to the human situation the power of the Spirit is at work, and as promised, the word will not return empty (Isa. 55:11). Given this fact, the temptation is to think of the Holy Spirit as a tool we can use. Rather He is the way God can use us. Our prayer must not be for the gift of the Spirit. We already have that. Our petition must be that we are submissive to His will.

IV. THE MESSAGE

We have no extant sermons of the apostolic preachers.[20] There is a *Reader's Digest* version of Peter's sermon to the Jewish audience on Pentecost, Paul's sermon of similar length at Antioch in Pisidia, and a condensed version of Paul's sermon to the Gentiles in Athens. Other than these three messages we are dependent upon summaries (Rom. 11:4,16-18; I Cor. 15:1-3) given by the New Testament writers. We have enough data, however, to know the essence of the apostolic message.

The gospel is *good news* to men who are aliens from God. The news is good because it reveals God is alive, not a stone idol (Acts 17:15). He is near and not distant. He loves them, rather than hates them. He wants to forgive, not punish them. He offers

---

19. Peters, p. 67.
20. Some regard Hebrews as a record of a previously spoken sermon.

them victory in this world, not failure. He assures them of the resurrection, not permanence in the grave. And he holds out the hope of heaven, not the despair of hell.

The gospel centers in *Jesus Christ* (Acts 2:22ff; 3:3-16; 4:10-12; 5:42; 8:5,35; 10:36-39; 11:19-20; 13:23-27; 17:3,18; 18:5; 24:24; 28:23). The message is summarized as "the word of God" on Cyprus (Acts 13:5) and in Antioch of Pisidia (Acts 13:46), and the "word of the Lord" in Antioch of Pisidia (Acts 13:48) and Asia Minor (Acts 13:49), "good news" in Derbe (Acts 14:21), the "kingdom of God" in Ephesus (Acts 19:8), and simply "the word" in Perga (Acts 14:25).The message is about the person of Christ, not a law to be obeyed (Acts 13:38-39). The preaching is about the person of Jesus, not a philosophy to be understood (Acts 17:19-21). It is a person, not a doctrine to believe. The salvation they preach is in the person of Christ, not in a ritual to be performed.

The gospel focuses on two events in the life of Jesus: his *death* and *resurrection*. The evangelistic preaching of the early missionaries did not include the virgin birth, the sermon on the mount, the miracles or the parables of Christ. There were only two points to their sermons: one, Christ died for our sins (Acts 2:23,36; 3:13-15; 4:10; 5:30; 7:52; 10:39; 13:28-37; 17:3), and two, Christ rose from the dead (Acts 2:24,31-32; 3:15; 4:2,10; 5:30; 10:40; 13:30-31; 17:18; 17:31; 13:6) to guarantee our resurrection.

The Jews, who should have been prepared to understand and accept the death on the cross because of the long history of animal sacrifice, found the cross offensive. This may have been in part because of their guilt in causing the execution of Jesus. The early preachers probably did not help their attitude by calling the Jews killers and murderers.

The Gentiles, on the other hand, could not believe in the resurrection and so sneered (Acts 17:32) and turned away.

However, in every place a few Jews and many Gentiles believed and a church was formed.

The gospel requires men to *act*. The original hearers were invariably told to repent (Acts 2:38; 3:19; 5:31; 20:21; 26:20) and to be baptized (Acts 2:38; 5:32; 8:27-38; 9:18; 10:47-48; 16:15; 18:8; 19:5). Nowhere in the New Testament do we find the language of the Twentieth Century preachers: "come forward," "receive Jesus," "pray the sinner's prayer," and "get religion."

V. THE CHURCH

Jesus said, "I will build my church" (Matt. 16:16). The church, then, is divine. It has a divine purpose, a divine name, members who are divinely called, divinely recorded scriptures, it worships the divine in a divinely approved way, is in-breathed with the divine Spirit, and has a divine hope in the future.

The Church is so integral in the thinking of the apostles, so identified with the Kingdom of Christ, and so much a part of Christianity, that it is inconceivable to think of Christians apart from the Church. This is not to say that a person cannot be a Christian in isolation. But the desire to convert others to Christ, to have fellowship with other believers, and to strengthen one another, is so strong that every Christian is expected to be a part of a church or to form a church.

The Book of Acts is a history of the Church. This history understood in this light may be outlined as follows:

1. The Foundation of the Church, Acts 1:1-2:41. The Church as having a solid foundation in revelation.

2. The Fitness of the Church, Acts 2:42-5:42. The Church as a qualitative community.

3. The Form of the Church, Acts 6:1-7. The Church forming an adequate and serviceable structure.

4. The Fulmination Against the Church, Acts 6:8-8:1. The Church being tested and challenged to a greater witness. This

259

chapter is a transition in which the Church is scattered and a new apostle is introduced.

5. The Function of the Church, Acts 8:1-12:25. The Church reaching out in aggresive evangelism in the local communities.

6. The Forwarding Church, Acts 13:1-3. The Church sending its members as missionaries to reap the harvest in other cultures.

7. The Focus of the Church, Acts 13:4-28:31. The Church concentrating its ministry on aggressive world evangelism.[21]

VI. TERMS OF SALVATION

The terms of salvation are the same for everyone. The major controversy in the early Church was whether to have different entrance requirements for the Gentiles and Jews. The first Church-wide, world-wide conference was held in Jerusalem to settle that issue. Some taught "unless you are circumcised you cannot be saved" (Acts 15:1). The conclusion of the meeting as stated by James was, "we should not make it difficult for the Gentiles who are turning to God" (Acts 15:19). Circumcision no longer was required as a term of salvation. The later circumcision of Timothy (Acts 16:3) had nothing to do with his salvation, but was an accommodation to the Jews to make him culturally acceptable to them.

There are seven cases of conversion that are reported in some detail in Acts. From these cases we can discover what the First Century Church considered essential for a man to do in order to be saved.

Six of these conversion experiences resulted in churches being established or in the converts being identified with the local body of believers. And it is reasonable to assume in the case of

---

21. Points 2, 3, 5, and 7 are from Peters, p. 134.

the treasurer of Ethiopia that he gathered a church when he returned home.

	Believe	Repent	Be Baptized
Pentecost 2:14-41	2:41	2:38	2:38
Samaria 8:4-13	8:12		8:12-13
Ethiopian 8:26-39			8:37-38
Saul 9:1-19*			9:18 22:16
Cornelius 10:23-48	10:43		10:46-48
Lydia 16:13-15	16:15		16:15
Jailer 16:25-40	16.31		16:33

*Parallels: 22:4-16; 26:9-18

Each of these incidents has something to add to our theology of mission. More lessons are learned from Pentecost, probably because it is the first. The following list is not exhaustive, but does point out some important factors in soteriology that influenced the growth of the Church in the New Testament era.

1. Pentecost

The proclamation that Jesus was crucified, buried, raised from the dead, and exalted to the right hand of God cut men to the hearts. That message is crucial to mission. Paul defines it as the "good news" (I Cor. 15:1-3). Dean M. Kelley points out that

261

when churches abandon the "meaning" of this message they quit growing.[22]

"And about three thousand were added to their number that day" (Acts 2:41). A genuine people movement started that continued as "the Lord added to their number daily those who were being saved")Acts 2:47). Pentecost was not a "multi-individual, mutually-interdependent conversion" as defined by McGavran.[23] No doubt some families did discuss the implications of Peter's sermon and responded as a family unit. But since the group numbered in the thousands, many of them visitors from seventeen other nations, it can be described best as a people movement. If a people movement can happen on one occasion, given the proper conditions, it can occur again. We can no more effect a people movement than the Twelve caused Pentecost. But we can be alert to evidence of its occurrence and at least not obstruct the work of the Holy Spirit.

They were told to repent (Acts 2:38). Although *metanoia* means "to change the mind" repentance was a break with the past. Simon's break was not complete (Acts 8:13,18-24). One wonders whether or not he destroyed his magical apparatus. Whether he did or not, he had not changed his mind completely about having power and being honored. So he coveted the power of the Holy Spirit. Peter commanded Simon to repent and pray (Acts 8:22-23). Similarly, the Christians in Ephesus continued to practice sorcery until, motivated by fear, they burned their scrolls (Acts 18:17-20). Christopaganism can be avoided if two things take place: One, a repentance that is thorough which may include the destruction of fetishes, amulets, gods, and spirit shelves. And, two, adequate instruction in the biblical record is given to the convert.

2. Samaria

---

22. Dean M. Kelley, *Why Conservative Churches Are Growing* (New York: Harper and Row, 1972), Chapters III and IV.
23. Pp. 302-303.

The unique feature of the evangelistic campaign in Samaria was the power encounter. The power of Satan was actively present. Many had evil spirits. All the people, both high and low, gave Simon their attention and exclaimed, "This man is the divine power known as the Great Power!" (Acts 8:10). In a situation where evil spiritual power dominates the lives of the people, the oral presentation of the gospel is essential, but may not be adequate to demonstrate the power of God over Satan. Many missionaries have testified that changed lives, and answers to prayer that could only have come from God, have allowed people to break with their false gods and turn to Christ.

3. Ethiopian Treasurer

Baptism is the one common denominator of the seven conversions in Acts. Probably each theological implication of baptism has relevance for cross-cultural church planting. But I will confine my remarks to two items.

One, baptism signals a complete break with the past and an identification with a new Master (Rom. 6:3-4). Those baptized are now members of a new family, a new brotherhood. New activities of fellowship and ritual replace pagan social and religious customs. Baptism not only washes away their past, it incorporates them into the body of Christ. One of the weaknesses of various kinds of evangelism today is that the new believer is asked to pray the sinner's prayer, but he is not asked to make the total commitment of life and body that occurs in baptism, and consequently is not brought into a local congregation of believers.

Two, the baptism of the eunuch took place immediately as did all the others recorded in Acts. Postponement of baptism in a culture alien to Christianity is understandable. The missionary wants to be sure the new follower understands the essential nature of Christianity. But delay can also be disastrous to the convert and to the growth of the church. The first flush of excitement may wear off, and with it, the evangelistic thrust that comes from enthusiasm. And, perhaps even more importantly, becoming a Christian becomes identified with the acquisition of a body of religious knowledge.

It is not without reason that Matthew's account of the Great Commission has this order, "make disciples. . . . baptize . . . teach" (Matt. 28:18-20). This has led some missiologists to assert that the content of teaching after baptism is more important than the teaching prior to baptism. McGavran refers to this post-baptismal care as "perfecting."[24] In the context of his theology this is an acceptable term to express maturation. But it probably is not a good choice of words for interdenominational use. He does not mean sinlessness as some use the word, nor does he identify perfection with salvation as Yoder does.[25] Much of the controversy can be avoided if a neutral term, such as "maturing" is used.

4. Saul

Seen through missiological eyes the most important conversion is that of Paul. There are two important lessons here that help correct two theological errors.

One, Paul was not converted on the Damascus road. This experience occurred to him so that he would be qualified to be an apostle (Acts 1:22). And although he was called to be an apostle to the Gentiles (Acts 26:16) this "call" cannot be considered normative for potential missionaries today since the vision was primarily to make him an apostle.

Two, Saul was sent to Damascus where Ananias "told him what he must do" (Acts 9:6). The Lord could have told him during the vision what was necessary for him to become a follower of Jesus. But the Lord chose to follow the normal method of conversion. He sent a *man* with the message. There is no shortcut to church growth. We cannot pray down a miraculous conversion. We cannot mechanize or computerize evangelism. Evangelism still requires the persuasive presentation of the gospel by one person to another.

---

24. Pp. 25-27.
25. P. 34.

5. Cornelius

Some Jews believed that God had made the Gentiles to be the kindling for the fires of hell. It is no wonder, then, that the Jewish preacher, Peter, needed a special vision — in triplicate — to persuade him to go to Cornelius. The sad thing is that although the Jerusalem church accepted Peter's report and praised God for the conversion of *this* Roman army officer, they did not subsequently launch a cross-cultural evangelistic program to reach other Gentiles. I. Howard Marshall suggests that it was this very failure that caused the Jerusalem church to fall from prominence and eventually to disappear.[26]

These lessons, repeated throughout two thousand years of church history, are clear: one, many churches have an opportunity for cross-cultural evangelism, Two, failure to harvest the new ripe fields in another culture will not only result in the church not expanding, it can result in the death of that church that refuses to reach out with the gospel.

6. Lydia

One of the issues that has been debated by missionaries is "with which group does one start a church in a new locality?" The question is, whether a church started in a lower class can ever break through to the upper classes? Or should one concentrate only on the leaders of society, with the assumption that the masses will follow them into the new religion? The conversion of Lydia may give a partial answer to that question. She was a woman, a member of a minority race, and an expatriot — not a promising person with whom to begin a church. However, from the inauspicious start in a women's prayer meeting a strong church that soon included the "brothers" assembled in a house church (Acts 16:40). Given the circumstances of Paul's trip to Philippi (Acts 16:6-10) the lesson seems to be that we should enter the door that God has opened.

---

26. I.Howard Marshall, *The Acts of the Apostles* (Grand Rapids: William B. Eerdmans Co., 1980), p. 198.

7. The Philippian Jailer

"Be prepared in season and out of season" (II Tim. 4:2). Paul practiced the advice he gave to Timothy. The middle of the night in a Roman jail was not a likely place to have an evangelistic meeting, but the results were great.

One of the more effective missionaries I know is a man in Honduras who is constantly talking about Christ — with the shopkeepers, waitresses, neighbors, everybody. And his witness to a cigar manufacturer opened the door to reaching a remote village which was the home of the man's wife.

SUMMARY

"The Church of What's Happening Now" is beginning to take shape as "The Church of What Ought to Happen Now."[27] We have seen the Church grow numerically, geographically, and culturally. It has grown because of the Divine Dimension, the Universally Valid Principles that only God can supply: the Purpose of the Church, the Power of Prayer, the Influence of the Holy Spirit, the content of the preaching, the divine nature of the Church, and the terms of Salvation.

---

27. A title given by Thomas Friskney in a private conversation.

11

THE STRATEGY OF MISSION PRACTICE

ACTS OF THE APOSTLES

The purpose of this chapter is to examine the missionary activity recorded in Acts and to learn what they did that advanced or retarded the growth of the church, and from these lessons to develop missionary strategies for today's mission practice. This chapter, then, will concentrate on the human dimension of mission. Of course, a complete separation of the divine and human elements is impossible, so, to some extent, this division is arbitrary.

The topics covered in this chapter are arranged somewhat according to their chronological appearance in Acts, and, therefore, the order does not necessarily reflect their relative importance.

I. MOBILIZED MEMBERSHIP

There was no "clergy" in the Church of the New Testament

era. In the very beginning the leaders consisted of the twelve apostles. As the Church grew, "deacons" were elected to distribute food (Acts 6:1-7), but they were not set apart for evangelizing. But they *did* evangelize. Following the appointment of the seven "deacons" Luke summarized the results in these words,

> The word of God spread. The number of disciples in Jerusalem increased rapidly, and a large number of priests became obedient to the faith (Acts 6:7).

Following the martyrdom of Stephen "all except the apostles were scattered throughout Judea and Samaria (Acts 8:2). Philip, one of the deacons, conducted a very successful evangelistic meeting in Samaria (Acts 8:4-25). He then converted an African who took the message of the new Savior to a new Continent (Acts 8:26-39). Philip's evangelism continued in a number of un-named towns (Acts 8:40). Others who were driven out of Jerusalem went as far as Phoenicia, Cyprus, and Antioch telling the message (Acts 11:19). The ripple effect continued as converts from Cyprus and Cyrene also went to Antioch telling the good news (Acts 11:20).

Luke records the preaching, actions, and journeys of the "professional missionaries": Peter and Paul and their associates. Their ministries alone could not account for the dramatic numerical and geographical growth of the Church. For reasons not disclosed Luke only opens tiny windows on the evangelism performed by the members of the Church. Thus although it is not documented, it is obvious that a large group of early Christians were excited about their new faith and were responsible for much of the growth of the Church.

The Church in the First Century grew rapidly because a large number of believers took seriously the responsibility to "make disciples." If there is any one strategy that is most important in the growth of the Church it is a mobilized membership. The numerous church growth studies conducted in the last two decades corroborate this statement.[1]

II. PERSECUTION

No sane person ever seeks to be persecuted. But even the persecution of the Christians can result in the growth of the church.

> And we know that in all things God works for the good of those who love him, who have been called according to his purpose (Rom. 8:28).

Driving the Christians out of Jerusalem backfired on the persecutors. The attempt to extinguish the flaming evangelistic zeal was like trying to beat out a brush fire with dry sticks. Few flames were put out, and many were scattered only to start new fires. The Church did not die, it spread. The effect on the Christians was to crystallize their convictions and to cause them to become more aggressive as evangelists. This effect has been repeated in the modern era.

> When . . . the Centenary Conference of Protestant Mission in China was held in Shanghai, it was found that for every missionary martyred in 1900 (in the Boxer rebellion) a thousand converts had been received into the churches and the visible results in baptized converts for the seven years following the Boxer uprising were actually double those of the preceding ninety-three years of the century.[2]

More recently in China it is estimated that the Church grew

---

1. Many have been published by William Carey Library. Dozens of unpublished studies, done as doctoral projects, are in the library of the School of World Mission, Fuller Theological Seminary.
2. Glover, p. 92.

remarkably in numbers and renewal since 1950 when the Church was outlawed during the Communist regime. It is estimated that there are now four million Protestants and three million Catholics (who have severed their ties with the Vatican), plus other millions who are worshipping in house churches.[3] There are over four thousand open churches, twenty thousand meeting points, a monthly church magazine, twelve seminaries, myriads of church-training schools, a printing house for the printing of Bibles and Christian literature.[4]

Church historian Glover calls our attention to the fact that,

> [t]he ascended Saviour's words to Ananias concerning Saul of Tarsus were *not* "I will shew him how great things he must *attempt*, or must *achieve*," . . . but "I will shew him how great things he must *suffer* for my name's sake."[5]

And persecution has been the frequent experience of the Church in the intervening two thousand years, and there is no reason to believe but that many more missionaries will continue to suffer for His name's sake.

III. MEETING HUMAN NEEDS

We have already seen that the Church had a food distribution program for Christian widows in Jerusalem. Following the appointment of the deacons "the word of God spread" (Acts 6:7) with a rapid growth in the number of disciples. The immediate cause was the preaching of the Seven. But is it not possible that

---

3. Charlene L. Fu, "Christian churches in China overflow with worshippers," *The Indianapolis Star*, January 24, 1988, p. G-3.

4. Ralph Covell, "God at Work in China," *Trinity World Forum*, Spring 1988, p. 1.

5. Pp. 87-88.

the receptivity of the Jewish population was increased because of the welfare program of the local church?

However, the church leaders did not limit their relief for human needs to the brethren. The practice of healing the sick was the handmaiden of evangelism. The first recorded instance of healing was of the crippled beggar at the Temple (Acts 3:1-10). Although this miracle brought a crowd and gave Peter and John an audience, it was not performed for this reason. It appears Peter healed him simply because the crippled man had a need. Other miraculous healings, mostly of non-Christians, occurred sporadically throughout the ministry of the Twelve and their colleagues (Acts 6:8; 8:6; 9:33-34,40-41; 14:9-10; 16:18; 19:11-12; 20:9-10; 28:8).

After Paul *healed* the father of the chief official on Malta (Acts 28:8) "the rest of the sick of the island came and were *cured*" (Acts 28:9 emphasis mine). The choice of the translators to use two different English words, *healed* and *cured*, was deliberate and reflects the fact that two different Greek words are used in the text. The second word, *therapeuo*, means to receive medical treatment. This is particularly important for the Twentieth Century missionary who does not have the gift of healing. Here, for the first time, we have a record of a medical doctor, Luke, treating the sick with medicine. Medical missions, then, has credibility not only because the sick are healed but because there is a biblical precedent.

IV. TRAINED LEADERSHIP

The Twelve could not be in all places at once nor could they remain in one place for long. So a high priority for them was to train leaders in each local church. We have treated this under the ministry of Jesus. And we will examine it again in the chapter on "Letters to Mission Churches." At this point we will only say that trained leaders were critical both to preserve the Church from

271

false teaching, and to promote its growth.

V. EFFECTIVELY ORGANIZED

Not much was said in Acts about organization in the Church or in the local church. During the first generation of the Church's existence she had apostles and prophets. They continue today through their writings in the Holy Scriptures. Other leaders mentioned in the New Testament are evangelists, pastor-teachers, elders, and deacons. The sphere of authority or assignment of these permanent leaders seems to be in the local church. The development of a hierarchy over more than one congregation seems to be a post-New Testament development. Super-congregational authority in the New Testament rested in a conference of leaders of differing opinions from many churches (Acts 15).

It was a local church, Antioch, not the apostolic conference in Jerusalem, that responded to the word of the Spirit and sent out the first church-sent missionaries (Acts 13:1-3).

The lesson for strategy is that the Church functions best in missionary activity if every congregation is free to follow its own Spirit-led leaders in sending out missionaries, and launching mission activities. Such a practice postulates two things: one, the local churches have leaders that are open to Spirit-led mission outreach, and, two, planning strategies need not, and must not, be limited to a few leaders in high ecclesiastical positions.

VI. OPEN DOORS

On Paul's second missionary journey, after having visited the congregations in Galatia which he had established on his first trip, he arrived at the border of the province of Asia which is about fifteen to twenty miles from Pisidian Antioch. Asia offered the possibility of a rich harvest for the gospel. There were two main roads to the west coast port of Ephesus. The usual route went through Metropolis, Apamea, Colosse, Laodicea, and Ephesus. The high road, which Paul may have taken later (Acts 19:1), went almost straight from Apamea to Ephesus without passing through any major cities. From a human point of view appropriate missionary strategy would require Paul and his companions to take the road through the population centers on their way west. However, they "were kept by the Holy Spirit from preaching the word in the province of Asia" (Acts 16:6). We are not told how the Spirit prevented them from preaching in Asia. The only course open to them was to go north toward Bithynia or to return to Antioch. There were a number of flourishing cities in Bithynia: Prusa, Nicaea, Nicomedeia, Chalcedon, and Heracleia. So they went north toward the border of Bithynia. The rich harvest there was not for Paul to reap. Numerous churches were started there later and their influence became so great that Pliny, the Roman governor in the beginning of the Second Century, wrote a letter stating that the worship of idols was falling into neglect.[6] It may have been Peter who planted these churches since he addresses his first epistle to them (I Pet. 1:1). Again, "the Spirit of Jesus would not allow" Paul to enter Bithynia (Acts 16:7). So they went west to Troas, a coastal city north of Ephesus, but close to the European city of Philippi.

> During the night Paul had a vision of a man of Macedonia standing and begging him, "Come over to Macedonia and help us" (Acts 16:9).

Paul's conclusion was that "God had called us to preach the gospel to them" (Acts 16:10). Paul and his party left at once for their first European campaign.

---

6. Richard Belward Rackham, *The Acts of the Apostles* (London: Methuen & Co. Ltd., 1947), p. 276.

273

Paul's commission was to preach the gospel to the Gentiles. He was making every effort to discharge that responsibility. But doors had been closed twice: the door to Asia, and the door to Bithynia. Another door, the door to Europe, had been opened for Paul (II Cor. 2:12). Divine leading is evident. God, Jesus, and Holy Spirit are all mentioned in this connection (Acts 16:6,7,10). However, the precise way that the Spirit showed that the door was open or closed is not disclosed in the text. Normally the Spirit spoke through prophets (Acts 21:11; 20:33). And there were two prophets in the company. The hand of God was also seen in the overruling of external events and circumstances.

In this age of the absence of living prophets, missionaries need to be aware of the lessons of the Spirit-directed writings of the prophets in the Scriptures, and be sensitive to the providentially opened and closed doors.

A point that is easily missed is that Paul and company responded with *alacrity* when the door opened to go to Macedonia. As Luke described it, "we got ready at once" (Acts 16:10). Alan Trippett points out that Christian missionaries have often delayed going to a responsive people until they became unresponsive to the gospel. One example he gives was of the Anglicans who had spent much money and time in establishing a beachhead. But when the population of Malaita became responsive to the gospel they continued to concentrate on developing leadership for the few congregations they had established, rather than sending evangelists through the newly opened doors. Other groups saw and entered the open doors.[7]

VII. SOUGHT BRIDGES

It has often been pointed out that Paul went to the cities. We

7. Alan R. Tippett, *Solomon Islands Christianity* (Pasadena, William Carey Library, 1967), pp. 46-50.

have no record of his evangelizing in rural areas. Unfortunately, Paul does not explain his strategy, so we are left on our own to examine the evidence and to induce the probable reason for evangelizing the cities to the apparent exclusion of the towns and rural areas. Three explanations have been offered.

One, perhaps the most popular hypothesis is that Paul, who could visit only a limited number of places in his lifetime, concentrated on higher density populations with the expectation that the churches that were established in the cities would then spread the word in the geographical region in which they were located. This is a nice theory and it may, indeed, have happened this way. But we have no record in the New Testament that Paul encouraged the churches to follow this strategy, and no record in the Scriptures that this pattern was followed.

Two, in a variation of the first view Charles McNeely argued that Paul spent little time in traveling but much time evangelizing in the cities of the Roman Empire. His contention is that Acts is not a record of Paul's travels but his urban evangelism.

> Paul called home ten of the Roman Empire's largest cities In this urban area alone, he had access to nearly ten percent of the Empire's estimated 50 million people. . . . It is time to go where the people of this planet live.[8]

Three, the first place Paul went in each city was the synagogue (or in Philippi, where there was no synagogue, the place of prayer). Why did the apostle to the Gentiles go to the Jews first? There appear to have been two reasons. First, Paul's desire was that the Israelites would be saved (Rom. 10:1). And, secondly, it was in association with the synagogues that he found the proselytes and godfearers — the Gentiles who would most likely respond to the gospel.

---

8. Charles A. McNeely, "The Myth of Paul's missionary journeys: The urban center of Paul's missionary activity," *One Body*, Spring 1988, p. 5.

The Diaspora had taken Jews throughout the Roman world. However, they were concentrated in the cities. Few of them could be found in rural areas.

Viewed this way, Paul's strategy was a natural one that followed his perception that the scattered Jewish population was a natural bridge[9] into the Gentile community. The modern missionary, who is without the benefit of synagogue, proselytes, and godfearers, needs to look for those bridges into a culture that already exist. Tippett points out one such set of bridges in the Solomon Islands: the existence of trade routes between local populations. Communication, as well as goods, moves along these natural roadways. And, as his study revealed, the Church expands along these same routes.[10]

VIII. CULTURALLY APPROPRIATE ACTIONS

All readers of the Bible are aware that Saul and Paul are different names for the same person. The best explanation for the name change seems to be that Paul changed his name when he began his cross-cultural ministry to the Gentiles. The change was culturally appropriate since Saul was a Hebrew name and Paul a Greek.[11]

When Timothy joined Paul and Silas at Lystra Paul circumcised him "because of the Jews who lived in that area" (Acts 16:3). Otherwise, Timothy would not have been accepted by the Jewish population.

In Athens Paul's sermon began with a reference to an altar

---

9. Donald A. McGavran, *Bridges of God* (New York: Friendship Press, 1955), pp. 31-36. Peters refers to these channels as "points of contact," pp. 112-113.

10. P. 187.

11. The change, recorded in Acts 13:9, occurred on Cyprus which was his first stop on his first missionary journey. Before that he is always called Saul. After that he is always called Paul.

with the inscription, "TO AN UNKNOWN GOD" (Acts 17:23). Such an introduction by Peter on Pentecost would have been unthinkable.

In each case Paul was adjusting his approach to conform to his policy to "become all things to all men so that by all means possible I might save some" (I Cor. 9:23).

The cultural differences between the Twentieth Century missionary and his target audience are potentially greater than the cultural distances Paul had to cross. Faithful preaching of the gospel does not require being a Bible College graduate, wearing a dark suit, white shirt, four-in-hand tie, standing behind a pulpit in a gothic church building, and giving a formal address.

IX. RESPONSIVE POPULATIONS

Paul could have spent a lifetime attempting to evangelize the Jews. His heart was in it (Rom. 10:1). However, he always turned to the Gentiles. There was more to that action than the fact he was called to be an apostle to the Gentiles. He was turning from a resistant population to a responsive people.

Other enigmas confront us in Paul's journeys. For instance, why did he spend three years in Ephesus and only a short time in Athens?

Responsiveness seems to be the answer. In those places where the people were more receptive a larger share of his time was spent. For Paul life was too short and the task too urgent to spend it in unprofitable pursuits.

The emphasis by the church growth school of thought on concentrating resources on the receptive people has its critics and especially from missionaries working in resistant fields. I find it interesting that Mark Maxey of Japan in defending the practice of working with resistant peoples has three chapters entitled, "What the Prophets say," "What the Gospels Say," and "What the Epistles Say," but he does not include a chapter on "What Acts

277

Says."[12]

But what are the marks of a receptive population?

Change contributes to conversion. The breakup of a former life style makes conversion to Christianity easier. People who are changing their residence are less under the control of family or tribe and in their new environment are more willing to accept a new faith. Political changes such as freedom of religion, freedom of movement, or freedom of association may for the first time allow people to make a change in religion. An upward social change such as increased education or a better job may make it possible for people also to move up to a more "advanced" religion. A change in marital status, especially when accompanied by another of the above changes releases a person from the hold of old family ways to establish his new home in a new faith.

Inadequacy of the old religion contributes to conversion. Cultural anthopologists have pointed out that every culture adequately, although not perfectly, meets the needs of the people who live within that culture. However, from time to time the people of that culture become aware that certain aspects of their culture no longer meet the needs of the people. When that occurs the culture changes. In fact every culture is constantly changing to meet new needs, or to meet more adequately the continuing needs. Consequently, at that point where the people perceive that their religion no longer adequately serves to cure their illnesses, to defend them from their enemies, to explain the existence of evil, to free them from the guilt of sin, or to provide them with an adequate hope for life beyond the grave, at these points they are open to a new religion. It is for this reason that animists, generally, are more responsive to the gospel than followers of a "higher" religion such as Islam, Hinduism, Buddhism, materialism, etc.

---

12. Mark Maxey, *Preaching the Gospel in Resistant Fields* (San Jose, California: Osaka Bible Seminary, n.d.).

X. HOMOGENEOUS CHURCHES

Probably the most often quoted statement of McGavran is, "Men like to become Christians without crossing racial, linguistic, or class barriers."[13] It is relatively easy to understand that people understand a sermon more clearly if it is preached in their mother tongue, that they prefer to sing the kind of songs the tunes of which are similar to those that they sing on other occasions, and that they prefer the people sitting next to them in church to be of their own tribe.

The issue is whether a case can be made for homogeneous churches from the New Testament. It is doubtful. For the first nine years all the congregations, except Caesarea where Cornelius was a member, were almost completely Jewish. That changed at Antioch where a large number of Greeks became Christian. Theoretically it is possible that the church in Antioch was composed of several house churches, and each of these was homogeneous. However, the text does not mention house churches, and the believers in that city are referred to as "the church" (Acts 13:1) not "churches." Whether one decides that Antioch was a heterogeneous church or whether one sees various homogeneous house churches being started will depend upon one's prejudice. For instance, Wagner would probably conclude there were homogeneous churches in Antioch since he conjectures that as many as five hundred to one thousand house churches existed in Jerusalem with a total membership of twenty thousand to twenty-five thousand people.[14] However, Luke refers to "the church," not "churches" at Jerusalem (Acts 11:22).

McGavran justifies the homogeneous unit principle on the fact that the Hellenistic widows in Jerusalem were treated separately

---

13. P. 198.
14. C.Peter Wagner, "Church Growth Principles and Procedures," a lecture given at the School of World Mission, Fuller Theological Seminary, Nov. 19, 1975.

from the Hebrew speaking widows. He may be correct in his observation, but it is a shabby exegetical basis for an argument of homogeneous churches. Antioch offers a more substantial rationale and even the situation there is inconclusive. However, from a sociological point of view McGavran is right. People can more easily move into a group of people who are like themselves.

McGavran is not very precise in his definition of homogeneous. In a rather casual way he defines homogeneous units as those people who have "some characteristics in common."[15] This lacks the precision of a scientific definition. Wagner does better but his usage is confining. At first he defines homogeneous in sociological terms and then in all following chapters uses homogeneous unity to refer to ethnic groups.[16]

I cannot help but think that Yoder overstates the case in his criticism of McGavran. Yoder sees as the major tension between the New Testament and the church growth school of thought that the New Testament stresses the unity of people in Christ (the implication being that unity must be achieved at the cost of church growth if necessary). On the other hand, McGavran stresses the growth of the church even if it means postponing the attainment of unity of behavior.[17] Yoder writes, "The New Testament does not, as far as I can see, record self-conscious strategy-making on the basis of concern for growth."[18] However, the book of Acts records a lot about the growth of the church, about crossing cultural barriers, and about the unity of believers. The whole fifteenth chapter is concerned with the report of a council convened to achieve unity. The difficulty between McGavran and Yoder seems to be that each stresses a point almost to the exclusion of

---

15. *Understanding Church Growth*, p. 85.
16. C.Peter Wagner, *Your Church Can Grow* (Glendale, California: Regal Books, 1976).
17. John H. Yoder, "Church Growth Issues in Theological Perspective," *The Challenge of Church Growth*, ed., Wilbert R. Shenk (Scottsdale, Pennsylvania: Herald Press, 1973), p. 44.
18. Ibid.

THE STRATEGY OF MISSION PRACTICE

the other equally salient messages of the book.

I see the homogeneous unit theory irrelevent in most situations. The very fact that a church is started in a specific geographical location is going to make it a homogeneous congregation in most instances. Yoder asks a pertinent question at this juncture.

> Does the concept of the 'homogeneous unit,' whose people can respond to the gospel all more or less in the same way, promise to become increasingly helpful and its contents increasingly defined in the development of urban societies, or is it a concept that applies best where there is least social movement so that its adequacy will decrease with proletarianization, urbanization, and the forming of personality by mass media?[19]

The churches that Paul established on his mission journeys, for the most part, had both Jewish and Gentile members. Even the church in Jerusalem which was composed almost entirely of Jews, encompassed at least two varieties of Jews — Hebrew and Hellenic.

SUMMARY

After examining the human dimension of missions in Acts we have found ten strategies employed by the First Century missionaries which can be appropriated by today's missionary when the circumstances are appropriate. They are: a mobilized membership, persecution, meeting human needs, trained leadership, effective organization, open doors, cultural bridges, culturally appropriate actions, responsive populations, and homogeneous churches.

Peters finds thirteen principles in mobilizing the strategy and

---

19. P. 45.

methodology of the growth of the church in Acts 8-12. They are:

1. A church grows to the degree that it is able to move from a state of introversion to a state of extroversion.
2. A church grows to the degree that it is able to overcome barriers that would naturally inhibit the expansion of the gospel.
3. A church grows best when it functions energetically in extensive and intensive evangelism.
4. A church grows best when the total body of believers is mobilized and trained in continued ministries of praying, sharing, witnessing, and evangelizing.
5. A church grows best where the soil has been carefully and prayerfully prepared for the gospel.
6. A church grows best when evangelism is undergirded by a Spirit-directed strategy and relevant structure that rests on biblical principles to guide the onward movement.
7. A church grows best when the work is properly people related.
8. A church grows best by homogeneous units of society.
9. A church grows best by corporate-personality decisions and conversions in cultures of family, tribe, community, and people groupings.
10. A church grows best when the church releases the ablest, most experienced, and most qualified men of God for evangelism and church expansion.
11. A church grows best by team ministries under the guidance of strong and wise leadership.
12. A church grows best where the gospel is clearly, relevantly, and persuasively preached, Jesus Christ is most honored as Savior and Lord, and the Holy Spirit is believed and obeyed.
13. A church grows best where men of divine calling and qualification, faith, and prayer are able to guide the church body to live in the experience of the reality of God in the midst of His people and meet their needs.[20]

In the preceding chapter we saw that the New Testament writer seems to be concerned with maintaining the constancy of a

20. Pp. 209-210.

few divinely given items of faith. However, virtually all the strategic activities uncovered in this chapter have been reported so briefly or have been inferred from the text so that they have not and cannot be normative for the church. Peters has written:

> While I fully realize that built into Acts are a cultural flexibility and adaptability in method of operation and communication, there are absolutes that define domestication and acculturation. They will not bend to any accommodation. They are diversely fixed principles for all times and cultures. To find the line of demarcation between what is absolute and what is relative is not always easy.[21]

Thus the council in Jerusalem made a distinction between a few basic concerns the Christians shared with Jews and the large number of traditional Jewish practices that the assembly in Jerusalem regarded as matters of opinion not binding on Christians. Interestingly, a portion of their reasoning for this judgment was "that we should not make it difficult for the Gentiles who are turning to God" (Acts 15:19). Nor should we.

---

21. P. 13.

12

ANTIOCH: THE MODEL MISSIONARY CHURCH

ACTS 11,13,14

I. ANTIOCH WAS A CHRISTIAN CHURCH

"The disciples were called Christians first at Antioch" (Acts 11:26). I have quoted this verse hundreds of times to prove that the biblical name for the followers of Jesus is Christian. And numerous times I have cited it as evidence that the New Testament name for the Church is Christian. However, this kind of proof-texting left a haunting question in my mind, "Why Antioch?" The Church had been in existence for nine years before anyone was called a Christian. There was a large congregation in Jerusalem of perhaps as many as twenty-five thousand members. They were not called Christians. A successful evangelistic crusade resulted in a significant church in Samaria but it was not known as a Christian Church. A new convert was going

285

to a new continent with a new gospel about a new Savior, but remarkably the Treasurer of Ethipia was not given the new name, Christian. Even Paul, the most celebrated missionary, was not called a Christian. And, perhaps most significant for most readers of this book, Cornelius whose conversion opened the door to all Gentiles to enter the church, was not called a Christian. Why was this new name, Christian given at Antioch?

The first clue is given in Acts 11:19.

> Now those who had been scattered by the persecution in connection with Stephen traveled as far as Phoenicia, Cyprus and Antioch telling the message *only to the Jews* (emphasis mine).

Except for the family of Cornelius, the Church up until Antioch was one hundred percent Jewish. The apostles were all Jews. The leaders were all Jews. Most members were Jews.

> Some of them, however, men from Cyprus and Cyrene, went to Antioch and began to speak *to Greeks also*, telling them the good news about the Lord Jesus (Acts 11:20 emphasis mine).

For the first time in the history of the Church there was a concerted, consistent program of cross-cultural evangelism. Then, and not until then, "the disciples were called Christians." The believers had been "made disciples" (Matt. 28:19) but *they were not Christians until they, in turn, evangelized the nations.* I doubt seriously whether we can call ourselves Christians unless we are involved in cross-cultural evangelism. That does not mean that only the missionaries are Christians. But it does mean that all believers must be involved in some way in the missionary program of the church. I doubt seriously whether we can call our churches Christian unless they have a vital and vibrant program of cross-cultural evangelism.

The word, Christian, means "of Christ," "belonging to Christ." The very purpose of Christ was to save the world. To be a part of him, to deserve to wear His name, means that we, too, must be involved in saving the world.

"Were called" is a translation of a Greek word, *krematizo*, that occurs nine times in the New Testament. In seven of these occurrences the calling is stated as being of God (Matt. 2:12,22; Luke 2:26; Acts 10:22; Heb. 8:5; 11:7; and 12:25). Only in Rom. 7:3 is God not specifically named as the one who called the woman an adulteress. But even here she is called an adulteress because of the moral standard that was given by God. Thus "were called" is a word that implies a divine naming. I am aware that many commentaries say that "Christian" is a nickname, or worse, a name hurled in derision at the believers and subsequently stuck with them. My father owned a lumber yard. One time after a rain when I was a boy I went out into the gravel street in front of the lumber yard and made mudballs from the mudholes and threw them against the facade of the building where they stuck. As I surveyed my handiwork I realized how ugly they looked and what I had done wrong. I ran home and hid because I knew what was coming next. Many see the name "Christian" as a mudball that has stuck to the followers of Christ. But as McGarvey has pointed out "Christian" is not an accident of history but a divinely given name.

Even Isaiah foretold it,

> you will be called by a new name
> that the mouth of the Lord will bestow (Isa. 62:2b).

The followers of Christ are called by many names in the New Testament: disciples, saint, those of the way, believer, brother, etc. All of these were existing names. Only one totally new name appeared — Christian. Note in the first half of the verse the events which Isaiah said would attend the giving of the name,

> The *nations* will see your righteousness
> and *all kings* your glory (Isa. 62:2a emphasis mine).

287

After the gospel is preached to the *nations*, and only then would the new name be given.

Antioch was a logical place for this cross-cultural evangelism to occur first. Jerusalem was a thoroughly Jewish city. A few Roman soldiers and government officials worked there but they spent as much time as possible in one of the more compatible Roman cities on the Mediterranean. Antioch, on the other hand, was a cosmopolitan city. It was the third largest city in the Roman Empire. Roman armies, stationed there, controlled the trade routes to the East, Commerce from the East flowed through Antioch on its way to Rome. Consequently, Antioch, unlike Jerusalem, was the location of several ethnic groups. It was possible for the church in Antioch to have a cross-cultural evangelistic program in a way that it was not possible in Jerusalem.

II. ANTIOCH WAS A GRACIOUS CHURCH

News of this reached the ears of the church at Jerusalem, and they sent Barnabas to Antioch (Acts 11:22).

Although Jerusalem had accepted Peter's report of the conversion of Cornelius they had not done anything about it. They did not launch a cross-cultural evangelistic program of their own. They were content to remain as they were, a Jewish enclave in a Jewish city. Much like their ancestors who had received the Abrahamic promise and the Mosaic kingdom, they did not conceive it as their responsibility to take the good news to men of other cultures.

This Jewish congregation in Jerusalem was suspicious of this "new" cross-cultural evangelism in Antioch. Accepting the uncircumcised Greeks into full fellowship seemed inappropriate, perhaps even heretical. In any case it deserved an investigation. And Barnabas was sent to evaluate the situation. The church at Antioch had reason to resent this intrusion into their affairs. The

288

text is not explicit at this point, but it seems clear that Antioch received Barnabas graciously in spite of the purpose of his visit. This may reflect the wisdom of the Jerusalem church in selecting Barnabas. He was from Cyprus, the very home of some of the men who began the program of cross-cultural evangelism in Antioch. It is possible that he knew of them, and perhaps actually knew them, from his life in Cyprus. In any case, he would not be considered a total stranger, or a lackey of the Judaizers in Jerusalem. He is described as a "good man, full of the Holy Spirit and faith" (Acts 11:24). And his very name, Barnabas, means Son of Encourager. He was a good choice for a delicate investigation. And Antioch made a wise decision in accepting him so graciously.

III. ANTIOCH WAS A GENEROUS CHURCH

Agabus stood up and through the Spirit predicted that a severe famine would spread over the entire Roman world. . . . The disciples, each according to his ability, decided to provide help for the brothers living in Judea. This they did . . . (Acts 11:27-30).

When did the disciples at Antioch respond to the need of the fellow believers in Jerusalem? Did they wait until several had starved to death? Did they wait until the church in Jerusalem sent an emergency appeal letter? As in many cases the text is an abbreviated record of what actually happened. However, the implication is that the Christians in Antioch did not even wait until the famine started to take up their offering. Rather, just as soon as they heard the prediction that there was going to be a famine they provided help.

This was a magnanimous gesture, considering the fact that the Jerusalem church had just sent an investigator to check on the doctrine and behavior of the Antiochan church.

Apparently the church in Antioch had one hundred percent

participation in this enterprise: "The disciples *each* according to his ability, *decided* . . ." (Acts 11:29 emphasis mine). There is no hint of coercion, no hint of an order given by Paul. Here was a church where generosity was a part of their new nature. Here was a church where unity meant each and every person was united in giving.

What a contrast to the modern American congregation, which with the motivation of a "successful" Faith Promise program can only get twenty-five to thirty-five percent of the members to make a financial commitment to missions. And even with an every member canvass for the support of the local budget, or a much needed building program, it cannot hope to obtain commitments from more than seventy-five to eighty percent of the members.

IV. ANTIOCH THE PRAYING CHURCH

While they were worshiping the Lord and fasting, the Holy Spirit said, "Set apart for me Barnabas and Saul for the work to which I have called them" (Acts 13:2-3).

"While they were worshiping. . . ." Worshiping is an interesting word. We have an English word, liturgy, derived from the Greek *leitourgia*. Liturgy is what we do in worshiping God. This causes me to ask, "Do we do those things in our worship that allow the Spirit to call people into missionary service?" Specifically, do we select hymns that will allow the Holy Spirit to challenge men and women to mission service? Do we select Scriptures in which the Spirit has directed people to give themselves as missionaries? Do we invite missionaries to speak, especially on Sunday morning when we have the largest audiences? Do we pray for missionaries to be sent out from our congregation? Jesus has given us a divine directive in this regard, "Ask the Lord of the harvest, therefore, to send out workers into his harvest field" (Matt. 9:38).

290

The leaders in the Antioch church were backing up their prayers with fasting. What would happen in local churches today if the leaders were praying earnestly, and fasting sincerely for workers for the harvest? Would the Lord honor and answer those prayers in the Twentieth Century as He did in the First? Our greatest need is for more missionaries. We have the answer to our need in the example of the church at Antioch. We lack the will to pray in a similar manner.

V. ANTIOCH WAS A SENDING CHURCH

So after they had fasted and prayed, they placed their hands on them and sent them off (Acts 13:3).

"They sent them off." How did they send them off? Did they take them to a ship and say, "So long Saul, so long Barnabas. If you are ever back this way, stop in"? Perhaps, but not likely. Who bought the tickets for the voyage to Cyprus and on to Asia Minor? The text does not tell us. But is it not reasonable to assume that the church did it as a part of their "sending" them?

Did the church at Antioch stop praying for Paul and Barnabas? Of course it is possible, but given the nature of the church leadership in Antioch it seems unlikely. In Lystra Paul was stoned and left for dead (Acts 14:19-20). Since this was before the days of the telegraph, telephone or fax there was no way the Christians in Antioch could have known about the stoning. But is it not possible that at that very moment the disciples in the sending church were praying for him and God heard and answered their prayers?

Sending missionaries today is much more than taking up an offering for a visiting missionary speaker and promptly forgetting him. Responsible sending includes regular financial support, continuing prayer, and frequent communication. In the last two decades of the Twentieth Century a lot has been said, and will continue to be said, about the responsibility of the mission and missionary. Perhaps as much needs to be said about the responsibility of the sending churches.

Churches sometimes drop the financial support of a missionary without telling him. They switch their support from one mission to another for no reason other than they want to give more money to the one. Their support checks are irregular and undependable. And when a church is having financial difficulties, the first people to be affected are those farthest from home — the missionaries. Few churches have the faith and resolution of one that has come to my attention. The church income was down seriously because of the moving away of several members. The church took out a loan to keep their support of missionaries current until they could make up for the loss of income.

VI. ANTIOCH WAS A RESPONSIBLE CHURCH

At the end of this first "missionary" trip Paul and Barnabas returned to Antioch.

> On arriving there, they gathered the church together and reported all that God had done through them and how he opened the door of faith to the Gentiles. And they stayed there a long time with the disciples (Acts 14:27-28).

Paul and Barnabas demonstrated their exercise of responsibility by reporting "all that God had done through them" to their sponsoring congregation. Today there is an increasing emphasis on the necessity of missionaries being responsible to their supporting churches.

But the issue that is getting little attention is the necessity of the churches being responsible to the missionaries they send out. Paul and Barnabas had been gone eighteen months[1] and had

---

1. Rackham, p. lxvii.

much to report. A complete report could not have been restricted to twenty minutes. The church came together to hear the report. No doubt they came because they wanted to hear what had taken place. Unfortunately, many members of the modern American congregation find convenient excuses to absent themselves from the services when they hear a missionary is going to speak. Part of the fault may lie in the fact that we often tell the missionary not to report but to preach a sermon. Perhaps as the church members hear exciting reports of accomplishments they, like the Christians at Antioch, will want to hear the reports.

Paul and Barnabas "stayed there a long time." The text does not tell us what they did on this long furlough. I cannot help believing that they took up the work of "teaching" that they had left off when they were sent on their first mission itinerary.

SUMMARY

The church in Antioch provides a superb model that should be emulated by every congregation today. It had a dynamic program of cross-cultural evangelism that allowed the Lord to call the members Christians — those who belonged to Christ. They manifested a gracious spirit that overcame the potential criticism of an older congregation. They, to a person, were generous in meeting the physical needs of fellow believers. They had an enthusiastic worshiping and fasting program that resulted in two of their best leaders being sent out as missionaries. And they not only acted responsibly in sending Paul and Barnabas, they acted responsibly when they returned. Antioch is the model missionary church.

13

LETTERS TO MISSION CHURCHES

ROMANS TO JUDE

The twenty-one books of the New Testament that are classified as epistles were all written by missionaries. Most of them were composed during a missionary tour. With the exception of Philemon they were all addressed either to mission churches or to missionaries.

Most of the lessons in these letters which are relevant to the topic of mission are taken from Paul's writing. There is little helpful information in the epistles of James, Peter, John, and Jude. And it is especially interesting to observe that the two books written to Jewish Christian audiences, Hebrews and James, contain no instructions for the Jews to practice cross-cultural evangelism.

The lessons to be examined in this chapter fall into four heads: The Underlying Principles of Mission, The Theological

Teaching, The Contemporary Crises, and Handling Cultural Conflict.

I. THE UNDERLYING PRINCIPLES OF MISSION

The apostles did not enumerate or elaborate on the principles upon which they carried out their mission activity. But these principles are easily inferred from the apostolic writings.

1. God wants the world to be saved.

For Paul "the gospel . . . is the power of God for the salvation of *everyone* who believes" (Rom. 1:16). However, he wrote to Timothy, "God . . . is the Savior of *all men*, and *especially* of those who believe" (I Tim. 4:10). Is Paul contradicting himself? This is not an acceptable solution to this paradox. There are two better solutions. One, God is capable of saving everyone, but His condition for salvation is faith so that only those who believe will be saved. Two, Don DeWelt suggests that "salvation" is used in different ways. In writing to Timothy Paul is writing of salvation in the physical world for without God all men would be lost physically, mentally, and morally. Forgiveness of sin and eternal life is given only to those who believe.[1]

This salvation to all nations was promised to Abraham (Rom. 4:17-18), prophesied by the prophets (Rom. 16:26), experienced by Paul (I Cor. 2:14-17), and spoken of as salvation for Jews and Gentiles alike (Rom. 2:10).

On two occasions Paul wrote of those who were being saved as predestined (Rom. 8:29-30; Eph. 1:11). "Predestined" must not be construed as an inexorable force that leaves the individual with no real choice as to whether or not he is saved. Such a view, although popular, contradicts virtually all the rest of Scripture that urges men to choose salvation. "Predestined" is better

---

1. Don DeWelt, *Paul's Letters to Timothy and Titus* (Joplin: College Press, 1961), p. 84.

296

understood as referring to the purpose of God in saving a people for himself. Throughout our study of the Bible we have noticed that God has chosen a people to be His people. Many, perhaps most, of the individuals chosen refused to obey God. Their refusal did not thwart God's plan. He was determined to have a people of His own. That people was destined, predestined, to be His people.

Paul divides the population of the whole world into two categories, Jew and Gentile. His underlying belief is that both will be saved.

2. God wants the Jews saved.

Paul, being a Jew, had a special concern for his ethnic brothers. He wrote, "Brothers, my heart's desire and prayer to God for the Israelites is that they may be saved" (Rom. 10:1). This desire was so great that he had

> great sorrow and unceasing anguish in my heart. For I could wish that I myself were cursed and cut off from Christ for the sake of my brothers, those of my own race, the people of Israel (Rom. 9:2-3).

"This is clearly the language of a *Christian*."[2] As important as being "in Christ" was to Paul, he was willing to give up all those benefits if, in some way, it would bring his brother Jews "into Christ." This spirit we saw earlier in Judah who asked to remain in Egypt in Benjamin's place (Gen. 44:33). And it was also the spirit of Moses, who asked to be blotted out of the book of life if God would not forgive the sin of Israel (Exod. 32:32). It echoes David's cry, "O my son Absalom! My son, my son Absalom! If only I had died instead of you; O Absalom, my son, my son!" (II Sam. 18:33). Even more appropriately Paul's desire focuses our attention on Jesus who actually did die for the sins of His people

---

2. William Hendriksen, *New Testament Commentary: Exposition of Paul's Letter to the Romans* (Grand Rapids: Baker Book House, 1981), p. 310.

(Rom. 3:24; I Cor. 15:3).

Paul, the model missionary, here demonstrates what is probably the single most important quality of a missionary — a passion to save the lost.

In spite of the fact that the Jews Paul encountered on his missionary expeditions generally rejected Jesus as the Messiah, Paul was convinced that "all Israel will be saved" (Rom. 11:26). "All Israel" cannot mean all the Israelites in all times. In fact no scholar, to my knowledge, has advocated that it does. However, this brief statement has generated a lot of controversy.[3] The most popular theory is that "all Israel" refers to a large number of Jews, living in the end-time, who will be saved. Hendriksen gives seven reasons why this theory does not conform to the text. 1) The Greek word *houtos* does not mean *then* or *after that*. As most translations reflect, it means *so, in this manner, thus.* 2) The phrase "all Israel" cannot refer to the fraction of the number of Jews who will be alive at the return of Christ. 3) The context indicates that Paul is not just writing about the events of the end-time but is including what is happening *now*. Compare verses 30-31. 4) Out of the entire history of the Jewish race it would be strange for God to single out one generation to be saved. 5) Paul has constantly stressed the salvation of a remnant (Rom. 11:5). 6) This interpretation contradicts I Thess. 2:14b-16. 7) The next two verses (Rom. 11:26b-27) refer to the first coming of Christ, making any interpretation of verse 26 to refer to the second coming out of harmony with the context.[4]

John Calvin advanced the theory that "all Israel" referred to all the elect, both Jews and Gentiles, throughout history who would be saved. However, "Israel, Israelites," occurs eleven times in chapters nine, ten, and eleven. In each case "Israel" is used in the literal sense. It is unlikely that it would be used in the

---

3. See Hendriksen, pp. 379-384, for an excellent summary of the three common interpretations of this text.
4. Pp. 379-380.

spiritual sense in this one verse.

An interpretation that is much to be preferred is that "all Israel" "*means the total number of elect Jews, the sum of all Israel's 'remnants.'* 'All Israel' parallels 'the fulness of the Gentiles.' "[5] Thus, "the fulness of the Gentiles," and "all Israel" means that all the elect of each group will be present when the roll is called.

This view is held by a number of recognized scholars.[6]

The apostle to the Gentiles could write, "I make much of my ministry in the hope that I may somehow arouse my own people to envy and save some of them" (Rom. 11:14).

3. Paul's ministry to the Gentiles

"Is God the God of Jews only? Is he not the God of the Gentiles too? Yes, of the Gentiles too" (Rom. 3:29). The One who created all men also planned to save all men. More than that, Luke also says, "there is only one God, who will justify the circumcised by faith and the uncircumcised by that same faith" (Rom. 3:30). Paul was specifically called to be the apostle to the Gentiles (I Tim. 2:7; 4:11; Gal. 1:17; 2:7; I Thess. 2:15-16; Col. 1:26; Rom. 15:14-16). "Through him and for his name's sake, we received grace and apostleship to call people from all the Gentiles to the obedience that comes from faith" (Rom. 1:5). "Grace and apostleship" probably should be translated "grace of apostleship" or "gift of apostleship." There are two reasons for the alternate translation. One, as the NIV now reads it appears that there are two gifts to Paul, grace and apostleship. But there is nothing in the context to cause the gift of grace to be introduced here. Two, this may be a *hendiadys*, a figure of speech wherein a single concept is expressed with two nouns connected by "and." If this is correct the alternative translation is not only possible, but

---

5. Ibid., p. 381.
6. S. Volbeda, H. Bavinck, H. Hoeksema, L. Berkhof, H. Ridderbos, R. Lenski, O.Palmer Robertson, and W. Hendriksen.

299

the better translation.

Luke records Paul's call to apostleship three times (Acts 9:1-19, esp. verse 15; 26:15-18; 22:21).

Of special interest is the fact that Paul stated that he was "to call . . . the Gentiles *to the obedience of faith*" (Rom. 1:5). Faith and obedience are inseparably linked in Paul's theology.

> The purpose for which Paul was appointed was to bring about *obedience of faith*. Such obedience is based on faith and springs from faith. In fact, so very closely are faith and obedience connected that they may be compared to inseparable identical twins. When you see the one you see the other. A person cannot have genuine faith without having obedience, not vice versa.[7]

An interesting illustration of this occurs in the beginning and ending of Romans. In parallel passages Paul writes, "your *faith* is being reported all over the world" (Rom 1:8) and "everyone has heard about your *obedience*" (Rom. 16:19).

But Paul says his task was to "call people from *all* the Gentiles" (Rom. 1:5). The introduction of "all" creates a problem for us. Paul did not go to every people group or geographical area of the Gentiles. Paul did not complete the task. Neither have we completed it. The task that was given to Paul has been passed on to the church that survived him. And until we have reached people "from all the Gentiles" our job is not yet done.

Paul uses another interesting figure of speech that is filled with implications for his ministry to the Gentiles in Romans 11:11-24. The Gentiles, like wild olive branches, have been grafted onto the stock in place of the natural branches, Israel, that were broken off. "Because of their (the Jews') transgression salvation has come to the Gentiles" (Rom. 11:11). Does this mean that it was necessary for the Jews to reject the gospel in order for the Gentiles to receive it? That it was necessary for some to be lost in

---

7. Ibid, p. 45.

order for others to be saved? Not at all. Rather, when the Jews resisted the invitation to become Christians, Paul and the other First Century evangelists turned to a more reponsive population, the Gentiles (Acts 13:44-48; 18:6; 28:23-28). It was a case "that in all things God works for the good of those who love him, who have been called according to his purpose" (Rom. 8:28). Paul asks rhetorically,

> Did they stumble so as to fall beyond recovery? Not at all. . . . But if their transgression means riches for the world, and their loss mean riches for the Gentiles, how much greater riches will their fullness bring (Rom. 11:11-12).

Paul warned the Gentiles that they faced the potential of being similarly broken off the olive tree.

> But they were broken off because of unbelief, and you stand by faith. Do not be arrogant, but be afraid. For if God did not spare the natural branches, he will not spare you either (Rom. 11:20-21).

4. All men are under sin.

The reason the Jews and the Gentiles needed the gospel is because both were sinners. "We have already made the charge that Jews and Gentiles are all under sin" (Rom. 3:9). Paul had just written that the Jews were sinners and under the sentence of condemnation (Rom. 2:1-3:8). He had also shown that the Gentiles (Greeks) were under the same sentence (Rom. 1:18-32). He then followed this charge with a series of quotations from the Psalms, Isaiah, and Ecclesiastes which supported his accusations. In the first strophe (Rom. 3:10-12) the quotations stated that all men, not just a particular class, were guilty of sin. It is as if Paul were being asked, "Is there no exception?" And he replied, "There is no one . . . no one . . . no one . . . no one . . . not even one." The second strophe (Rom. 3:13-14) showed that all men by nature are under the power of sin. He demonstrated this by speaking about the evil throat (voice), tongue, lips, and mouth. In the third strophe (Rom. 3:15-18) he advanced from their evil speech to their evil actions and demonstrated that by their wars and murders men have demonstrated that they are sinners today as in Isaiah's age. The conclusion is that "all have sinned and fall short of the glory of God" (Rom. 3:23).

John told us that the purpose of the death of Christ was "for the sins of the *whole* world" (I John 2:2). Man's greatest need was met by God's greatest sacrifice, which led to the Church's greatest task.

5. The Purpose of the Church

The two paragraphs found in II Corinthians 5:11-6:2 are probably the most succinct and helpful summary of the purpose of the church. There are two words used in this paragraph, the understanding of which will give significant help to the understanding of the purpose of the church.

"We are therefore Christ's ambassadors" (II Cor. 5:20). The Greek word, *presbutes*, translated "ambassador" translates in Latin as *legatus*. In the Roman government the *legatus*, or *presbutes*, had two functions that contributed to Paul's meaning. Rome divided her provinces into two types: imperial and senatorial. The imperial provinces were those which had seditious people living within them and were therefore potentially dangerous to the government. As a consequence army troops were stationed within them to maintain the peace. The man who was the chief administrator in such a province on behalf of the Emperor was called the *legatus*, or in Greek, *presbutes*. This ambassador had a direct commission from the Emperor. And so Paul regarded himself as having a direct commission from his Emperor, Christ. The senatorial provinces were those which were peaceful and were under the direct supervision of the Roman Senate. The Senate also had ambassadors (*legati*, or *presbutai*) who had an interesting function. When a country was conquered and the Senate determined that the newly acquired territory should become a province, they sent ten *legati* along with the conquering general who arranged the terms of peace, established

302

the boundaries of the new province, and drew up the constitution of the new province. These men were responsible for bringing new people into the family of the Roman Empire. Paul saw himself as such an ambassador who took the offer of pardon and the terms of citizenship to new peoples and brought them into the family of God.

The ambassadors of the United States (or of any sovereign nation) have at least four characteristics. One, they live in a foreign land. Every Christian, in a sense, lives in an alien world. His citizenship is in heaven. But he lives in this world, works in this world, and witnesses in this world. The Christian missionary, like Paul, crosses the cultural barriers of the world in order to serve as an ambassador of Christ. Two, an ambassador of the United States speaks on behalf of his government. He has no message of his own. But he does speak officially on behalf of his nation. The Christian, and the Christian missionary, have no message of their own. They are ambassadors of Christ. As Paul wrote, "he has committed to us the message of reconciliation" (II Cor. 5:19). Three, the ambassador not only speaks on behalf of his sovereign government, he speaks in place of the sovereign who sent him. In verse twenty Paul twice wrote "on behalf of Christ." In each case the preposition is *huper*, which can be translated, "in place of."

It is his (the ambassador's) duty to proclaim faithfully and precisely the message entrusted to him by his sovereign. Accordingly there is a real sense in which the voice of the ambassador may be said to be the voice of the sovereign he represents Here, therefore, Paul boldly urges this analogy: when Christ's ambassador entreats it is equivalent to the voice of God entreating through him. His message, his authority, his power are all imparted to him by his Lord.[8]

And, four, the honor and reputation of the United States are

<hr>

8. Philip Edgcumbe Hughes, *Paul's Second Epistles to the Corinthians* (Grand Rapids: Wm. B. Eerdmans Publishing Co., 1962), p. 210.

vested in the ambassador. The host country judges the sending nation by the behavior of the ambassador.

It is no wonder then that Paul so severely criticizes the church in Corinth, "you are still worldly" (I Cor. 3:3), "are you not mere men" (I Cor. 3:4), "that kind of behavior does not occur even among the Gentiles" (I Cor. 5:1). And to a young missionary, he writes "train yourself to be godly" (I Tim. 4:7), "set an example for the believers in speech, in life, in love, in faith, and in purity" (I Tim. 4:12).

The second key word is reconciliation. "All this is from God, who reconciled us to himself through Christ" (II Cor. 5:18). Reconciliation begins with God. Just as in the first creation all things were called into being by the word of God, so in the re-creation it is the Word of God who makes reconciliation possible. Man may desire to be in harmony with God. Man's efforts in building the tower of Babel, in molding the golden calf, and in creating a variety of religions demonstrate his interest in achieving reconciliation. But there is nothing man can do. Reconciliation was made necessary by sin. Sin is not a minor aberration in behavior. It is the assertion of self in rebellion against God. It is not a small misunderstanding that can easily be corrected. It is mutiny. This rebellion brought the wrath of God upon man. It is an inadequate and truncated theology that speaks of the love of God but omits the wrath of God. The cross is the place where the wrath of God and the love of God meet. The wrath of God makes the cross necessary. The love of God makes it possible. And reconciliation is made possible.[9] But reconciliation can not take

---

9. Paul wrote that Christ was made "to be sin" (II Cor. 5:21) not that He was "made a sinner." It is clear from other passages that Jesus was not a sinner (Heb. 4:15; I Pet. 2:22; I John 3:5; Heb. 7:26). If He had been a sinner He could not have served as the perfect sacrifice and would have destroyed the very foundation of redemption. But, as sin, He was subject to the wrath and judgment of God with the result that sin and its consequences for the whole world were taken away (Isa. 53:5-12). Similarly, we are not said to be "righteous" but "the righteousness of God" (II Cor. 5:21). We have more than a right relation with God. The sinlessness of Christ's perfection has been transferred to us.

304

place until men accept the sacrifice of the cross and its benefits. So he "gave us the ministry of reconciliation. . . . And he has committed to us the message of reconciliation" (II Cor. 5:18-19). Paul makes it clear that the ministry of reconciliation is a ministry of proclamation. The ambassadors of Christ are the messengers, not the agents, of reconciliation. The word translated "message" is *logos* which can also be translated "word." Paul frequently uses "word" for the message of the gospel (Eph. 1:13; Col. 1:5; I Cor. 1:18). The task is cosmic in scope. "God was reconciling the *world* to himself in Christ" (II Cor. 5:19). God's love was not limited to the Chosen People, He loved the *world* (John 3:16). Christ did not die just for the elect. He died for the *ungodly* (Rom. 5:6). The very scope of the benefits of the death of Christ requires His missionaries to "go into all the world and preach the good news to all creation" (Mark 16:15).

6. The apostolic method was preaching.

The ambassadors of Christ were to deliver a message from their Sovereign. An experienced ambassador wrote to a youthful ambassador, "Preach the word; be prepared in season and out of season; correct, rebuke and encourage — with great patience and careful instruction" (II Tim. 4:2). "Preach" (*kerusso*) has the sense of "herald."[10] The herald in the Greek world was a messenger sent by the king to proclaim a royal message or law. Thus, "to herald" originally meant to "make known officially and publicly a matter of great significance."[11] "Preach" is a perfectly good translation as long as it is understood in its primary and etymological meaning of "to proclaim before the public." Preaching, in the New Testament, was not as it has sometimes become today: a moral discourse, a religious lecture, or a book review.

In the epistles the content of preaching is Christ (Phil. 1:15; II

---

10. See a fuller treatment of *kerusso* in the Introduction.
11. William Hendriksen, *New Testament Commentary: Exposition of the Pastoral Epistles* (Grand Rapids: Baker Book House, 1957), p. 309.

Cor. 4:5; 11:4), the gospel (Gal. 2:2; Col. 1:23; I Thess. 2:9), or more specifically the death (I Cor. 1:23), burial, resurrection of Christ (Rom. 15:11).

Four other imperatives tell Timothy how to preach. "Be prepared" can more consistently be translated, "be on hand in season, out of season."[12] The ambassador for Christ is to be "on the spot" where the unreached people are. He is to proclaim, not to play games. He is to be there whether he is wanted or not.

To "correct" is to emphasize the positive. It is not so much pointing out the wrong direction one is taking (that is "reproof") as it is setting one on the right path.

"Rebuke." This is the negative side of preaching. The sinner must not be allowed to think his sin is of no consequence. He must be brought to the conviction, by the Holy Spirit, that he is a sinner and in need of grace.

"Encourage." This word originally meant "to call aside." It may have as its purpose encouraging, comforting, exhorting, entreating, appealing to, or admonishing.

The spirit of the ambassador is characterized by "patience and careful instruction." These twin virtues are vital for the cross-cultural evangelist. People of another culture and religion normally have great difficulty and require a long period of time to grasp the meanings and implications of the Christian faith.

Paul asked the church in Rome, "How can they hear without someone preaching to them? And how can the preach unless they are sent?" (Rom. 10:14-15).

7. It is God who causes the growth of the church through men who are His agents.

The church in Corinth was composed of immature people (I Cor. 3:1-4). They were not only made of flesh (*sarkinoi*), they were dominated by the flesh (*sarkikoi*).[13] One result of this

---

12. Everywhere else in the New Testament *epistethi* is translated in the sense of "arrive," "come near," "be present," "be on hand."

13. William Barclay, *The Letters to the Corinthians*, (Edinburgh: The Saint Andrew Press, 1954), p. 33.

childishness was that they quarrelled, each claiming that he was following a specific spiritual teacher. Paul's response (I Cor. 3:5-9) not only addresses the situation directly, but, in so doing, gives us an insight into one of the underlying principles of his apostleship: growth of the church is the result of the action of God, not the work of the preachers. "However important the work of these men may be, their work is not the real work."[14] "What, after all, is Apollos? And what is Paul? Only servants" (I Cor. 3:5). Paul planted and Apollos watered. But they did not cause the seed to grow — that was the work of God. In spite of the humility expressed in this passage Paul does not denigrate the ministry. Quite the opposite. These missionaries were "God's fellow workers" (I Cor. 3:9). For Paul, the highest calling in the world was to be God's servant, fellow worker.

Paul changes the figure of speech. From describing the church as the field of God, he calls the church the building of God (I Cor. 3:9). Within this figure he says that he laid the foundation and others built on it (I Cor. 3:10). Paul had stated on another occasion (Rom. 15:20) that he preferred to lay foundations, not build on them. He makes it clear here that one phase of the building process is not more important than another. The one who lays the foundation is merely the first in time, not in importance. If the foundation is properly laid, those who follow need not relay it but should build upon it. Then each will receive his reward (I Cor. 3:11).

8. God opens doors of opportunity.

We saw on Paul's second missionary trip the closed doors in Asia Minor an the open door to Europe. In the epistles Paul is even more specific in referring to the open door. He wrote to the Colossians asking them to pray that "God may open a door" (Col. 4:3) so that he may preach the gospel even though he was a prisoner in Rome. Open doors, obviously, do not necessarily

14. F.W. Grosheide, *Commentary on the First Epistle to the Corinthians* (Grand Rapids: Wm. B. Eerdmans Publishing Company, 1953), p. 81.

mean personal freedom. By extension neither are political freedom nor religious freedom necessary to have an open door to evangelization.

In fact, open doors are often accompanied by difficulties. Paul was uncomfortable in Troas where he had an open door, because Titus was not there (II Cor. 2:12-13).[15] And in Ephesus, in spite of the fact that "a great door for effective work has been opened" (I Cor. 16:8), there were many who opposed Paul. It cannot, therefore be expected by the Twentieth Century missionary that he will find a comfortable place to work with lots of opportunity and no problems.

II. THE SIGNIFICANT THEOLOGICAL ISSUES

The letters of the apostles are not systematic theological treatises. Rather, they are issue oriented. Systematic theology is a western style of theology. Had the writers of the New Testament been schooled in western seminaries the New Testament would have been systematized and we would have monographs on theology, Christology, pneumatology, ecclesiology, eschatology, ad infinitum. We would have topics on "everything you ever wanted to know about religion, but were afraid to ask." Such letters probably would not have met the needs of the early church. They would not have scratched where the people were itching.

Are there lessons here for modern missionary teaching? I think so. One, teaching should be issues oriented. The missionary teacher should be primarily concerned with teaching on the topics that are of concern to the people on the field more than with covering topics of interest to the missionary. Two, the teaching

---

15. He was anxious to receive Titus' report on the situation in Corinth.

should be contextualized. That is, the method of teaching should be appropriate to the culture, and the shape of the church should be culturally relevant. This may be diagrammed as follows:[16]

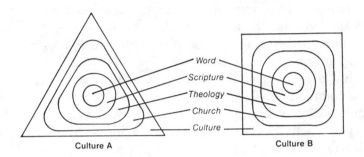

Culture A   Culture B

The core of the gospel does not change. It must not be changed or it no longer is the gospel. But the external shape of the church, the issues that are matters of opinion, not faith, may be different in each culture. Paul addressed seven theological issues at length in his epistles. Let's look at each one briefly.

1. The Lord's Supper, I Cor. 11:17-34.

Paul does not fully describe the situation in Corinth so we must make some conjectures about the Corinthian practices, and to that extent we are uncertain about our conclusions. Fortunately, however, the points that Paul makes are clear and there is no reason for doubt in those areas. Apparently the church in Corinth had "carry-in" dinners on a regular basis. It is possible that these

---

16. Adapted from Dean S. Gilliland, *Pauline Theology & Mission Practice* (Grand Rapids: Baker Book House, 1983), p. 212. He adapted these diagrams from Stephen C. Knapp, "Contextualization and its implications for U.S. Evangelical Churches and Missions," a paper delivered at the Institute of Mennonite Studies, Elkhart, IN, 1977, p. 23.

meals were served each time the church met.[17] Commentators usually have called these dinners "love feasts." Perhaps that was their purpose, but in Corinth very little love was shown on these occasions. Corinth must have been a heterogeneous congregation in at least one respect. The poor, who had little to bring to the suppers, frequently went away hungry, whereas the well-to-do were glutted and drunk. Paul makes the point that if the only reason they are coming together is to eat they would be better off staying at home.

The pot-luck dinners were followed by the observance of the communion. The practice of incorporating the sacramental meal into a common meal was instituted by the Lord Himself in the upper room. Paul refers to the Lord's Supper in verse twenty, but it is not clear whether he is referring to the common meal or to the sacramental portion of the celebration. Supper was the main meal of the Greeks and was served in the evening. We cannot be certain whether Paul referred to that meal as the "Lord's" because of the Christian character given to it by the practice of sharing food with those less fortunate, or because it became the Lord's by association with the Communion, or because Paul is referring only to the sacramental portion of the meal.

Paul made the point that the lessons he was giving about the Lord's Supper were not his own, they came from the Lord Himself. "Jesus on the night he was betrayed, took bread" (I Cor. 11:23). The bread was the unleavened bread of the Passover meal. And He said, "This is my body" (I Cor. 11:24). Since Jesus was present in His body when He referred to the bread in His hand as "my body" we are prevented from taking His words in a literal sense. There is, however, a very close connection between "bread" and "body." And that connection is made for us by Jesus Himself when He says, "do this in remembrance of me" (I Cor. 11:24). William Robinson, once when discussing the relative merits of the arguments for transubstantiation, consubstantiation,

---

17. *Sunerchomenon* is a present participle.

and symbolism said: "They are saying the right thing in the wrong way. The right thing is that Christ is present!"[18]

In the context of the Corinthian situation it was easy to fail to recognize the body of the Lord and so bring judgment on himself (I Cor. 11:29). Paul's concern was that they come to the table with the right attitude and behavior. It is probably nearly as difficult for Christians today, especially new believers without a history of church services behind them, to concentrate their thoughts on the spiritual reality behind the physical components of the communion.

2. The Work of the Holy Spirit, I Cor. 12,13,14

The church in Corinth had placed an unhealthy emphasis on speaking in tongues. It is understandable that problems with the gift of tongues would arise in Corinth. All Greeks knew of the wild ecstacies of the cult of Dionysius. Grosheide said "The Corinthians overestimated glossolalia and considered those who lacked that gift to be incomplete Christians."[19] It is possible that someone in Corinth had written Paul to get a clarification of glossolalia.

Paul does not take the opportunity to develop a full-blown pneumatology. He confines his comments to spiritual gifts, but he does that in some detail, devoting three chapters to the subject. He makes the following points: one, although speaking in tongues is to be desired, it is the least important of the nine gifts he lists in these chapters (I Cor. 12:10,30; 13:2). Two, those with the gift of speaking in tongues should only use it when there is someone present to interpret (I Cor. 14:13). Three, the miracle of speaking in tongues is a sign for the unbeliever (I Cor. 14:22). Four, the gifts are for communication or confirmation of the message from God (I Cor. 14:1-12,22-25). Five, the special gifts are temporary, they are to cease when the perfect comes (I Cor. 13:8-12). There are three gifts that every Christian has — faith,

18. William Robinson in "The Shape of the Eucharist," lectures at the School of Religion, Butler University, Fall 1955.
19. P. 327.

311

hope, and love — and they are much to be preferred over the special gifts.

Paul does not define speaking in tongues. A definition would have been pointless to his readers. But it has left Christians in succeeding centuries debating whether glossolalia is a foreign tongue or a "miraculous spiritual language that had its own sounds."[20] The preferred interpretation is given in other passages where the meaning is clear. On Pentecost, for instance, people from seventeen different language groups heard "in his own native language" (Acts 2:1-13). Tongues (glossa) can either mean the "physical tongue or its figurative meaning of that which the tongue is used for, a language."[21] When used in the figurative sense of a language, it is always "the *language* used by a particular people in distinction from that of other nations . . . to *speak with other* than their native i.e. in *foreign* tongues."[22] The idea of a "spiritual language" is a recent invention and unknown to the New Testament writers.

A second term that Paul did not define is "perfect." All agree that the special gifts were temporary, and would last only until "perfection comes" (I Cor. 13:10). But does this refer to the perfect gift, love, or to a perfect, complete, revelation; or does it refer to the ultimate perfection, heaven, or to the establishment of a mature church? The confusion created by the commentators is unnecessary. Four lines of evidence converge to provide us with a clear answer. One, the word "perfect" (teleios) literally means "having reached its end (telos)."[23] Used of persons it has the idea of mature, fullgrown. Of things, it has the idea of good working

20. Ibid., pp. 288-89.
21. Tom Friskney, Solving Church Problems (Cincinnati: Tom Friskney, 1987), p. 203.
22. Joseph Henry Thayer, "glossa," A Greek-English Lexicon of the New Testament (New York: American Book Company, 1886).
23. James Hope Moulton and George Milligan, "teleios," The Vocabulary of the Greek New Testament (London: Hodder and Stoughton, Limited, 1930).

order or condition. It also has the concept of complete, final.[24] Two, the purpose of the supernatural gifts was the establishment of the church.

> The supernatural gifts were very helpful in the establishment of the church. They were employed in receiving revelation from God, in knowing facts, in preaching the gospel in one's own language and in foreign languages, in credentialing the message, in having wisdom for the applying of the gospel, in governing the early church, etc.[25]

Three, the spiritual gifts were imparted by the laying on of the hands of the apostles (Acts 8:18; I Tim. 4:14). Consequently, these gifts would naturally come to an end with the infancy of the church and the death of the second generation of Christians. Four, prophecy was a more desirable gift than tongues (I Cor. 14:1). And although there were many prophets in the early church it is a rare case that someone will even claim to be a prophet today. The conclusion of the matter is that perfection refers to the condition when the church arrived at that point of maturity where it no longer needed men with special gifts to guide it, because it had the continuing testimony of the apostles and prophets through their writings. Paul's illustration was,

> [w]hen I was a child, I talked like a child, I thought like a child, I reasoned like a child. When I became a man, I put childish ways behind me (I Cor. 13:11).

Friskney used the illustration of a building, comparing the supernatural gifts to the temporary scaffolding that is removed when the building is completed.[26]

---

24. Ibid.
25. Friskney, p. 220.
26. P. 221.

3. The Resurrection, I Cor. 15; II Cor. 5:1-10

Some of the Corinthians said "there is no resurrection from the dead" (I Cor. 15:12). Although they apparently did not say it, the direct implication of that teaching was that "Christ has not been raised" (I Cor. 15:17). This view denied the very core of the gospel (I Cor. 15:1-3), made preaching useless (I Cor. 15:14), made faith meaningless (I Cor. 15:14), left the Christians still in their sins (I Cor. 15:17), and made Paul a liar (I Cor. 15:15).

Although the number who denied the resurrection was a minority ("some") in the church this false doctrine emasculated the gospel and threatened the existence of Christianity. This teaching had to be dealt with.

The resurrection was a special problem to the Greek people. There were Greeks who believed the body was evil. Death for them was the escape of the spirit from an evil incarceration.[27] The Greek philosophers were in disagreement, however, whether the soul perished with the body, or whether it lived on in a bodiless state.

Paul used two major arguments to establish his point. One, he marshalls more than five hundred eyewitnesses to the resurrection of Christ (I Cor. 15:3-8), this proving not only that Christ was raised from the dead, but that through His resurrection it is possible for all His followers to rise from the dead. Two, the resurrected body is a spiritual body (I Cor. 15:35-36). Since flesh and blood cannot inherit heaven (I Cor. 15:50), the perishable body must be replaced by a spiritual one (I Cor. 15:50), the tent with an eternal home (II Cor. 5:1-5). When the American astronauts landed on the moon they had to take an artificial atmosphere with them, contained in space suits, because their bodies could not survive in the atmosphere of the moon. Likewise, men in earthly bodies cannot live in heaven. But instead of taking a bit of earth's atmosphere with them, they will be given new bodies that are capable of thriving in the new eternal home. Paul calls them

---

27. See Pythagoras, Plato, and the Gnostics.

"spiritual" bodies.
Only Christ, through His own resurrection, can give hope for the resurrection of the dead.

Six young men in Central India recently committed suicide when they, with their spiritual guru, failed to restore the life of a companion. With implicit faith in the "tantra" (Black Magic) of his guru and his companions that they would be able to restore his life, Sahu jumped into a pile of burning logs. When restoration of his life with 'tantra matra" proved to be unsuccessful, they panicked and fled the area fearing capture and harrassment by the police.
Subsequently during the week, five more disciples of the Guru committed suicide by swallowing pesticides, whereas two of them lay down on the tracks before an approaching passenger train. Incense sticks and pieces of coconut meat were found beside their lifeless bodies as offerings to the goddess, Ghato Shakti. Guru Gokul is presently in police custody and his "powers" to produce scorpions from neem leaves, candy from clay and ten rupee notes from the air have suddenly and mysteriously disappeared. Gokul had been serving in a local Primary School as an errand boy. He is now charged with abetting six suicide cases.[28]

1. Stewardship, I Cor. 16:1-4; II Cor. 8,9
Paul did not hesitate to ask the Christians to give money to support the work of the church. There were at least four reasons why the Christians should give: one, God had given them the supreme gift (II Cor. 8:9; 9:15). Two, they needed to give for their own spiritual welfare (II Cor. 8:7-8; 9:6-7,11-12). Three, missionaries needed to be sent to unreached people (Phil. 4:10-19; II Cor. 9:13). And, four, other people, especially Christians needed help (I Cor. 16:1-4; II Cor. 8:1-7,13-15).
Perhaps the most difficult thing for the American missionary to do is to teach stewardship to new congregations in the Third

---

28. Bernel and Joan Getter, "Resurrection Failure," *The Evangel* (San Bernardino: Church of Christ Mission in India, July 1988), p. 3.

World. And consequently, it is my observation, that the New Testament teaching that is most neglected on the mission field is stewardship. This hiatus is understandable, but not defensible. The missionary, although poor by American living standards, is wealthy by local standards. He may have a weekly salary that exceeds a year's wage of a national. He sees people starving for want of money. He sees people dying because they cannot afford to buy medicine. It is easier for him to build a church, or pay a preacher, than it is to ask the poor members of a new church to do it. He must not forget "it is more blessed to give than to receive" — even for an impoverished native. And the church will never become indigenous until it learns to give.

We will leave an in-depth discussion of stewardship until the next chapter, "Financial Support of Missions."

5. The God of Comfort, II Cor. 1:3-11

Paul begins the second letter to Corinth with a vindication of his change of plans to visit the Corinthian brethren. But in so doing he tells us a great deal about the nature of God. Here again, a specific problem elicits from Paul an important theological statement. Ten times in five verses he writes about the "comfort" of God (II Cor. 1:3-7). Comfort (*parakaleo*) means in its basic sense the standing beside a person to encourage him while he is undergoing severe testing. It is from this word the English word, paraclete, is derived to refer to the Holy Spirit. Indeed, it is the Father who works through the Paraclete to strengthen and to guide (John 14:16; 15:26; 16:7).

Paul points out that we are not comforted strictly for our own benefit. We are comforted so we can comfort others (II Cor. 1:4-6). The Christian is blessed, not for selfish reasons, but in order to serve others. We have seen this principle beginning with Abraham (Gen. 12:1-3) and running throughout the divine record.

Suffering is endemic to the Christian life. To be a follower of Jesus is to follow Him into suffering (II Cor. 1:5; Phil. 3:10; I Pet. 4:13; John 15:20; Matt. 20:23; Rom. 8:17f.; Acts 14:22; II Tim.

2:12). But as we suffer for Christ we will also be comforted through Christ (II Cor. 1:5). "In the service of Christ, therefore, there may be disappointments, but there cannot be despair; there may be conflicts, but never doubt; there may be afflictions, but never without comfort."[29]

Paul was accused of not keeping his word by his critics in Corinth. He suffered such affliction in the province of Asia that he despaired of life (II Cor. 1:8). Paul did not identify the affliction, and the various speculations as to its nature really do not provide us with a sure explanation.

The Twentieth Century missionary need not feel that he is better than Paul, or expect that he is going to be exempt from the suffering of Christ. He can, however, have the hope that the comfort of God is greater than his suffering.

6. The Return of Christ, I Thess. 4:13-5:11; II Thess. 2:1-12

It is the propensity of man to be certain about the uncertain, to speculate about matters that have been withheld from man, to want to know what Jesus himself did not know, and to major in minors. Someone, professing to be Paul, wrote that the Lord had returned (II Thess. 2:2 3). Paul said six things about the return of Christ: one, Jesus would return (I Thess. 4:16; II Thess. 2:1). Two, no one knows when (I Thess. 5:1). Three, His return will come unexpectedly (I Thess. 5:2-3). Four, it will be after the revealing of the lawless one (II Thess. 2:5-9). Five, the dead in Christ will be raised, and those Christians living will join Him (I Thess. 4:15-17). And, six, we should live in anticipation of His coming (I Thess. 4:4-11).

7. Christian living: faith or law? Galatians

The major cultural barrier within the early church was between Jewish and Gentile members. The wall was raised higher because it was also a religious barrier. The problem of circumcision had been dealt with at the council in Jerusalem (Acts 15). But some of the Jews were still insisting on observing the law

29. Hughes, p. 15.

(Gal. 3:5,10). Paul wrote the troubled churches in Galatia explaining that the law had led to Christ (Gal. 3:24), and Christ, in turn, set men free from the law (Gal. 5:1), and made them sons of God (Gal. 4:7). Consequently, any insistence that the Christians continue to observe the law was to fall from grace (Gal. 5:4), make Christ of no value (Gal. 5:2), to be alienated from Christ (Gal. 5:4), and become a slave again (Gal. 4:9). The lifestyle of the Christian is to be determined by the Spirit (Gal. 5:16) and to be lived in faith (Gal. 5:8).

Every people has a religion. One of the problems every missionary faces is how much of the former religion may he allow the converts to retain? And what parts of it must be rejected? The missionary at the same time must preach a culturally relevant message, and avoid preaching "another gospel." The blending of unacceptable practices of the former religion with the new concepts is known as syncretism, or Christopaganism.

III. THE CONTEMPORARY CRISES IN THE CHURCHES

1. Division, I Cor. 1:10-17
Life in Corinth was a life of freedom to do as one pleased. It was a life without self-discipline. It was a life without moral constraint. It, indeed, was selfishness carried to the extreme. Unfortunately that independence carried over into the church. There were divisions within the church. *Schismata* is a word for tears, or rents, in a garment (Matt. 9:16). In the figurative sense it refers to differences between people (John 9:16). To make matters worse the word is plural indicating many divisions. Paul names four groups (I Cor. 1:12), and there may have been more. The sin of division was compounded by the sin of quarrelling (I Cor. 1:11) about their differences. *Erides* means strifes, wranglings, quarrels. The present tense *(eisin)* indicates that there was no let up in their arguing. The picture is of a very unpleasant situation, and one that could not contribute to effective evangelism. There is a spark

of hope. Corinth is still one church; she had not divided into separate congregations.

The Corinthian Church "had been enriched in every way — in all your speaking and all your knowledge . . . you do not lack in any spiritual gift" (I Cor. 1:5,7). Having supernatural gifts, however, did not guarantee Christian behavior.

Paul appeals to them. To appeal (*parakaleo*) is to "call to one's side," "invite," "urge," "exhort," "encourage," "request," "comfort." His appeal is based on the authority of Jesus Christ, "in the name of our Lord Jesus Christ" (I Cor. 1:10). "The starting point for the Corinthian Christians, if they are going to solve their problems, is to submit to the authority of Christ."[30]

2. Sexual Immorality

One thousand sacred prostitutes served the Corinthian men and Aphrodite, the goddess of sex, who had her enormous temple on Acrocorinth. This is the equivalent of having one thousand legalized prostitutes in Cincinnati. Promiscuity was commonplace. The habits of fornication were not easily dropped even when one became a Christian. The temptations were real and strong and ever present.

There was a case of incest within the church, "a kind that does not occur even among pagans" (I Cor. 5:1-13). The sin was bad and brought disgrace on the church. But the neglect, or refusal, to discipline the man was worse.

In I Cor. 6:13-20 Paul pointed out the principle that made sexual sin so heinous. Sexual union made two individuals one flesh. That kind of unity was reserved for marriage in the Judeo-Christian morality. And although Paul did not complete the statement that sexual union with a prostitute makes the man in union with the prostitute, he is also in union with the goddess she represents. Man's body is for the Lord. This is an interesting concept. Christianity is not exclusively a "spiritual" religion. The Christian religion has to do with the body as well. It is the body

---

30. Friskney, p. 35.

319

that is raised from the dead. It is the body of Christ that is consumed in the Lord's Supper.

This problem of immorality caused Paul to launch into a discussion of marriage for the Christian (I Cor. 7:1-16). For those who did not have the gift of continence marriage is good. Marriage, as defined by Paul, was monogamous. Paul also gives some guidelines for a married couple. Each should recognize and fill the sexual needs of the spouse. They should not divorce. However, if one of them becomes a Christian and the other leaves the Christian partner is free.

The practice of fornication may be as prevalent in many places in today's world as it was in Corinth.

In the United States television programming both reflects and shapes the behavior of the population. The popular series, *L.A. Law* represents what I am saying. Nearly every attorney in the firm, except the senior partner, has been shown having an affair with one, or more, people who are not their spouses. The obvious message the writers are conveying is that lawyers, who determine what is right and wrong, what is legal, show by their actions that sexual intercourse between consenting adults is not sin.

In India, Siva, who is one of the three principal gods of the Hindu religion, is a fertility god. Scholars have identified her with Baal of the Canaanite religion.

Some of the pastoral tribes in east Africa are known for their promiscuity. Beginning at puberty boys and girls become sexually active indiscriminately. After marriage, when the men follow the cattle to greener pastures, their wives stay home to tend the gardens and children. But the prostitutes travel with the men.

Immediately following the presentation of the high moral standards for the Christians, Paul said that "circumcision is nothing and uncircumcision is nothing" (I Cor. 7:19). And of food that had been sacrificed to idols, "food does not bring us near to God" (I Cor. 8:8). The conclusion I reach is that in the matter of ethics there are some issues for which moral absolutes are given, and other issues that are determined by personal preferences. Because of the culture in which we have been raised we each have strong opinions about the rightness or wrongness of certain activities. Other Christians, with different backgrounds, will have contradictory opinions concerning dancing, drinking alcohol, smoking, card-playing, attending movies, watching TV, wearing clothes, wearing certain kinds of clothes to a church service, etc. The new missionary will immediately see many events in his chosen field that are offensive. He probably will be tempted to preach against all or most of these "immoral" actions. The cause of evangelism will be better served if he 1) declares as absolute only those things that the New Testament absolutely states as absolutes. 2) That he carefully examine every "trait" in his new home in order to learn the "meaning" of each "form" he sees.[31] A frequent and startling lesson is that the form does not have the meaning to the nationals that it does to the cross-cultural worker. 3) He is patient and lets the congregation of new Christians determine what is proper Christian behavior in their society.

Dean S. Gilliland wrote,

One of the regrets of my earlier days of missionary work was the lack of charity about what was really important and what was secondary. Things that should have been treated as matters of purely personal preference were often made the subject of hard-and-fast rules. . . . I recall the way in which it was insisted that schoolboys remove their hats whenever they came into the school building or stood before a teacher. Yet in some parts of Africa it is considered good manners to wear a hat at all times. . . . Some

---

31. These are technical terms of cultural anthropology. A "trait" is that minimal constituent of a culture which is functionally organized and regarded as having an independent existence. "Form" is a thing as it is seen or heard. It includes the shape, color, size, sound, etc. "Meaning" is the significance attributed to the form by the members of a society. The same form may have different meanings to different cultures. An overcoat, for instance, to a European means warmth. To someone in tropical Africa it can mean prestige, resulting in it being worn on public occasions in sweltering weather.

churches said the betel nut must not be chewed because it alleged-
ly contains a narcotic, yet the sharing of a betel nut between
friends is a traditional symbol of hospitality and fraternity. . . . At
one point there was a long discussion about a certain word that
contained the Arabic word for God. One group of elders banned
the use of the word to its flock, while the rest said it was merely an
explicative and should not be taken as profanity. There was one
topic that seemed equally important to all; this was the question of
seasonal rites. Should Christians attend dances that were organized around the traditional values? Could they be permitted to
honor the ancestors by a libation or "feed" them by leaving food at
their shrines?[32]

3. Lawsuits against brethren, I Cor. 6:1-11

The contentiousness mentioned in chapter one went beyond
verbal wrangling and frequently (*krimata* is plural) ended up in
trials in civil court. Paul's solution is totally unacceptable to the
selfish man: "Why not rather be cheated?" (I Cor. 6:7). In one
society cheating in trading, buying, and selling is a normal way of
life. The meek person, the missionary who takes Paul's injunction
seriously, will be regarded as a fool by the people he is trying to
win. Are we to allow ourselves to be taken advantage of? Is Paul's
statement, "We are fools for Christ" (I Cor. 4:10) applicable
here? Is this what Jesus meant when He said, "be as shrewd as
snakes and as innocent as doves" (Matt. 10:16)?

IV. LEADERSHIP TRAINING: I & II TIMOTHY, TITUS

"And the things you have heard me say in the presence of
many witnesses entrust to reliable men who will also be qualified
to teach others" (II Tim. 2:2). First Christian Church in Troas
could not write to Jerusalem Bible College or Antioch Christian
Seminary to get a preacher. The Church of Christ in Antioch
could not telephone the School of World Mission for recruits for

32. Pp. 167-68.

their proposed missionary team to Asia Minor. How were the leaders selected and trained in the early church?

1. Selection

One, apparently some men volunteered for cross-cultural evangelism. Men from Cyprus and Cyrene came to Antioch (Acts 11:19).

Two, Paul and Barnabas were chosen by the Spirit (Acts 13:2).

Three, Paul chose Silas (Acts 15:20) and Timothy (Acts 16:3). Barnabas chose John Mark (Acts 15:37).

Four, the church chose seven "deacons" (Acts 6:5).

There seems to be no "standard" way of calling men to leadership. The only thing they seem to have in common is the potential of being good leaders. In some places it is stated, in others implied, that they had already demonstrated their qualities by the service they were performing.

2. Preparation

One, the education of these leaders was done in an apprenticeship. In this they followed the example of Jesus, although perhaps more unwittingly than deliberately. Certainly in the Greek culture they had the example of the master-pupil relation.

Two, specific teaching was done (II Tim. 2:2). Since there were no schools we must conclude the teaching was on an informal basis.

Three, the training included project assignments. This especially can be seen in Paul's ministry, for example, as he left Aquila and Priscilla in Ephesus (Acts 18:19). He sent Sopater, Aristarchus, Secundus, Gaius, Timothy, Tychicus, and Trophimus on ahead to Troas to lay the groundwork for Paul's ministry there (Acts 20:4-5).

This model of leadership training can be adapted in any culture and undoubtedly is the most effective plan. The Bible College is a western phenomenon and the exportation of the American Bible College is probably one of the most inefficient and ineffective ways to train leaders. For instance, in many

African cultures only the older men are respected as leaders. But by the time they could be respected as leaders in their cultures, they have families and find it impossible financially to spend four years in college. And, on the other hand, to train young men is futile, because while they have learned the scriptures, they will not be accepted as legitimate leaders.

SUMMARY

It is not to be expected that a missionary writing to mission churches is going to make a case for mission. The very existence of the churches is proof of the validity of mission. But the concept of mission underlies and penetrates these letters, especially those of Paul, and, hence, several lessons about mission can be learned from these epistles.

The principles underlying the practice of mission are: God wants the world to be saved, God wants the Gentiles to be saved, all men are under sin and need to be saved, the purpose of the Church is to save the world, preaching is the apostolic method of saving the world, God causes the church to grow through men, and God opens the doors of opportunity to save the world.

The mission letters are issue oriented, addressing contemporary problems in the churches. If Twentieth Century missionaries are to follow Paul's example, they, too, will be more concerned with addressing current issues that concern the converts than teaching a western type systematic theology. Some issues Paul addressed were, the Lord's Supper, the work of the Holy Spirit, the resurrection of the body, stewardship, the nature of God, and the return of Christ.

The contemporary crises that threatened the life of the churches were division, sexual immorality, and lawsuits.

Although not an issue or crisis, a serious situation in these new congregations was the lack of leadership. Consequently a major concern was the selection and preparation of leaders for the churches.

14

FINANCING MISSIONS

I CORINTHIANS 16; II CORINTHIANS 8,9

Paul had seen the suffering of the Christians in Jerusalem which was a result of their persecution (I Thess. 2:14) combined with the famine in Judea (Acts 11:29-30). They had little food. They had difficulty finding housing. This, in turn, was because they had little money because few of them could get work. He was determined to do something about it. So he wrote the first letter of what may be the first fundraising by mail campaign in history. It reads, in part,

> Now about the collection for God's people. Do what I told the Galatian churches to do. On the first day of every week, each one of you should set aside a sum of money in keeping with his income, saving it up, so that when I come no collections will have to be made (I Cor. 16:1-2).

Since a specific Sunday is not designated it must be concluded that Paul was commanding (*poiesate* is imperative) the believers to bring their gifts to the regular meeting of the church on the first day of the week. No one was exempt from this Christian obligation: "*each one* of you should set aside a sum of money." Even the poorest saint and the youngest member could give "in keeping with his income." Paul, even with his Pharisaic background, is not a legalist. He does not specify the proportion each should give.

Paul was a practical theologian. He could write erudite and profound theology as he did in Romans. But theology was a resounding gong and a clanging cymbal unless it was applied to the real issues of life in this world. The letters to Corinth reflect this practical application of Christian doctrine. Christianity is not just a philosophy, not just a way of meditation, it is a way of life. At this point Paul is saying that the Christian helps another Christian in need. One result of this action is the welding of the Gentile community in Corinth into one brotherhood with the Jewish community in Jerusalem.

The Corinthian Christians apparently were long on promise and short on delivery. They had not continued to collect the benevolent funds although they had been the first church to send money to Jerusalem (II Cor. 8:10). There really was no excuse. Corinth was a commercial city with a lot of money flowing through it. It is reasonable to assume that many, if not all, of the church members were gainfully employed or were in business. In all their problems we do not read that one of them was persecution. So Paul writes a second letter urging them to "finish the work" (II Cor. 8:11).

One of the best motivations, one of the best teachers is example. So begins his appeal, "And now, brothers, we want you to know about the grace that God has given the Macedonian churches" (II Cor. 8:1). Three churches in Macedonia are named in Acts: Philippi, Thessalonica, and Berea. They were in "severe trial" (II Cor. 8:2). For instance the Jews in Philippi were filing

326

charges against the believers who then were thrown in jail. They
were also extremely poor (II Cor. 8:2). Most of us have said we
were poor but have never been really poor. One-third of the
world's population goes to bed hungry every night. They have no
food in the house (if they have a house) for breakfast the following morning and no money to buy food. The Macedonian
churches were not only poor, they were extremely poor. Yet out
of their trial and poverty "their overflowing joy . . . welled up in
rich generosity" (II Cor. 8:2).

First they gave "as much as they were able" (II Cor. 8:3). This
was all that Paul had asked. It is inconceivable that they could
give more or that the Lord would expect more. But Paul told us
they gave "even beyond their ability" (II Cor. 8:3). But how could
they give what they did not have? What Paul is saying they did is
impossible to do. It is impossible for man. Paul gave us the clue in
verse one: "We want you to know about the grace that God has
given." God made it possible. When they had given all they
could, God provided more for them to give. The Twentieth Century name for this kind of giving is "Faith Promise." Charles Lit-
toll, missionary on Mindanao, Philippines, has a two-phase
stewardship program that he has implemented among the
churches he has planted. Phase one, which he labelled, "First
Step," teaches the stewardship of one's income and possessions.
Phase two is the practice of "Faith Promise Mission Programs."

To look into our billfold, purse or checkbook and give what
we already have requires no faith. This kind of giving is giving by
sight. It does not require us to trust God to supply the need.

Abraham is cited more often in the New Testament as an example of faith than any other Old Testament hero. When
Abraham left Ur he did not know where he was going. He did not
even have a map. He went in faith trusting that God would lead
him to his destination. When he offered Isaac he did not see the
lamb caught in the brush. He believed in the resurrection
although up to that time no one had ever been raised from the
dead.

The principle of making a promise to God to give money that we do not have but trust that God will supply has been the basis of the Faith Promise programs conducted in local churches to provide money to support missions.[1]

How does God provide the means for the individual to give more? There are many ways.

Funds may come from an unexpected source. A young widow with three small children made a Faith Promise of $100 per week over and above her current giving. It was a real step of faith for a woman in her position. A few weeks later she received a letter from the insurance company that read, in part, "We made a mistake when we calculated your husband's death benefits. Here is a check for $5200!"

Extra funds may be freed up from re-ordered priorities. As we make the evangelization of the world the most important thing in our lives we may discover that we do not really need what we wanted. We may find that we do not really need to spend as much on recreation. We do not need to eat out as often. We do not really have to drive an expensive car. In such cases the Lord provides, not by giving us more money, but by changing our perspective on what is really important.

New opportunities may be offered us. I knew a factory worker who was just getting by on his wages. He made a Faith Promise not knowing where the money was coming from. Within a few days his foreman offered him the opportunity to work overtime. The extra money he received was almost identical to the amount he had promised to give to missions.

The source may not be clear. There was a young preacher who was giving substantially to the church and to missions. He was in debt. He stretched his commitment by promising still more to missions. The very next Sunday he increased his giving as pro-

---

1. For a procedure manual on the "how to's" of a Faith Promise program, see Robert Reeves, *Faith Promise for Church Growth* (Cincinnati: Standard Publishing, 1972).

mised. A few weeks later he had to take a $1700 cut in salary! It seemed the Lord was not giving, but taking away. Nevertheless, he kept on giving according to his promise. By the end of the year he had kept his promise and was farther out of debt with less money coming in. He could identify no factor with more money going and less money coming in that allowed him to be better off.

Is it not possible that the Lord can allow us to give more because He prevents expenses from occurring? This is one of those things that cannot be known. But is it not possible that He could prevent an expensive hospitalization, or other catastrophic cost and so allow us to keep our commitment? There is no way to know.

I also knew a man who made a Faith Promise of $100 per week over and above his current giving. But he never gave any of it. Apparently he was waiting for the Lord to miraculously drop the money in his lap. But the Lord never did. Faith Promise also means *giving*. And giving before the funds come in is really giving in the faith that they will come.

There is a fine line between faith and foolishness. It is possible to make a commitment that is not an act of faith, but of foolishness. It is also possible to give foolishly. The line between the two has to be drawn by the giver.

Almost every church that has had a Faith Promise Program has doubled its missionary giving the first year of the program. And with rare exceptions the giving for missions has increased in each of the following years.

Pessimists will say that the total giving will not increase, but the members of the church will just take money out of one pocket and put it in another. They will say if the missions giving goes up because of a Faith Promise program, the general fund or the building fund will suffer. Several years ago I did a study of all the churches I could find who had held a Faith Promise Missionary Conference specifically to learn if this is true. The clear statistical answer was that every church not only increased the mission giving but at the same time increased the money available for other purposes. Jesus gave the principle, "Seek first his kingdom and his righteousness, and all these things will be given to you as well" (Matt. 6:33).

The offering given by the Macedonian churches was not strictly a missionary offering. It was a benevolent contribution to the suffering saints in Jerusalem. The Twentieth Century Faith Promise Program is a missionary program based on the principles of the giving in Macedonia. The similarity is that in both cases the giving is for *others*. It is then more than a stewardship program. It is a program of outreach. On several occasions churches have attempted to have Faith Promise programs for local expenses. Most of those times the program has failed because they have not understood the principles involved. Such churches have confused an outreach program for a stewardship program. There is no doubt churches need stewardship programs but the Faith Promise idea does not fit that need. Church members need to support the local program — out of what they have.

What constitutes a mission-minded church? One factor has to be substantial giving to mission activities. Historically, churches have practiced tithing, giving ten percent of their income to missions. However, generally only about one-third of that amount is sent to cross-cultural missionaries. The result is only about three percent of the budget is actually spent on cross-cultural evangelism. It is my opinion that a church cannot consider that it has a viable mission program and can be considered a mission congregation unless it is spending at least as much on others as it is spending on itself. And certainly we are not going to win the world until we make world evangelism the top priority in the local churches.

The greatest missionary need is not for money, but for people. Is it not appropriate to also have a goal for missionary recruits in our Faith Promise conferences? What would happen if the mission committee and eldership set a goal for a specific number of recruits, then the church prayed fervently for a number of weeks leading up to the commitment service for recruits? Would the

Lord answer the prayers? Is this not what Jesus asked us to do (Matt. 9:38)? Was it not while the leaders of the church in Antioch were praying that the Holy Spirit directed them to send Paul and Barnabas to the mission field? We have the solution to our greatest need. We need only to put it into practice. I saw it done once. I was holding a Faith Promise meeting in a church that set a goal for two recruits. I did not see any possibility for a response, but before the week was over one young couple stepped forward.

Paul gave the key to the Macedonian generosity, "they gave themselves first to the Lord" (II Cor. 8:5). The first, and most basic, human sin is selfishness (Gen. 3:6). As long as we regard our money and our possessions as "mine" we will not give generously. Only after we have given *ourselves* to the Lord will we be able to see that everything I have does not belong to me but to Him.

15

THE ACTS OF THE ALMIGHTY

REVELATION

If I were given the privilege of renaming the books of the Bible I would call Revelation, "The Acts of the Almighty." At the time[1] that Christ revealed Himself to John in exile on Patmos the church was undergoing the most severe persecution to date. The Roman emperor was Domitian (c. 81-96) who is known "as the one who bathed the empire in the blood of Christians."[2] His predecessors, Julius Caesar and Augustus, had claimed to be deities, but Domitian carried the claim to his divinity further than the others. His subordinates knew him as *deus et dominus*.

---

1. I accept the date of 96 A.D. which is generally held by conservative scholars.
2. Ray Summers, *Worthy Is the Lamb* (Nashville: Broadman Press, 1951), p. 83.

Suetonius said that Domitian began his letters, "Our Lord and God commands that it should be done. . . ." He had gold and silver images of himself erected throughout the empire to facilitate his worship. These were removed and melted down to be used for more useful purposes by his successor, Nerva. The Roman subjects were expected to offer a pinch of incense annually to one of these idols with the words, "Caesar is Lord." The population could worship other gods as well since the religion was polytheistic. However, worship of Domitian was required as a test of loyalty to the emperor. The Christians could respect and obey the emperor (Rom. 13:1-7) but they could not say, "Caesar is Lord." They had only one Lord, Jesus. Domitian saw their refusal as a personal affront to his deity and as a sign of disloyalty to the government. Many of the Christians were executed as a result of the exercise of their faith. This persecution was particularly severe in Asia Minor, the location of the seven churches of Revelation. The Church was about to be extinguished. The Church was holding onto life as if clinging by her fingernails to the end of a rope. Her situation was desperate. Only an act of God could save her.

The Revelation was given to John who had been exiled to Patmos, possibly to serve in the salt mines, and to the churches to give them encouragement and to tell them that ultimately Christ, not Caesar, would prevail.

The word "Almighty" (*pantokrator*) occurs only ten times in the New Testament, nine of these in Revelation. This name for God, therefore, is peculiar to the apocalypse. "The one who holds sway over all things"[3] will take action and give victory to His Church.

Since "Acts of the Apostles" is the title of the book describing the actions of the Twelve, "Acts of the Almighty" seems to be an appropriate title for the book that records the actions of the all-

---

3. Joseph Henry Thayer, *A Greek-English Lexicon of the New Testament* (New York: American Book Company, 1886), s.v. *pantokrator*.

powerful God.

Revelation is not the most common source for lessons about mission. So far as I know, no books have been written on this topic and only one chapter in one book.[4] Although little has been written about mission in Revelation, it is the climax of the work of mission. Consequently there are some important lessons about mission in the Apocalypse. I will try to bring them out.

The book begins, "The revelation of Jesus Christ" (Rev. 1:1). "Of Jesus Christ" is genitive and it has both the idea "from" and "about" Jesus.

It is written "to show what must soon take place" (Rev. 1:1). These words are critical to a correct understanding of Revelation. "To show" (deixai) is an aorist infinitive denoting its application at whatever time it is needed. "Must (dei) involves a moral necessitry. Jesus used dei when He said "he must go to Jerusalem . . . and that he must be killed" (Matt. 16:21). "Soon take place" (en takei) may also be translated "quickly," or "short-ly." This is also the word Paul chose when he wrote Timothy, "Do your best to come to me quickly" (II Tim. 4:9 emphasis mine). The Church, at least in Asia Minor, was about to be destroyed. They needed a message that would help them "now" not to be told about events hundreds, or thousands, of years in the future. Domitian was about to stamp out Christianity. If they did not get help immediately, there would be no Church. A message that would help them in their persecution would also help the Church in any future persecution and suffering. And if it would not be relevant to their current needs, it would likely not be helpful to the Church at any future time.

They needed a revelation from God which would say: "Christ is alive. He is in the midst of his people. We are going to see to it that

---

4. James C. Smith, who wrote that chapter, could find no books after extensive research. See James C. Smith, "Missions in Revelation: Research in Progress," *Unto the Uttermost*, ed. Doug Priest, Jr. (Pasadena: William Carey Library, 1984).

his cause triumphs over those who are trying to stamp it out. And he is going to do it *now*. Therefore, be comforted and hold your own." There was a moral necessity that these things be fulfilled "quickly." The need was an urgent one, and the message was one to meet this urgency.[5]

The Acts of the Almighty is not a calendar of future events, although the ultimate future, judgment and heaven, concludes the book. It is an account of what God is doing.

We must look briefly at the method of interpretation. The book itself gives the key. If we use the key that John has given us, the Acts of the Almighty will no longer be a "maze or a mystery but revelation."[6] In the very first verse John wrote, "The *revelation* of Jesus Christ, which God gave him to *show* his servant what must soon take place, He *made it known* by sending his angel to his servant John . . ." (emphasis mine). The three underlined verbs make it clear that Jesus intended to disclose, not hide, the message of the book. The third word "make known" (*semaino*) is sometimes translated "signified." However, the signs, or symbols, that are given are not to obscure but to enlighten the Christian reader. John even gives us an example in chapter one of a proper understanding of one of these pictures (Rev. 1:12-20). The colors, images, beasts, cities, etc. must all be taken symbolically. To interpret Revelation literally is a sure way to misunderstand it.

I. VICTORY

The soldier in the trenches will fight more aggresively, more courageously, if he is confident his army is winning. If defeat seems inevitable, he will be more inclined to retreat, surrender, to

---

5. Summers, p. 33.
6. Tom Friskney, *Strength for Victory* (Cincinnati: Tom Friskney, 1986), p. 205.

save his own skin. The missionary is on the front line where the enemy's territory is being invaded, the fighting fiercest, and casualties highest. Of all Christians he needs the confidence of being on the winning side. The Commander-in-Chief, in His revelation to His troops, gives assurance of victory in two ways: the defeat of the enemy, and the victory of the forces of righteousness.

Four themes are intertwined like a braided rope throughout Revelation. For our purposes I am going to attempt to separate them into individual strands.[7] Those individual ideas are: the Christian suffers in the present, God is in control, Satan will be defeated, Victory is assured.

1. The Christian Suffers in the Present.

There were many congregations in Asia Minor other than the seven addressed in Revelation chapters two and three. No doubt they were all suffering persecution, and these seven were a synecdoche for all of them. They suffered "wicked men" (Rev. 2:2), "hardships" (Rev. 2:3), "afflictions" (Rev. 2:9), "poverty" (Rev. 2:9), "slander" (Rev. 2:9), "prison" (Rev. 2:10), "persecution" (Rev. 2:10), "Satan" (Rev. 2:12), "martyrdom" (Rev. 2:13), "sexual immorality" (Rev. 2:21), "spiritual death" (Rev. 3:1), "lukewarmness" (Rev. 3:16), and "material riches" (Rev. 3:17).

The opening of the fifth seal shows "under the altar the souls of those who have been slain because of the word of God and the testimony they had maintained" (Rev. 6:9). The "altar" is a

---

7. A verse by verse exegesis needs to be done before attempting this exercise. Space forbids such a study in this book. The reader is referred to the following commentaries: Tom Friskney, *Strength for Victory* (Cincinnati: Tom Friskney, 1986); James Strauss, *The Seer, the Savior, and the Saved* (Joplin: College Press, 1973); Ray Summers, *Worthy Is the Lamb* (Nashville: Broadman Press, 1951); William Hendriksen, *More than Conquerors* (Grand Rapids: Baker Book House, 1939); Henry Barclay Swete, *The Apocalypse of St. John* (London: Macmillan and Co., Ltd., 1909); Albertus Piters, *Studies in the Revelation of St. John* (Grand Rapids: William B. Eerdmans Publishing Company, 1950).

metonymy for the benefits gained by the sacrifice of Jesus. Thus the altar is not a place, but the relation one has with God. Careful reading of the text suggests that these "souls" are not the disembodied spirits of martyrs. Rather *psyche* is the life principle and may refer to those, dead or living, who are opposed by "the inhabitants of the earth" (Rev. 6:10) who are the wicked men. "How long" (Rev. 6:10) before the Lord takes revenge? As in Matthew twenty-four Jesus does not provide a time table for future events but tells them how to handle the present situation.

The great dragon who is also the "ancient serpent," "the devil," and "Satan" (Rev. 12:8) pursues the "woman . . . the male child" (Rev. 12:13), "and the rest of her seed," (Rev. 12:17) all of whom represent the people of God. This persecution is to take place on earth. So long as Satan is loose on earth, and men are living there, conflict is inevitable.

The image changes to "a beast coming out of the sea" (Rev. 13:1). The purpose of the sea beast is clear. "He was given power to make war against the saints and to conquer them" (Rev. 13:7). His authority and power are limited because they are from the dragon (Rev. 13:4) and are temporary — for forty-two months (Rev. 13:5).

A third animal, the land beast, who resembles the Lamb because of his horns (Rev. 13:11), comes with the same purpose as the sea-beast — to persecute the people of God. In spite of the presence of the enemies and their apparent victories, God reigns.

2. God Is in Control.

Chapters four and five contain a vision of the throne, its Occupant, and its surroundings. This vision gives us a much clearer picture of the person, the position, and the power of God.

The church needs what is herein revealed, for it is vital to comprehend the Lord of history so that God's people will receive strength to face the future and be assured of victory. It is the touchstone of our faith. Trials and tribulation may take our eyes from the throne. It is too true that sometimes we are so involved with God's "footstool" that we do not see His throne. Christians are fortified for their tests by a clear vision of God on His throne and what it means to them.[8]

The same voice, one like a trumpet, that John first heard (Rev. 1:10) spoke (*laleo*) again (Rev. 4:1). Domitian may be seated on an earthly throne, but his rule is temporal. "The Lord God Almighty, who was, and is, and is to come" (Rev. 6:8) is the only One who is "worthy . . . to receive glory and honor and power" (Rev. 6:11). Domitian may demand worship from his Roman subjects, but he is not worthy of the praise thay are forced to give.

Also in the middle of the throne (a literal impossibility with the Almighty seated there, Rev. 5:6) is the One who is at the same time a Lion, a Root of David, and a Lamb (another physical impossibility, Rev. 5:5). He is "standing," indicating that although He had been slain He is very much alive. Thus He "overcame" (Rev. 5:5)[9] His trial and gives hope that the Christians will overcome and sit with Him on the throne (Rev. 3:21).

The Lamb made men "to be a kingdom and priests" (Rev. 5:10). These are not two different roles. Rather, this is a hen diadys which may be translated "kingdom of priests." This was the promise first made to Israel (Exod. 19.6) and has its an titypical fulfillment in the Church (I Pet. 2:5,9).

God is in control. He has four angels holding back the "four winds of the earth" (Rev. 7:1) which are the forces of evil which desire to destroy the people of God. And again, God sends "another strong angel" (Rev. 10:1) who with "his right foot on the sea and his left foot on the land" (Rev. 10:2) asserts his control over the entire world and shouts so that "the voices of the seven thunders spoke" (Rev. 10:3).

---

8. Friskney, p. 54.
9. The NIV clouds the meaning by translating *nikao* as "triumphed." It is accurate but does not allow the English reader to see this is the same verb translated "overcome" elsewhere in Revelation.

3. Satan will be defeated.

The announcement of the defeat of the forces of evil begins with the opening of the seals in chapter six. The first four disclose four horses, each of a different color. These, like the somewhat similar vision in Zecariah 6:1-8, are going forth to conquer the enemies of the people of God. The rider on the white horse "held a bow" (Rev. 6:2) which is a military weapon, a synecdoche for war. The white horse and the crown symbolize victory.[10] Together we are shown military conquest of Rome. The rider of the red horse has a great sword so as to make war. Famine is portrayed by the black horse and the balance in the rider's hand. Barley, the food of the poor, and wheat are selling at twelve times the normal prices reflecting the inflation that resulted from war.[11] Pale, the color of the fourth horse, "is used especially in reference to the grey, ashen color of a face bleached by fear.[12] And no wonder — the rider was named "Death" (Rev. 6:8). From the Old Testament we learn that death means pestilence.[13] Conquest, war, famine, pestilence — actions that are beyond the control of the Christians, or their enemies — were under the control of Him who sat on the throne of heaven and can, at will, be used to bring about the defeat of Satan and his cohorts.

The judgment meted out in the first four seals reaches its climax in the sixth. The disastrous effects of earthquakes are brought to the attention of the world with the earthquake in Armenia on December 7, 1988. Earthquakes were frequent in Asia Minor. In fact the one that hit Armenia also hit Turkey. The readers of Revelation would have understood the terrible destruction that was coming. The whole picture is that of final judgment

---

10. For the reasons that this seal should not be interpreted as Christ going forth to conquer, see Summers, Swete, et. al.

11. See the details in Swete.

12. Swete, p. 88.

13. See Ezek. 14:21; Lev. 26:23ff; Jer. 21:7; Ezek. 5:1,2-17; 24:5; 30:27; 34:28.

THE ACTS OF THE ALMIGHTY

upon those who dwell on earth, that is upon the wicked.

The seventh seal is opened to display seven angels, each with a trumpet. Trumpets are used to give orders to armies. What are they going to announce? When the seal is first opened "there was silence in heaven for about half an hour" (Rev. 8:1). Suspense builds. The first four trumpets announce natural calamities. Destruction is not complete as one-third earth, trees, sea, living creatures, ships, rivers, springs, waters, sun, moon, stars, day, and night were affected. Many people and all of the green grass died.

The fifth trumpet calls forth the locusts from within the earth. From this we get the idea of hellish rottenness coming from the heart of the earth, from the Abyss. "It symbolized the hellish rottenness, the internal decadence in the Roman Empire."[14]

In the beginning of chapter seven we see four angels standing at the four corners of the earth holding back the winds of destruction. The sixth trumpet allows us to hear the voice from the horns of the altar. This is no doubt the altar of incense since it is golden, which is a symbol of the prayers of the saints. Their petitions, seemingly unheard for a long time, are now going to be answered. The voice directs the angel with the trumpet to release the four angels who are at the extreme eastern boundary of the Empire so that the "mounted troops" can advance to "kill a third of mankind" (Rev. 9:15).

Christians have been persecuted in some locality by oppressive governments in every age. They can have the assurance that Jesus gave the Christian in Asia Minor: that God, in due time, will bring about the downfall of powerful enemy governments, as He destroyed Rome, through natural calamity, internal rottenness, external invasion, or such other methods He deems appropriate. No evil emperor, or empire, can thumb his nose at the eternal God and continue to get by with it.

---

14. Summers, p. 158.

341

One would think that men who escaped this devastation would see the hand of God in it all, repent, and turn to God. Unfortunately, it did not happen. It does not happen.

> The rest of mankind that were not killed by these plagues still did not repent of the work of their hands; they did not stop worshiping demons, and idols of gold, silver, bronze, stone and wood — idols that cannot see or hear or walk. Nor did they repent of their murders, their magic arts, their sexual immorality or their thefts (Rev. 9:20-21).

Either they do not see that God is on His throne and is behind it all, or they are unwilling to change. Either way, the Christian is aware that Satan is alive, although not well, and is working aggressively through his agents to destroy the Church.

John was given a reed to use as a measuring stick (Rev. 11:1). Although he was told to measure the temple, he was specifically told not to measure the "outer court . . . because it has been given to the nations" (Rev. 11:2).[15] Many from the nations (Matt. 28:19) have entered the temple, that is, have become the People of God. So "nations" is not to be taken literally but understood as "those who dwell on earth" that is, those who not only do not believe but are enemies of the Church. These enemies "will trample on the holy city for forty-two months" (Rev. 11:2). The length of time is not to be taken literally. The point is that the persecution will be limited in duration. The two witnesses are the two olive trees that provide oil for the lamps and at the same time are the two lampstands which give light. Whether known as witnesses, olive trees, or lampstands their purpose is to prophesy, to give light. The beast from the abyss attacks the witnesses and kills them. Their bodies are in the "great city" and "the inhabitants of the earth" gloat over them

---

15. The NIV translates *ethnesin* as Gentiles. Here again, while accurate, this translation may confuse the English reader.

342

(Rev. 11:10). Both represent the opposers of God's people and are set over against "the holy city" and "the two prophets." "The enemy is very real, just as his hurt is. Yet he is never really the power in control."[16] God gave them life "and terror struck those who saw them" (Rev. 11:11). And a great earthquake came and "a tenth part of the city collapsed. Seven thousand people were killed . . . and the survivors were terrified and gave glory to the God of heaven" (Rev. 11:13). The persecuted church is to take heart. The power of the gospel will prevail. Divine retribution will come. Many will embrace Christianity.

Chapter sixteen contains six of the seven bowls of God's wrath. There are similarities between the bowls of wrath and the plagues of Egypt. There are also parallels with the seven trumpets. But there are differences. The trumpets called for repentance. The bowls are poured out in judgment when it is too late to repent. The trumpets bring destruction to one-third of the objects, but the bowls touch the whole of the objects. Further, the trumpets do not touch man until the fifth trumpet; whereas, all of the bowls affect mankind. In effect the bowls are a repetition of the trumpets, but worse.

One item, because of popular misunderstanding, requires some attention. In the sixth bowl "they gathered the kings together to the place that in Hebrew is called Armageddon" (Rev. 16:16). As with the rest of Revelation Armageddon must be understood as a symbol and is not to be interpreted as a literal battle. Armageddon is the place where Gideon and a company of three hundred men defeated the Midianites. King Saul was defeated by the Philistines here. Barak and Deborah defeated the army of Jabin in this valley. Ahaziah died here after being wounded by Jehu. Here Pharaoh-Necho overthrew Josiah. Thus "Armageddon," the most famous battleground of Israel, becomes a by-word for a terrible battle. And in Revelation "Armageddon" becomes the symbol for the tremendous spiritual war between the

---

16. Friskney, p. 104.

forces of righteousness and evil. Armageddon is not some future physical war. Jesus rejects physical warfare as a strategy for His kingdom (John 18:36; Matt. 26:52-53). Further, a physical battle between the forces of righteousness and the forces of evil is antithetical to His purposes.

The seventh bowl is in chapters seventeen and eighteen and vividly portrays God's wrath being poured out on the great harlot who was drunk on the blood of the saints. Since the harlot, also known as Babylon, sits on the seven hills (Rev. 17:9) which are the seven kings (Rev. 17:10), she is commonly interpreted to represent Rome, the church's persecutor that was located on seven hills and had seven kings. Whether or not this is correct, the point is that Satan with all his forces are ultimately defeated.

> And the devil . . . was thrown into the lake of burning sulfur, where the beast and the false prophet have been thrown. They will be tormented day and night for ever and ever (Rev. 20:10).

4. Victory is assured.

Victory for the suffering saints is possible. One thing each of the letters to the seven churches has in common is a promise, "to him who overcomes." Swete wrote,

> the book is a record of and prophecy of victories won by Christ and the Church. The note of victory is dominant in St John, as that of faith in St Paul; or rather, faith presents itself to St John in the light of a victory (1 John 5:4).[17]

"The hands of the ascended Christ are full of gifts" (Eph. 4:7-13).[18] To the victorious Christians in Ephesus He promised "the right to eat from the tree of life which is in the paradise of God" (Rev. 2:7). To those from Smyrna He promised "some of

---

17. P. 29.
18. Ibid.

the hidden manna . . . (and) a white stone with a new name written on it" (Rev. 2:17). To those from Thyatira He promised "authority over the nations . . . (and) the morning star" (Rev. 2:26,28). The victors from Sardis "will be dressed in white. I will never blot out his name from the book of life, but will acknowledge his name before my Father and his angels" (Rev. 3:5-6). He said of the overcomer from Philadelphia "him . . . I will make a pillar in the temple of my God. Never again will he leave it. I will write on him the name of my God and the name of the city of my God . . . and . . . my new name" (Rev. 3:12-13). And of the overcomer from Laodicea (even a Laodicean Christian could overcome!) He promised, "I will give the right to sit with me on my throne" (Rev. 3:21).

The four angels at the four corners of the earth were holding back the destructive winds until the servants of God could be sealed (Rev. 7:1-4). A seal is a mark of ownership. And in contrast to the "mark of the beast" later, this seal shows the relation of the Christian to God who will provide protection to those who are His. The one hundred forty-four thousand out of Israel must not be taken literally. It is a symbol of the large number who constituted the People of God. The next verse repeats the idea but in contrasting words, "a great multitude that no one could count from every nation, tribe, people and language" (Rev. 7:9).

When the seventh angel sounded his trumpet,

> there were loud voices in heaven, which said: "The kingdom of the world has become the kingdom of our Lord and his Christ, and he will reign for ever and ever" (Rev. 11:15).

This, for me, is the single most important verse in Revelation. Victory is here already! It is incredible but true. The forces of evil are represented as "the kingdom of this world." Note the voices do not speak of the "kingdoms of this world." *Basileia* is singular. John is not writing about political powers although they are included. He is speaking of the underlying power of the "prince of this world" (John 14:30; 16:11; Eph. 2:2; 6:12). This deceiver is a usurper. Final victory cannot be achieved by overthrowing Rome, Berlin, or Moscow. The power behind the evil rulers must bow to the Lord (Phil. 2:10). This spiritual war has been a long one (Psa. 2; Acts 4:26; Eph. 6:12). "Has become" (egeneto) is aorist indicative, indicating that this has already occurred in a single action in the past. The reign of the usurper (Matt. 4:8-9) has now passed into the hands of the true "ruler of the kings of the earth" (Rev. 1:5). "And he will reign for ever and for ever" (Dan. 2:44; 7:14,28). But how do evil men still rule and persecute the Church if the kingdom of this world has been defeated?

A few years ago I read through Winston Churchill's six massive volumes, *The Second World War*. The first two volumes were most depressing. Hitler had overrun Rhineland, Austria, Sudetenland, Bohemia, Moravia, and Czechoslovakia. The Nazis wre joined by Italy who invaded Albania and Greece. Poland and France succumbed. Norway came under the control of Hitler. Most of North Africa was lost. Yugoslavia was pummelled into submission. The German Navy dominated the Atlantic and the Mediterranean. The German Air Force controlled the air. Russia stood by oblivious of any but her own interests and the United States seemed by its cumbersome democracy to be muscle bound into inaction. Only England and the people of the British Commonwealth were resisting Hitler's apparently irresistible juggernaut.

The Japanese bombed Pearl Harbor and overran everything touching the South China Sea, the Philippines, New Guinea, Borneo, Sumatra, Singapore, and French Indochina. They had the mastery of the Pacific Ocean, and were threatening Australia, New Zealand and India.

I lived through World War II as a school boy. I knew the outcome before I read Churchill's account but it still was depressing to read. Only sheer determination kept me going through the first two tomes.

Then the Battle of Alamein in North Africa was fought. Before that the Allies had lost virtually every battle. After that the Allies were the victors in virtually every battle. Churchill called that battle, "The Hinge of Fate" because the outcome of World War II turned on that battle. The reading of the last three volumes was interesting and exciting because the Allies were winning!

Christians are Allies in a far more significant war — the war between the prince of the earth and the King of Kings. The Allies are definitely in the minority as far as numbers of people are concerned. There are times the tide seems to be turning against us. Some of us may even be in doubt as to the ultimate outcome. You may find it depressing to be slugging it out alone in a tiny church in a great metropolis. But the decisive battle — the battle of the cross and the tomb — has been fought. It is not the Hinge of Fate but the Hinge of History. Although that battle was fought two thousand years ago, and skirmishes continue, the war is over.

> Revelation is a series of apocalyptic images given for the assurance of the people of God that Christ is going to be victorious over all opposition. For the Christians of John's day the assurance was given by showing the victory of Christ over the system of emperor worship because that was the greatest enemy of Christ in that day. The same assurance is given to Christians in every age. Find the greatest enemy of Christ (whether corrupt religion, godless government, social anarchy, or any other) put it in the place of emperor worship, and see its eventual failure as the living Christ, the redeeming Lamb, marches to victory over chaotic world conditions.[19]

The kingdom of Christ has both come and is coming.[20] It is here now in the form of the church, it is in the future as heaven,

---

19. Summers, p. 205.
20. See C.H. Dodd on "realized eschatology" in "Appendix: Eschatology and History," *The Apostolic Preaching and its Developments* (London: Hodder & Stoughton, 1936).

The Acts of the Almighty moves from the first earth to the new heaven and new earth (Rev. 19,21,22) and we are allowed to see the eternal home for those who overcome. This hope, more than any other motive, keeps the persecuted Christians faithful, knowing that death is not the end.

II. GOD THE CREATOR

The four living creatures and the twenty-four elders worship God saying,

"you created all things, and by your will they were created and have their being" (Rev. 4:11).

However, the NIV does not follow the word order of the original. Perhaps this is to be expected since the order of the Greek words is surprising in that *esen* is placed before *ektisthesan*: "*kai dia to thelema sou esan kai ektisthesan*," "and through your will they are, and were created." Paul used a more natural order, "in him we live and move and have our being" (Acts 17:28), an order adopted by the translators of the NIV. Swete suggested that the order of John

makes good sense. It places the potential existence of the universe before its creation. The divine will had made the universe a fact in the scheme of things before the Divine Power gave material expression to the fact.[21]

John leaves unanswered the question, "Why did God create the universe? And, especially, why did He create man?" Paul gave the answer in his sermon at Athens: "God did this so that men would seek him and perhaps reach out for him and find him, though he is not far from each one of us'"(Acts 17:27). The very

---

21. P. 75.

purpose of creation was evangelism — to bring men into the relation with God that they would praise Him. Inherently this evangelism was cross-cultural for in the preceding sentence Paul said ,"[f]rom one man he made every nation of men, that they should inhabit the whole earth; and he determined the times set for them and the exact places where they should live" (Acts 17:26). The Creator God is a Missionary God!

Domitian, who commanded worship of himself, was not worthy of it. He had created nothing. The Lord God Almighty, however, deserves praise because of what He has created. And mankind, seeing this creative power, voluntarily worship Him.

III. THE REDEEMING LAMB

The Creator who made man to be His worshipper also planned from the beginning that the Lamb of God would make man's redemption possible, for "the Lamb . . . was slain from the creation of the world" (Rev. 13:8). An explanation is found in a similar word order in I Peter 1:20: "He was chosen before the creation of the world, but was revealed in these last times for your sake."

The purpose of the Lamb was sung by the four living creatures and the twenty-four elders,

you were slain, and with your blood you purchased men for God from every tribe and language and people and nation (Rev. 5:9).

Three lessons are quickly noted in this verse. One, men were purchased *for God*. The purpose of Christ's sacrifice was to redeem mankind so they could serve Him as a kingdom of priests (Rev. 5:10), by worshipping Him (Rev. 5:13), and by reigning on earth (Rev. 5:10). Two, this redemption was accomplished through the blood of Christ. Three, all men are to be included. Redemption is unlimited in scope.

The death of Christ, then, is the heart of mission, the basis of mission, and the motivation for mission.

IV. ALL MEN

Four words, "tribe, language, people, and nation" define the people who are objects of redemption. These four words occur six times in Revelation but in a different order each time (Rev. 5:9; 7:9; 10:11; 11:9; 13:7; 17:15).

"Tribe" (*phule*) originally meant a group of people bound together by blood relationship or common descent. It is used in this sense frequently of the twelve tribes of Israel. It can also mean a subdivision of a people.

"Tongue" (*glossa*) refers to the tongue, the organ of speech. From that it means the language of a people in distinction from the language of another people.

"People" (laos) are all the people of the same stock and language.

"Nation" (*ethnos*) is a multitude living together, a race, a nation, Gentiles (as opposed to Jews).

These are four terms saying the same thing in different ways. That is, each term embraces the whole of humanity but viewed as divided in different ways. To make sure we do not miss the point the terms are prefaced by *every*. Even though John uses the singular "every," the reader thinks plural by synecdoche. The kingdom of God is to be universal embracing every person who will accept its conditions.

Jesus died for "men . . . from every tribe and language and people and nation" (Rev. 5:9). A great multitude in white robes and holding palm branches "from every nation, tribe, people and language" shouted praises to God (Rev. 7:9-10). John was given the repsonsibility to prophesy "about many peoples, nations, languages and kings" (Rev. 10:11, *basileus* is substituted for *phule*). "Men from every people, tribe, language and nation"

350

(Rev. 11:9) will gaze on the bodies of those killed in the persecution. The beast was given authority over "every tribe, people, language and nation" (Rev. 13:7). Where the prostitute sits, there are "peoples, multitudes, nations, and languages" (Rev. 17:15 *ochloi* is substituted for *phule*).

The responsibility of the Christian pictured in Revelation remains the same as in the Great Commission — "make disciples of every nation."

SUMMARY

Revelation, the neglected book, has not neglected the purpose of the Church — mission. The Church may be persecuted but she still has the supreme purpose to evangelize the world. The most important lesson, and the one that occupies the most space, is victory. The Christian, although threatened with death, can have confidence that he is victorious because God is in control, Satan will be defeated, and Christ is Victor.

God, the Creator, created man in order that he could serve God. This fact requires the Church to be missionary and invite men into this service.

Jesus, as the Lamb of God, died to redeem men from their sins and to make them a kingdom of priests. His faithful servants have an abiding relationship with Him to provide what they *need* as long as they "keep the Word of God and the testimony of Jesus."

Men from every tribe, language, people, and nation   in short , every person is to have the opportunity to live for God on this earth and to live with God in His eternal home.

The Spirit and the bride say, "Come!" And let him who hears say, "Come!" Whoever is thirsty, let him come; and whoever wishes, let him take the free gift of the water of life (Rev. 22:17).

CONCLUSION

We have now learned that mission is a major theme of the Bible. Mission, we have seen, runs from the first verse to the last chapter. And it is found, in some form, in most of the books between Genesis and Revelation.

The Old Testament which, for many Christians, has been viewed as irrelevent to Christian mission, now has been demonstrated to have an important place in the historical development of mission.

Out of the mass of biblical data that we have examined, can the many facts and concepts be reduced to a single word or idea? At the risk of oversimplification, I say, "yes." That word is purpose.

The purpose of God both before the creation of the world and in the development of salvation history is to bring all men into fellowship with Him.

The purpose of God for the patriarchs was to provide a people through whom the Messiah would come, to provide a people who would be the evangelists of the good news, and to provide a people who would be a bridge to the nations.

The purpose of God for the nation of Israel was to be a kingdom of priests who would serve as intermediaries between God and the Gentiles. They were a vehicle for God's revelation, people to propagate God's message, and a nation through whom the Messiah would come.

The purpose of God in the kingdom of Israel was to possess the promised land, which was strategically located for the launching of the world-wide kingdom of Christ.

Throughout this period the psalmists and prophets made it clear that God's purpose was universal in scope. That is, people of all nations were to be included in the new Reign of God.

The purpose of Jesus was to "seek and save what was lost." His birth, life, teaching, death, resurrection, and ascension were all focused on the singular purpose of the redemption of mankind.

The purpose of the Church is a continuation of the purpose of Jesus. The Church is to grow numerically, geographically, and culturally until ultimately "the kingdom of the world has become the kingdom of our Lord and his Christ."

In spite of opposition and persecution the purpose remains constant and victory shall be ultimately achieved.

The purpose is mission. The purpose is the sending across cultural barriers by Christ through the church of evangelists whose primary function is to make disciples of Jesus Christ by proclaiming the good news about Jesus. They require faith in Jesus as Lord, changed lives, and baptism of penitent disciples. The disciples receive the promise of forgiveness of sin and entrance into the eternal kingdom. These disciples are to be taught the principle of the kingdom and, in turn, are to become evangelists, making other disciples.

The book of Acts, the major source of our mission lessons, ends with an interesting sentence. Paul had met with the leaders of the Jewish community in Rome on two occasions. He used his most persuasive arguments from the Law of Moses and the Prophets in order to convince them of the claims of Jesus. Although some believed, Paul was convinced that Isaiah was correct,

For this people's heart has become calloused; they hardly hear with their ears, and they have closed their eyes (Acts 28:27).

So he announced "God's salvation has been sent to the Gentiles" (Acts 18:28). And he added, *"they will listen"* (Acts 28:28 emphasis mine).

This is also true today. There are millions of unreached people *who will listen* if we will just tell them the message!

We have examined what the Bible says about missions. What we need now is the *practice* of missions. "Go and make disciples of all the nations. . . ."

Bibliography

ACMC, *The Local Church Can Change the World*, Pasadena: Association of Church Missions Committee, 1977.

Anderson, Gerald H., ed. *The Theology of Christian Mission*, New York: McGraw Hill, 1961.

Barclay, William, *And Jesus Said: A Handbook on the Parables of Jesus*, Philadelphia: The Westminster Press, 1970

_____, *The Letters to the Corinthians*, Edinburgh: The Saint Andrew Press 1945.

Bavinck, J. H., *An Introduction to the Science of Missions*, Grand Rapids: Baker Book House, 1960.

Beasley-Murray, G.R., *Jesus and the Kingdom of God*, Grand Rapids: William B. Eerdmans Publishing Company, 1986.

Blauw, Johannes, "The Biblical View of Man in His Religion." In *The Theology of Christian Mission*, Edited by Gerald Anderson, New York: McGraw-Hill Book Company, Inc., 1961

Boer, Martin, *Pentecost and Mission*, Grand Rapids: Wm. B. Eerdmans Publishing Co., 1981.

Bright, John, *A History of Israel*, Philadelphia: The Westminster Press, 1959.

Butler, Paul, ed., *Best Sermons*, New York: Trident Press, 1968.

Butterick, George Arthur, ed., *The Interpreter's Dictionary of the Bible*, 4 vols, New York: Abingdon Press, 1962.

Covell, Ralph, "God at Work in China." *Trinity World Forum*, Spring 1988, p.1.

Cullman, Oscar, *Baptism in the New Testament*, Translation by J. K. S. Reid, Chicago: Alec R. Allenson, Inc., 1950.

DeRidder, Richard R., *The Disperson of the People of God*, Kampen: J. H. Kok, Co., 1971.

DeWelt, Don, *Paul's Letters to Timothy and Titus*, Joplin: College Press, 1961.

Dodd, C.H., *The Apostolic Preaching and its Development*, London: Hodder & Stoughton, 1936.

Donovan, Vincent J., *Christianity Rediscovered*, Maryknoll: Orbis Books, 1978.

Douglas, J.D., ed., *Let the Earth Hear His Voice*, Minneapolis: World Wide Publications, 1975.

Edersheim, Alfred, *The Life and Times of Jesus the Messiah*, 2 vols. Grand Rapids: William B. Eerdmans Publishing Company, 1947.

Friskney, Tom, *Solving Church Problems*, Cincinnati: Tom Friskney, 1987.

_____, *Strength for Victory*, Cincinnati: Tom Friskney, 1987.

Fu, Charlene L., "Christian Churches in China overflow with worshippers." *The Indianapolis Star*, January 24, 1988, p.G-3.

Gerber, Virgil, *God's Way to Keep a Church Going and Growing*, Glendale, California: Regal Books, 1973.

Getter, Bernel, and Getter, Joan, "Resurrection Failure," *The Evangel*, July 1988, p. 3.

Glasser, Arthur F., *Theology of Mission I*, Pasadena: Fuller Theological

Seminar, n.d.

Glasser, Arthur F., and McGavran, Donald A., *Contemporary Theologies of Mission*, Grand Rapids: Baker Book House, 1983.

Gilliland, Dean S., *Pauline Theology & Mission Practice* Grand Rapids: Baker Book House, 1983.

Glover, Robert Hall, *The Bible Basis of Missions*, Chicago: Moody Press, 1946.

Grosheide, F.W., *Commentary on the First Epistle to the Corinthians*, Grand Rapids: Wm. B. Eerdmans Publishing Company, 1953.

Haenchen, Ernst, *Acts of the Apostles: A Commentary*, Philadelphia: The Westminster Press, 1971

Hahn, Ferdinand, *Mission in the New Testament*, Naperville: Alec R. Allenson, Inc., 1965.

Harris, R. Laird, ed., *Theological Wordbook of the Old Testament*, 2 vols. Chicago: Moody Press, 1980.

Hastings, James, ed., *A Dictionary of the Bible*, 5 vols. Edinburgh: T. & T. Clark, 1902.

Hendriksen, William, *More Than Conquerors*, Grand Rapids: Baker Book House, 1939.

_____, *New Testament Commentary: Exposition of the Gospel According to Luke*, Grand Rapids: Baker Book House, 1978.

_____, *New Testament Commentary: Exposition of the Gospel According to Matthew*, Grand Rapids: Baker Book House, 1973.

_____, *New Testament Commentary: Exposition of Paul's Epistle to the Romans*, Grand Rapids: Baker Book House, 1981.

_____, *New Testament Commentary: Exposition of the Pastoral Epistles*, Grand Rapids: Baker Book House, 1957.

Hesselgrave, David S., *Theology and Mission*, Grand Rapids: Baker, 1978.

Hoven, Victor E., *Shadow and Substance*, St. Louis: The Bethany Press, 1934.

Howe, Allen H., "The Church: Its Growth and Mission", In *The Challenge of Church Growth*, Edited by Wilbert R. Shrenk, Scottdale, Pennsylvania: Herald Press, 1973.

Hughes, Philip Edgcumbe, *Paul's Second Epistle to the Corinthians*, Grand Rapids: Wm. B. Eerdmans Publishing Co., 1962.

Kane, J. Herbert, *Christian Missions in Biblical Perspective*, Grand Rapids: Baker Book House, 1976.

_____, *A Global View of Christian Missions from Pentecost to the Present*, Grand Rapids: Baker Book House, 1975.

Keil, and Delitzsch, *Old Testament Commentaries*, 6 vols., Grand Rapids: Associated Publishers and Authors, n.d.

Kelley, Dean M., *Why Conservative Churches are Growing*, New York, Harper and Row, 1972.

Kittel, Gerhard, gen. ed., *Theological Dictionary of the New Testament*, 8 vols. Translation by Geoffrey W. Bromiley, Grand Rapids: Wm. B. Eerdmans Publishing Co., 1964.

Kraybill, Donald B., *The Upside-Down Kingdom*, Scottdale, Pennsylvania:

Herald Press, 1978.

Lapierre, Dominique, *The City of Joy*, Translated by Kathryn Spink, New York: Warner Books, 1985.

Leupold, H.C., *Exposition of Genesis*, Grand Rapids: Baker Book House, 1950.

Lindsell, Harold, *An Evangelical Theology of Missions*, Grand Rapids: Zondervan Publishing House, 1970.

Lingenfelter, Sherwood G., and Mayers, Marvin., *Ministering Cross-Culturally: An Incarnational Model for Personal Relationships*, Grand Rapids: Baker Book House, 1986.

The Local Church Can Change the World., Pasadena: Association of Church Missions Committees, 1977.

Lockyer, Herbert, *All the Parables of the Bible*, Grand Rapids: Zondervan Publishing House, 1963.

Luther, Martin, *Luther's Works*, ed. Hilton C. Oswald, Vol. 25: *Lectures on Romans*, St. Louis: Concordia Publishing House, 1972.

McCracken, Robert, "The Human Touch", In *Best Sermons, 1968*, Edited by G. Paul Butler, New York: Trident Press, 1968.

McGavran, Donald A., *Bridges of God*, New York: Friendship Press, 1955.

_____, *Understanding Church Growth*, Grand Rapids: William B. Eerdmans Co., 1970.

_____, *Understanding Church Growth*, Revised edition, Grand Rapids: William B. Eerdmans Publishing Company, 1980.

McNeely, Charles A., "The Myth of Paul's Missionary Journeys: The urban center of Paul's missionary activity," *One Body*, Spring 1988, p.5.

Marshall, I. Howard, *The Acts of the Apostles: An Introduction and Commentary*, Grand Rapids: William B. Eerdmans' Publishing Company, 1980.

Maxey, Mark, *Preaching the Gospel in Resistant Fields*, San Jose, California: Osaka Bible Seminary, n.d.

Messenger, John C., Jr., "The Christian Concept of Forgiveness and Anang Morality", In *Reading in Missionary Anthropology*, Edited by William A. Smalley, Pasadena: William Carey Library, 1974.

Morgan, G. Campbell, *The Great Physician*, London: Marshall, Morgan and Scott, 1937.

_____, *The Parables of the Kingdom*, London: Hodder and Stoughton, 1907.

Moulton, James Hope, and Milligan, George, *The Vocabulary of the Greek New Testament*, London: Hodder and Stoughton, Limited, 1930.

Naisbitt, John, *Megatrends*, New York: Warner Books, 1982.

Newbigin, Leslie, *Sin and Salvation*, Naperville: SCM Book Club, 1956.

Nida, Eugene A., *Customs and Cultures*, New York: Harper and Brothers, 1954.

Niles, D.T., *Studies in Genesis*, Philadelphia: The Westminster Press, 1958.

Olson, Bruce E., *Bruchko*, Carol Stream: Creation House, 1973.

Pentecost, Edward C., *Issues in Missiology: An Introduction*, Grand Rapids:

Baker Book House, 1982.

Peters, George W., *A Biblical Theology of Missions*, Chicago: Moody Press, 1972.

————, *A Theology of Church Growth*, Grand Rapids: Zondervan,1981.

Pieters, Albertus, *Studies in the Revelation of St. John*, Grand Rapids: William B. Eerdmans Publishing Company, 1950.

Pusey, E.B., *The Minor Prophets*, New York: Funk & Wagnalls, Publishers, 1885.

Rackham, Belward Richard, *The Acts of the Apostles*, London: Methuen & Co, Ltd., 1947.

Ravenhill, Leonard, *Why Revival Tarries*, Minneapolis: Bethany Fellowship, 1961.

Reeves, Robert, *Faith Promise for Church Growth*, Cincinnati: Standard Publishing, 1972.

Richardson, Alan, *A Theological Wordbook of the Bible*, New York: The Macmillan Company, 1955.

Robinson, William, *The Devil and God*, New York: Abingdon-Cokesbury Press, 1945.

Rowley, H.H., *The Missionary Message of the Old Testament*, London: The Carey Press, n.d.

Senior, Donald, and Stuhlmueller, Carroll, The Biblical Foundations for Mission, Maryknoll: Orbis Books, 1983.

Shenk, Wilbert R., *The Challenge of Church Growth*,Scottsdale, Pennsylvania: Harold Press, 1973.

Simkins, Cyril, *Salvation in the Early Church*, Lincoln, Il: Lincoln Christian College, 1979.

Smalley, William A.,*Readings in Missionary Anthropology*, Pasadena: William Carey Library, 1974.

Smith, James C., "Missions in Revelation: Research in Progress", In *Unto the Uttermost*, Edited by Doug Priest, Jr., Pasadena: William Carey Library, 1984.

Smith, Mont W., *What the Bible Says about Covenant*, Joplin: College Press, 1981.

Snowden, James, It., *The Coming of the Lord*, New York: The Macmillan Company, 1919.

Spurgeon, C.H., *The Treasury of David*, 5 vols., Byron Center: Associated Publishers and Authors, Inc., 1970.

Stott, John R.W., *Christian Mission in the Modern World*, Downers Grove: Intervarsity Press, 1975.

Strauss, James, *The Seer, the Savior, and the Saved*, Joplin: College Press, 1973.

Summers, Ray, *Worthy is the Lamb*, Nashville: Broadman Press, 1951.

Sweet, Henry Barclay, *The Apocalypse of St. John*, London: Macmillan and Co., Ltd., 1909.

————, *The Parables of the Kingdom*, London: Macmillan and Co., Limited

1921.

Taylor, William M., *The Parables of the Savior*, New York: A.C. Armstrong & Sons, 1886.

Thayer Jospeh Henry, *A Greek-English Lexicon of the New Testament*, New York: American Book Company, 1886

Thielicke, Helmut, *How the World Began*, Translated by John W. Doberstein, Philadelphia: Muhlenberg Press, 1961.

_____, *The Waiting Father: Sermons on the Parables of Jesus*, Translated by John W. Doberstein, New York: Harper & Brothers, 1959.

Tippet, Alan R., *Introduction to Missiology*, Pasadena: William Carey Library, 1987.

Tippett, Alan R., *Solomon Islands Christianity*, Pasadena: William Carey Library, 1967.

Trench, Richard Chenevix, *Notes on the Parables of Our Lord*, New York: N. Tibbals & Sons, 1879.

Verkyl, Johannes, *Contemporary Missiology*, Grand Rapids: William B. Eerdmans Publishing Co., 1978.

Wagner, C. Peter, *Your Church Can Grow*, Glendale, California: Regal Books, 1976.

White, Paul, *Jungle Doctor*, London: The Paternoster Press, 1942.

Winter, Ralph D., "The Highest Priority: Cross-Cultural Evangelism", In *Let the Earth Hear His Voice*, Edited by J.D. Douglas, Minneapolis: World Wide Publications, 1975.

_____, *The 25 Unbelievable Years, 1945-1969*, South Pasadena: William Carey Library, 1970.

Rad, Gerhard, *Old Testament Theology*, 2 vols., New York: Harper and Row, 1956.

Yoder, John H., "Church Growth Issues in Theological Perspective", In *The Challenge of Church Growth*, Edited by Wilbert R. Shenk, Scottsdale, Pennsylvania: Herald Press, 1973.

361

Index of Scriptures

Old Testament
Genesis

1:1	54
1:7	64
1:26	56
1:26,27	59
1:28	60,61
1-11	53-76
2:8	59
2:15	59
2:16,17	65
2:20	64
2:18	65
2:18-25	59
2:25	65
3	66
3:3	67
3:6	65,331
3:8,9	56
3:10	68
3:15	54,58,71
3:16	68
3:17	64
3:19,20	68
3:20	64
3:22	56
3:23	57
3:23,24	69
4:1	64
4:2-5	67
4:11	57
4:13	35
4:13,14	66
5:1	64
5:2	64
5:3-5	64
6:3	68,178
6:4	57
6:5	69
6:7	57
6:11	57
6:14	71
7:24	71
8:20,21	72
9	73

Genesis

9:8	73
9:11	73
9:27	73
10	78
10:5	90
10:20	90
10:31	90
11:4	74
11:7	66
12	77
12:1	78
12:1-3	54,109,114,120,316
12:2	90
12:3	80,184
12:15	120
17:4-6	90
17:16	90
17:20	90
18:16-33	92
21:8	90
21:11-13	84
26:1-6	84
27:29	84
27:42	14
28:3,4	84
28:13,14	142
31:4	14
40:10	85
41:8	14
41:43	27
44:33	297
49:9-12	85

Exodus

2:24	110
3:14	91
4:10	26
6:2,3	91
12	100
12:43	108
12:48	108
19:4-6	88
19:6	116,339
20:30	92

Exodus

24:13	18
25:1-7	105
25:8-55	105
25:15	32
25:22	32
29:26-28	99
30:10	99
30:38ff	99
31:18	32
32:5	27
32:15	32
32:23	95
32:32	35,297
33:3	95
33:11	18
33:13	43,90
33:14	95
33:16	95
34:15,16	108
36:6	27

Leviticus

4:1-5:13	99
4:20	35
5:10	35
5:13	35
5:14-6:7	99
7:15ff	136
11:32	38
14:8	109
16	99
17:11	72,99
23:26-32	99
24:10	108
25:9	99

Numbers

3-4	103
6:13-20	99
8:7	109
10:29-32	108
11:28	18
11:29	177

Numbers

14:19	35
15:25	36
20:1-13	106
27:15-23	19
28:1-8	99
29:7-11	99

Deuteronomy

4:12	93
4:32	93
4:38	90
6:4	92
7:6	43,88
13:5	89
14:2	88
15:1-18	105
17:14-20	116
21:10-14	109
23:1	250
26:5	79
31:19	40
31:22	40
32:6	93
32:11	88
32:18	94
32:21	96
32:43	151

Joshua

1:2	98
2	108
2:21	90
2:23	90
5:14-6:27	108
12:17	108
12:24	108
14:13ff	108
15:13	108
15:16-19	108
17	108
23:13	90

Judges

1:1-21	120

364

Judges

1:10-20	108
1:11-15	108
1:16	108
2:23	90
4:11	108
5:15-17	106
5:23	106
8:22-24	115
12:1-6	107
17:6	115
18:1	115
19-20	107
19:1	115
21:25	115

I Samuel

4:7	101
4:6,7	102
8:6-9	115
8:7	115
8:10-17	118
9:2	117
10:1ff	117,133
10:17-19	115
11:6	117
11:14	117
12:12-17	115
14:47,48	118
14:50	118
14:52	118
15:6	108
16:13	119
22:6	118
27:10	120
30:14	120

II Samuel

2:1-4	119
2:8-10	119
4:10	22
5:1-4	118
5:2	119
5:6-10	120

II Samuel

5:11	165
5:17-25	120
6:2	101
6:17	157
7:11-16	121,165
8:1	120
8:12	120
11:11	157
12:31	122
18:20	22
18:22	22
18:25	22
18:27	22
18:33	297
22:38-51	124
22:50	125
23:13-17	120

I Kings

1:28-52	121
1:39	157
5:13-18	123
8:41-43	123
8:59,60	124
9:4-7	117
9:26 28	121
10:1ff	121
10:15	121
10:22	121
10:26-29	122
14:6	15
18	160
20:20	14

II Kings

1:42	22
2:1-13	121
6:18	90
7:9	22
5:14	38
6:1ff	19
17:7-23	167

II Kings
22:1-23:30 168
22:35 40

I Chronicles
14:17 120
34:1-35:19 168

II Chronicles
4:29 27
20:3 27
24:2 188
28:9 140
36:22 27

Ezra
4:14 14
5:17 14

Nehemiah
2:5 14

Esther
6:9 27
6:11 27

Psalms
2 129,346
2:1,2 131,132
2:4-6 132
2:7 132
2:7-9 133
2:10-12 133
3:8 130
5:5 57
9:7-8 153
9:19,20 154
22 129,136
22:25,26 136
22:27,28 137
22:29 137
22:30 138
22:31 138
24 129,148,155
24:1,2 54,156

Psalms
24:3 156
24:4 156
24:3,4 55
24:5,6 155
24:7-10 157
24:18 35
27 133
31:5 35
33 129
33:1 129
33:9-15 130
33:15 131
33:18 131
47 129,140,143
47:1 141
47:3 141
47:4 142
47:5,6 143
47:7 143
47:8,9 144
50 129,153
50:1 153
50:4,5 154
51:7 38
66 129,144
66:1,2 144
66:3 144
66:4 145
66:5,6 145
67 129,140
67:1 138
67:2 139
67:3-5 139
67:6,7 140
68 157
72 129
72:8 135
72:9a 135
72:9b 135
72:10,11 135
72:12-14 135
72:16 134
73:12 139

Psalms

86:9	109
93:10	40
96	129,145,152
96:1,2	146
96:3	146
96:4,5	147
96:6	148
96:7-9	148
96:10	148,153
96:11,12	149
96:13	149,153
97	129,152
97:1-3	152
97:4-7	152
97:8	153
98	129,145,149,152
98:1	149
98:2	149,185
98:3	150
98:9	153
117	129,151
117:1,2	151
145	129,155
145:5,6	155
145:8,9	155
146	129
146:7	134
146:7c-9	134

Ecclesiastes

11:4	213

Isaiah

1:15ff	38
2:1-4	167,168
4:4	38
11:1-11	167
11:3	139
11:9	173
11:10	109
22:14	36
25:1-9	167
25:6	137

Isaiah

25:20	224
40:3-5	185
40:5	22
40:9	22
41:1	174,186
41:8,9	166
42:1	39,109
42:1-9	166
42:6	109,167
42:19	166,167
43:9-13	31
43:10	166,167
43:12	167
44:1,2	166
44:7-11	31
44:8	167
44:21	166
44:26	166,167
45:4	166
45:23-25	22
48:20	166
49:1	22
49:3	166
49:6	43,166,167
50:10	166
51:4	22
52:10	185
52:13-53:12	167
55:7	36
55:11	257
60:6	22
61:1	27
61:11	90
62:2	167,287

Jeremiah

1:6	26
2:22	38
4:14	38
10:25	44
20:15	22

Ezekiel

17:23	219

Ezekiel
31:6 219
36:25 38

Daniel
1 176
2-12 176
2:31 174
2:44 174,346
4:12 219
5:9 .27
5:18-24 109
7:14 176,346
7:24 176
7:28 346

Joel
2:1 .27
2:28-32 177
3:6 198

Amos
1:9 198
2:9-11 164
3:1 164
3:2 164
9:10 164
9:11 165
9:12 165

Jonah
1:2 .27
3:2 .27
3:4 169
3:5 .27
3:6-9 170
3:10 170

Micah
4:1-5 168

Nahum
1:1 171
1:13-15 171
3:19 172

Habakkuk
1:4 172
1:5,6 172
2:4 173
2:5-14 173
2:8 173
2:14 173
2:20 174

Zephaniah
1:1 168
1:1-3 168
1:18 168
2:1-3 168
2:11 168
3:4 168
3:9,10 169
3:14 27
4:6 133
6:1-8 340
9:9 .27
12:3 90
13:1 38

New Testament
Matthew
1:15 198
2:1-12 185
2:12 287
2:13-18 197
2:22 287
3:2 .34
3:6 .35
3:7-10 34
3:11 35,186
3:15 38,186
3:17 39,132
4:1-11 188
4:2,3 188
4:4 193
4:8 .45
4:8,9 346
4:14 198
4:15 197

Matthew

4:17 34
4:18-20 194
4:23-25 237
5-7 198
5:14 46,193
5:26 199
6:7 199
6:12 36
6:14ff 36
6:24 193
6:23 44,199
6:33 330
8:5 198
8:5-13 199
8:11 73,185
8:28-34 199
9:1 198
9:11 205
9:12-22 236
9:13 183
9:16 318
9:29 235
9:34 205
9:36 240
9:38 290,331
10:1,2 16
10:5,6 198
10:7 30
10:14 249
10:16 322
10:27 29
11:3 202
11:5 23
11:20-24 198,205
11:23 198
11:28ff 192
12:2 205
12:14 205
12:46 171
13:1-9 207-213
13:3-9 249
13:11 205,207
13:12 206

Matthew

13:14,15 206
13:16 207
13:17 207
13:18 207
13:18-23 207-213
13:19 209,211
13:20 209
13:21-23 211
13:22 209
13:23 209
13:31-35 214-223
13:33 217
13:38 46
13:52 17
15:21-28 199
15:24 199
15:29-31 199
15:63 32
16:15 30
16:16 259
16:18 175,203
16:21 202,335
16:22 202
18:3 34
18:11-14 249
18:17 46,199
18:18 16
18:21-34 36
20:23 316
20:28 202
20:38 185
21:33-45 226
21:43 193,226
22:1-14 225
22:14 148
24:9 44
24:14 29,44,135,196,199,
200,203,215
25:31-46 229
25:32 44
25:41 232
25:43 232
26:13 199

Matthew

26:18 36
26:52,53 344
27:57 17
28:5-8 201
28:18-20 110,264
28:19 17,37,44,286,342
28:19,20 54
28:20 40,43

Mark

1:4 34,35
1:11 38
1:12,13 188
1:15 34
1:16 198
1:23 198
1:28 200
1:31 198
1:34 198
1:35 242
1:38 28
1:40-45 231-243,233
1:43,44 238
1:44 240
2:5ff 36
2:13ff 20
2:13-15 194
2:27 193
3:7 200
3:14,15 30
4:1-9 207-213
4:30-32 214-223
5:1-29 199
5:22 198
5:28 236
5:35 236
6:12 29
6:30-44 189
6:34 189
6:56 236
7:22 199
7:24-30 199
7:27 199
7:31-37 199

Mark

8:1-13 189
8:2 189
8:37 193
10:38 187
10:42 199
10:45 182,201
10:52 236
11:17 44
11:25 36
12:1-12 226
13:10 33,44,200,203
14:9 193
16:15 21,24,45,196,305
16:15,16 37
16:15-20 33
16:16 36,237

Luke

1:51-53 184
1:55 155
1:16 34
1:67 184
1:68-79 184
2:10-14 184
2:26 287
2:32 185
3:6 185
3:11 34
3:14 38
4:1-3 188
4:2 188
4:5 45
4:13 188
4:18 22,30
4:18,19 28
4:21 191
4:43 30
4:43,44 28
5:4-11 249
6:20 192
7:1-10 199
7:2 192
7:5 44,197
7:17 217

Luke

7:21,22 192
7:22 23
7:47ff 36
8:4-8 207-213
8:26-37 199
9:1-6 23
9:2 30
9:47-50 198
10:9 231
10:16 182
10:24 192
10:25 227-229
12:30 46
12:50 187
13:6-9 249
13:16 192
13:18-21 214-223
14:14 224
14:15 224
14:15-24 223-225,249
14:18 224
15:1ff 20
15.8 10 249
17:3ff 34,36
17:6 217
17:19 236
19:10 182
19:11 202
20:9-19 226
21:24 44
22:45 20
22:50,51 235
23:2 44
24:13-49 21
24:21 202
24:25 37
24:26,27 202
24:27 44
24:47 32,33,35,36
24:48 32

John

1:1-14 183

John

1:9 193
1:14 185,241
1:18 185
1:29 185,193,201
1:35-42 194
2:4 201
2:13-17 199
2:22 37
3:3 207
3:16 46,182,305
3:16,17 185
4:1-42 198
4:24 193
4:42 46
4:43-54 199
4:46 198
5:22,23 204
6 198
6:26 189
6:33 46,193
6:60-71 20
7:30 201
7:37 192
7.39 203
8:12 46,193
8:20 201
8:28 11
8:13ff 192
9:1 233
9:1-12 195
9:3 233
9:16 318
9:28 18
10:16 193
11:48 44
11:50 44
11:51 44
11:52 44
12:23 201
12:32 185,193
12:47 46,193
13:1 201
14:1-3 202

John

14:6,7	258
14:12	203
14:16	316
14:30	346
15:18	47
15:20	316
15:26	316
16:7	203,255,316
16:8	193,256
16:11	346
17:1	201
17:11	47
17:14	47
17:21	193
18:35	44
18:36	344
20:21	12,13
20:23	36

Acts

1-12	246
1:1-2:41	259
1:6	202
1:7	203
1:8	30,32,33,95,145,151, 229,249
1:9-11	203
1:14	254
1:15	247
1:22	202,264
1:22-26	32
2	29
2:1-13	312
2:4	254
2:10,11	250
2:11	251
2:14-41	261
2:17	167
2:22ff	258
2:23	258
2:24	258
2:29-36	132,202

Acts

2:31,32	258
2:36	258
2:36-38	37
2:38	34,35,36,40,95,178, 255,259,261,262
2:38,39	40
2:41	247,261,262
2:42	254
2:42-5:42	259
2:47	247,262
3:1-10	224,271
3:3-16	258
3:13-15	258
3:15	258
3:19	34,259
3:26	35
4:2	41,258
4:4	247
4:9	236
4:10	258
4:10-12	258
4:18	41
4:25	44,133
4:26	346
4:27	44
4:27,28	132,200
5:14	247
5:30	258
5:31	259
5:32	259
5:42	23,258
6:1	20
6:5	250,251,323
6:7	270
6:1-7	259,268
6:3,4	263
6:7	17,247,268
6:8	271
6:8-8:1	259
6:13	32
7:52	258
8-12	282
8:1-12:25	260

Acts

8:2	268
8:4-8	166,224
8:4-13	261
8:4-25	264
8:5	258
8:5-24	224
8:6	271
8:10	263
8:12	23,261
8:12,13	37,261
8:13	262
8:18	313
8:18-24	262
8:22	35
8:26-40	224,261
8:27-38	259
8:34-38	37
8:35	23,258
8:37,38	261
8:40	268
9:1 19	224,261,300
9:6	264
9:15	300
9:18	37,259,261
9:31	247
9:33,34	271
9:35	247
9:40,41	271
10	224
10:2	251
10:22	44,287
10:23 48	261
10:36-39	258
10:39	258
10:40	258
10:42	29,33
10:43	261
10:44-48	37
10:46-48	261
10:47-48	259
11	285-293
11:18	34
11:19	268,286,323

Acts

11:19,20	258
11:20	23,224,268,286
11:22	279,288
11:24	248,289
11:27-30	289
11:29	290
11:29,30	325
12:24	248
13	285-293
13-28	246
13:1-3	16,260,272
13:2	254,323
13:2,3	290
13:3	13,291
13:4-28:31	260
13:5	258
13:6	258
13:9	276
13:14	34
13:23-27	258
13:24	35
13:28-37	258
13:30,31	258
13:33	132
13:38,39	258
13:44	248
13:44-48	301
13:46	258
13:48	258
13:49	248,258
14	285-293
14:1	248
14:1	16
14:7	23
14:9,10	271
14:14	16
14:21	248,258
14:22	316
14:25	258
14:27,28	291
15	224,272,317
15:1	260
15:14	44

Acts

15:16,17 166
15:19 260,283
15:20 323
15:21 23
15:37 323
16:3 260,323
16:5 248
16:6 273,274
16:6-10 224,264
16:7 273,274
16:9 273
16:10 23,273,274
16:13-15 261
16:14,15 37
16:15 259,261
16:16-18 160
16:18 271
16:25-40 261
16:40 264
16:31 261
16:33 261
17:3 258
17:4 248
17:15 257
17:17-20 262
17:18 23,258
17:19-21 258
17:23 277
17:24-31 55
17:26 44,349
17:27 348
17:28 348
17:30 34,35
17:31 258
17:32 258
18:5 258
18:6 301
18:8 248,259
18:19 323
18:28 355
19:1 273
19:4 34,35
19:5 259

Acts

19:8 258
19:10 248
19:11,12 271
20:4,5 323
20:9,10 271
20:21 34,35,259
20:33 274
21:11 274
21:20 248
22:4-16 261
22:14-16 37
22:16 40,261
22:21 300
24:2 44
24:10 44
24:14 44
24:14 37
24:17 44
26:4 44
26:9-18 261
26:15-18 300
26:16 264
26:20 34,35,259
26:27 37
28:8 271
28:9 238,271
28:19 44
28:23 258
28:23-28 301
28:28 355
28;31 42

Romans

1:1-6 201
1:4 132
1:5 37,299,300
1:8 45,300
1:11 24
1:15 24
1:16 23,37
1:17 173
1:18-32 301
2:1-3:8 301
2:14 70

INDEX OF SCRIPTURES

Romans

3:3	97
3:9	301
3:10-12	301
3:13,14	301
3:15-18	302
3:19	46
3:20	173
3:21-26	58
3:23	302
3:24	298
3:25	37
3:29	299
3:30	299
4:13	45
5:	100
5:12	46
5:18,19	39
6:1-6	39
6:3,4	187
8:1	154
8:2	173
8:9-11	177
8:17ff	316
8:28	269
9:	169
9:2,3	297
9:5	98
9:30	169
10:1	275,277,297
10:4	30
10:9	37
10:11	37
10:14,15	306
10:17	37,67
10:15	30
11:4	257
11:5	298
11:11	300
11:11,12	301
11:11-24	300
11:16-18	257
11:20,21	301
11:26	298

Romans

11:26,27	298
11:30,31	298
12:7	42
12:16	161
15:9	198
15:11	44,151,306
15:14-16	299
15:20	23,307
16:7	16
16:19	300

I Corinthians

1:1	161
1:3-7	316
1:5	316,317
1:5-7	319
1:8	317
1:10	319
1:10-17	318,319
1:11	318
1:12	318
1:18	305
1:18ff	161
1:22ff	29
1:23	306
2:4	29,30
3:1-4	306
3:3	304
3:4	304
3:5 9	307
3:9	307
3:10	307
3:11	307
4:10	322
4:13	46
4:15	23
5:1	304
5:1-13	319
6:1-11	253,322
6:7	322
6:11	40
6:13-20	319
7:1-16	320

I Corinthians		II Corinthians	
7:19	320	2:12,13	308
8:8	320	2:14ff	161
9:12-18	24	3:8	178
10:1,2	89	4:5	306
11:17-34	309	5	253
11:23	310	5:1-5	314
11:24	310	5:11-6:2	302
11:29	311	5:14	185
12-14	311-313	5:17-19	252
12:10	311	5:18	304
12:13	178	5:18,19	305
12:30	311	5:19	46,303,305
13:2	311	5:20	15,302
13:8-12	311	7:9ff	34
13:10	310	8-9	315,316,323-331
13:11	313	8:1	326
14:1	313	8:1-7	315
14:1-12	311	8:2	326,327
14:13	311	8:3	327
14:18	161	8:5	331
14:22	311	8:7,8	315
14:22-25	311	8:9	315
15	201,314	8:10	326
15:1,2	23	8:11	326
15:1-3	16,257,261,314	8:13-15	325
15:2	23	9:6,7	315
15:3	298	9:11,12	315
15:3-8	314	9:13	315
15:12	314	9:15	315
15:12-28	58	10:16	23
15:14	37,314	11:4	306
15:15	314	11:7	23
15:17	37,314		
15:35,36	314	**Galatians**	
15:50	314	1:6-9	253
16	325-331	1:8	23
16:1,2	325	1:11	23
16:1-4	315,316	1:17	299
16:8	308	1:19	16
		2:2	306
II Corinthians		2:7	299
1:3-11	316	3:5-10	318
2:12	274	3:8	44

Galatians

3:10 173
3:11 172,173
3:24 318
3:27 225
4:4 81
4:7 318
4:9 318
4:13 23,24
5:1 318
5:2 318
5:4 318
5:8 318
5:16 318
5:22 256
6:10 236

Ephesians

1:4 28,182
1:13 23,305
1:20-23 203
2:2 346
2:8,9 229
3:6 73
4:7-13 344
4:13 217
5:26 40,102
6:12 346
6:15 23
6:17 256

Philippians

1:10 203
1:15 305
2:10 346
3:10 316
4:10-19 315

Colossians

1:5 305
1:18 203
1:19 185
1:23 23,33,306
1:26 299

Colossians

1:28 42
2:13-15 185
3:16 42
4:3 307

I Thessalonians

1:8 37
2:3ff 25
2:9 306
2:14 325
2:14-16 298
2:15,16 299
4:5 44
4:4-11 317
4:13-5:11 317
4:15-17 317
4:16 317
5:1 317
5:2,3 317

II Thessalonians

2:1 317
2:1-12 317
2:2,3 317
5:5-9 317

I Timothy

2:7 299
3:1-13 195
3:16 37
4:7 304
4:11 299
4:12 304
4:14 313

II Timothy

1:11 25,30
2:2 322
2:7 25,30
2:12 316
3:16 150,256
3:16,17 70
4:2 24,29,266,305

II Timothy

4:9 335
4:10 213

Titus

1:5-9 195
3:5 102

Hebrews

1:2 167
1:5 132
3:12 35
4:14-16 203
6:1 35
6:4-6 35
8 .89
8:5 287
9:12-14 201
9:28 100
10 89
10:1-4 72
10:22 40,102
10:26 35
10:37,38 173
11 37
11:1 37
11:4 67
11:7 287
11:8 79
11:9 85
11:13 37
11:31 108
12:1 32
12:25 287

James

1:18 23
2:14-17 229

I Peter

1:1 273
1:20 349
1:23 23
2:5 339

I Peter

2:9 44,339
2:25 35
3:20,21 72
3:21 36
4:13 316
5:9 45

II Peter

2:5 25,46
3:6 46
3:9 34,74

I John

1:8 36
2:2 302
2:18 167
2:27 41
3:7 229,242
3:8 185
4:14 185
5:4,5 47

Revelation

1:1 335
1:5 346
1:9 89
1:10 339
1:12-20 336
2:2 337
2:3 337
2:7 344
2:9 337
2:10 337
2:12 337
2:13 337
2:17 345
2:21 337
2:22a 35
2:26 345
2:28 345
3:1 337
3:5,6 345
3:12,13 345

Revelation

3:16 337
3:17 337
3:21 339,345
4:1 339
4:11 348
5:5 339
5:6 339
5:9 349,350
5:9,10 73,151
5:10 339,349
5:13 349
6:2 340
6:8 339,340
6:9 337
6:10 338
6:11 339
7:1-4 345
7:1 339
7:9 345,350
7:9,10 350
8:1 341
9:15 341
9:20 35
9:20,21 342
10:1 339
10:2 339
10:3 339
10:11 350
11:1 342
11:2 342
11:9 350,351
11:10 343
11:11 343
11:13 343
11:15 71,215,345
12:5 133
12:8 338
12:13 338
12:17 338
13:1-7 334
13:1 338
13:4 338
13:5 338

Revelation

13:7 338,350,351
13:8 349
13:11 338
16 343
16:9 35
16:11 35
16:16 343
17:9 344
17:15 350,351
17:17 344
18:5 69
19 348
19:11-16 133
20:7-10 58
20:10 344
21 348
21:1-4 58
22 348
22:17 351